Globalization and the American South

Globalization
and the American South

EDITED BY JAMES C. COBB
AND WILLIAM STUECK

The University of Georgia Press / *Athens and London*

© 2005 by the University of Georgia Press
Athens, Georgia 30602
www.ugapress.org
All rights reserved
Designed by Sandra Strother Hudson
Set in Minion by G&S Typesetters, Inc.

Printed digitally in the United States of America

Library of Congress Cataloging-in-Publication Data
Globalization and the American South / edited by
James C. Cobb and William Stueck.
xvi, 229 p. ; 24 cm.
Includes bibliographical references and index.
ISBN 0-8203-2647-X (hardcover : alk. paper) —
ISBN 0-8203-2648-8 (pbk. : alk. paper)
1. Globalization—Congresses.   2. Industrial promotion—
Southern States—Congresses.   3. Investments,
Foreign—Southern States—Congresses.   4. Industrial
location—Southern States—Congresses.   5. Minorities—
Southern States—Congresses.   6. Southern States—
Economic conditions—Congresses.   7. Southern
States—Social conditions—Congresses.   I. Cobb, James C.
(James Charles), 1947–   II. Stueck, William Whitney, 1945–
HC107.A13G54 2005
337.75— dc22
2004016160

Paperback ISBN-13: 978-0-8203-2648-1

British Library Cataloging-in-Publication Data available

CONTENTS

TABLES

ACKNOWLEDGMENTS

The essays in this volume were originally presented at a conference on globalization and the South held at the University of Georgia, June 21–22, 2002. This conference was made possible in part by grants from the Georgia Humanities Council, the State-of-the-Art Conference Grant Program, and the Center for Humanities and Arts at the University of Georgia. Additional funding came from the offices of the vice president for instruction and the dean of the Franklin College of Arts and Sciences, as well as the Department of History at the University of Georgia. Needless to say, we are deeply grateful for this support.

We are also indebted to the commentators on the various sessions at the conference: Professors Cary Frasier, Joseph A. Fry, Lloyd Gardner, Mark Lytle, Tennant S. McWilliams, Robert Pratt, and Thomas Zeiler. Their suggestions and criticisms helped not only to enrich the conference but the essays that follow. We must also thank Sherry Dendy, whose conscientious supervision and assistance helped to make this meeting such a success.

We appreciate the support of the editorial, production, and marketing staff at the University of Georgia Press, as well as the excellent work of our copy editor, Mindy Wilson. Finally, and most of all, we are grateful to our contributors for the wonderfully cooperative spirit in which they responded to our questions and suggestions and demonstrated to us that they truly shared our determination to make this collection as good as it could possibly be. If, as we surely hope, this book facilitates a greater understanding of the impact of globalization on the American South, the lion's share of the credit should be theirs.

James C. Cobb
William Stueck

James C. Cobb and William Stueck

Like the overwhelming majority of the South-watching scholars of his generation, when David M. Potter wrote in 1967 that the southern historian's job is to "identify and investigate the distinctive features of southern society," he effectively defined southern distinctiveness only in relation to the rest of the United States. More specifically, the South has traditionally been measured against its longtime nemesis and counterpoint, "the North," which was actually a partly imagined regional embodiment of the overarching American legends of success, enlightenment, virtue, and innocence. Most of those who exhorted southerners to bring their region up to national, that is, northern, standards acted out of a genuine desire to incorporate the South into the mainstream of American life. Still, their insistence on examining the southern experience almost exclusively through the lens of an idealized northern one ignored profound differences in factors such as timing, technology, resources, comparative economic advantage, climate, and topography. Instead of being studied and understood on its own terms, southern history was written with an eye toward explaining what did not happen, or put another way, why what happened (or was believed to have happened) in the North had not happened in the South.[1]

This approach to studying the South was driven by a desire to understand both why the South acquired its problematic characteristics and how they might be eliminated. However, a northern white backlash against the civil rights movement and the decline of the traditional northern manufacturing belt, coupled with the South's emergence as the nation's most racially integrated and economically dynamic region, has cast serious doubt on the assumption that the South's peculiarities were really all that peculiar even in the American context. Moreover, a number of scholars have shown recently that, as historian C. Vann Woodward suggested more than fifty years ago, when viewed against a broader global backdrop, the South's experience seems far less distinctive. Likewise, international scholars from both Europe and Asia see much in the region's troubled history of tragedy, poverty, war, and oppression that seems quite familiar.[2]

All of this suggests a growing conviction that there is more value in studying the South as a part of the world than as a world apart. Certainly, this volume is premised on that belief. Over the last half century the South has had dramatically increasing exposure to and impact on areas and peoples well beyond the borders of the United States. The essays in this volume encourage us to think more broadly by considering the South's place in the rapidly evolving global economy and culture. As it emerges in the pages that follow, the essence of globalization is the transnational flow of people, capital, technology, and expertise that is initiated and sustained by the desire to capitalize on natural or human resources or attractive investment opportunities available somewhere else. Our authors use a variety of approaches and perspectives to ask both "How has life in this region been influenced by these crisscrossing currents of global interaction?" and "What role is the South likely to play in the new global economoculture?"

James C. Cobb's wide-ranging survey of what southerners and others can learn from the South's experience with globalization argues against a simplistic model of continuity versus change, showing that global forces were often at work on both sides of this matchup, simultaneously reshaping the South while adapting to and exploiting its peculiarities within the American context. For example, the persistence of the meager wages and lower taxes that were often cited both as symptoms and causes of southern backwardness relative to the rest of the United States have been the key to the South's attractiveness to foreign industrial investors. At the same time, a legacy of institutional and infrastructural weakness has left many southern communities struggling to recover from the loss of other low-wage jobs to even cheaper labor markets elsewhere in the world. Above all, Cobb believes the South's experience illuminates globalization not as a fixed universal reality but as an ongoing process of accommodation and interaction between the local and the global.

In "Globalization before Globalization," Peter A. Coclanis demolishes the traditional vision of an isolated South dragged kicking and screaming into the international marketplace. The South was "born of global forces," Coclanis reminds us, "as an expression of the outward expansion of the European economy during the early modern period." As Coclanis shows, by the eve of the American Revolution, the southern colonies accounted for nearly two-thirds of the total value of colonial commodity exports. Cotton and tobacco would help to sustain the South as a major contributor to American exports right up to World War II, and though the principal southern industry, textiles, was never heavily oriented toward exports, it was extremely sensitive to shifts in markets and production throughout the world economy. Meanwhile, the South's agricultural and rural mercantile economy reacted to the slightest twitches in world cotton demand, even as its laggard (by U.S. standards) industrial sector reflected not the exploitive machinations of external would-be colonializers but the legacy of a regional economy dominated by the production of agricultural staples for export.

Picking up where Coclanis leaves off, Alfred E. Eckes surveys the dramatic consequences of the changing nature of southern global involvement since the middle of the twentieth century. Although Eckes finds more pluses than minuses among these consequences, like Cobb, he notes the propensity of globalization to reinforce a long-standing southern reliance on cheap nonunion labor. He also points to the loss of thousands of jobs, white collar as well as blue, to distant but much cheaper labor pools. Eckes links the sustainability of globalization as we now know it to variables such as the proliferation of terrorism, and he emphasizes the crucial role of international currency valuation as well. Likening the experiences of the South to the accelerating economies of nations like China and India, he implies that certain social shortcuts taken in the interest of speeding up the South's pursuit of economic modernity may well result in a bumpy and erratic journey toward the promised land unless southern leaders put greater emphasis on educational and infrastructural improvements.

Raymond A. Mohl's discussion of Latino immigration to the South challenges the traditional wisdom that the region is still primarily about black and white. In a sense, many Hispanic immigrants have become the key players in a southern Horatio Alger story. For many of them, even entry-level employment in a low-wage region has actually been a springboard to upward mobility, and their willingness to take jobs that others disdain has not been lost on southern employers. The result has been an accelerating and self-sustaining flow of Hispanic immigrants, trickling into even the tiniest and most remote towns in the South. There is evidence that the American Dream is becoming a reality for a growing number of these newcomers whose buying power manifests itself in merchandise displays and on grocery shelves throughout the region.

Not all of the story is pretty, however. Head-to-head job competition with blacks has brought tension and, in some cases, open hostility. The same is true to a lesser extent between Latinos and blue-collar whites. Meanwhile, less affluent school systems are sometimes hard pressed to respond to an influx of children whose acquaintance with English may be sketchy at best. Finally, growing voter participation is beginning to change the face of state and local politics. Traditionally, the diverse origins of Hispanic immigrants have militated against the kind of political cohesion often exhibited by African Americans, but with Hispanics now officially designated as the nation's largest minority, southern black leaders are understandably wary. If W. E. B. Du Bois correctly predicted that the problem of the twentieth century was the color line, the problem for the twenty-first-century South may lie in determining where that line actually runs.

Hispanics represent the largest but not the only significant new minority presence in the South. As David M. Reimers points out, the region's smaller but growing Asian population is introducing another layer of ethnic complexity to the increasingly multicultural South. While there have long been Asian enclaves in some cities and even a few rural areas like the Yazoo-Mississippi Delta, the more recent Asian influx is most visible in and around major metropolitan areas. With higher educational levels and greater income expectations, Asian immigrants have generally entered the region's economic pecking order well above their Latino counterparts. The relative absence of severe language barriers has facilitated their sociocultural assimilation, while their greater professional expertise has allowed more freedom to choose the nature and extent of that assimilation. Asians have actually helped to enhance the South's image as a bulwark of evangelical Protestantism, and in larger metropolitan areas some congregations project a definite Asian identity. Settings like the Buford Highway corridor outside Atlanta reflect a remarkable clustering of Asian-owned and -operated businesses. Though they are less visible, new residents from the Indian subcontinent are also making their economic and political presence felt in other parts of suburban Atlanta and elsewhere in the South.

The South has witnessed an influx of Asian capital as well. Sayuri Guthrie-Shimizu's assessment of Japanese investment in the South demonstrates that, like politics, globalization can make for some pretty improbable bedfellows. Japanese textile and apparel manufacturers had long been cast as the archenemies of their southern competitors (and their workers), but other Japanese industrialists became the apple of many a southern developer's eye during the last third of the twentieth century. Guthrie-Shimizu's essay helps us understand the complex process that produced this seemingly unlikely outcome. Guthrie-Shimizu presents a most useful perspective on the economic and geopolitical considerations that led Japanese investors to consider expanding their operations into the American South even as she notes the influence of the exuberant and generous courtship of these investors by southern industrial recruiters.

Marko Maunula offers a tightly focused analysis of the highly successful industrial recruitment efforts of development leaders in Spartanburg, South Carolina. Maunula's essay leaves no doubt that the generosity as well as the enthusiasm and organizational quality of industrial recruitment efforts not only matters but matters a great deal. Although he sees some striking European influence on the local culture, Maunula also finds that the influx of foreign immigrants has not destroyed traditional racial and class attitudes among some Spartanburg whites and even suggests that some of the incoming European employers may be accommodating themselves to local mores in this regard.

Most interest in southern global interaction has focused on Europe and Asia, but Andrew DeRoche directs our attention to Africa, a continent whose economic and cultural connections to the South reach back to the early seventeenth century. DeRoche stresses the importance of Andrew Young's personal reputation and his more affirmative and inclusive vision of the South in strengthening the region's ties to Africa, and he explores the legacy of Young's actions as well. His essay points to the crucial role of the civil rights movement in removing the racial system that stood as the major barrier to greater involvement in the South not only by Africans but also by other members of the international community. By emphasizing Young's pivotal role in securing the Olympics for Atlanta, DeRoche joins the other essayists in reminding us that globalization has not been totally a product of impersonal economic forces but has been shaped and altered by individuals like Young and his fellow Atlanta boosters or their counterparts in Spartanburg and elsewhere in the South. The globalization process has also been influenced by countless human decisions on policy and programs, from President Richard M. Nixon's moves to devalue the dollar to the often ad hoc generosity of southern subsidy offers.

Taken together, these essays suggest that globalization cannot be fully understood as simply the march of indomitable economic forces that crush cultural distinctiveness and neutralize individual initiative. Although our authors raise some notable concerns, none of them suggest that globalization in the southern United States has shown itself to be the hydra-headed monster its critics seem to describe. For all the talk about globalization exacerbating inequalities of wealth, the extent of a nation's global economic involvement correlates positively with a rise from day-to-day subsistence to a more stable and secure existence for many of its people. It is no coincidence that Africa, the world's least globalized continent, is now its poorest, sickest, and most strife ridden as well. If we reject globalization because it is exploitive, we reject the simple realities of capitalism, which, for all its manifold shortcomings, remains the only modern economic system that has demonstrated the capacity over time to improve the lot of those whom it exploits.

A number of our essayists suggest that states, regions, or communities may reap significant benefits from the exploitation of the resources and opportunities they offer. As several of our contributors also make clear, however, the long-term impact of such exploitation depends on the willingness of state and local leaders first to maximize the public gains derived from it and then to reinvest them in ways that generate new and even more attractive and beneficial opportunities for the future. Indeed, all the essays in this volume provide new and broader insights into the South's recent and long-term historical experience that should be useful to those who would chart the course of any region, nation, or community in the much wider and increasingly fluid global context where the future is always now.[3]

Notes

1. David M. Potter, "Depletion and Renewal in Southern History," in *Perspectives on the South: Agenda for Research,* ed. Edgar T. Thompson (Durham, N.C.: Duke University Press, 1967), 78; C. Vann Woodward, "The Search for Southern Identity," in *The Burden of Southern History,* 3rd ed. (Baton Rouge: Louisiana State University Press,

1993), 3–26; Richard N. Current, *Northernizing the South* (Athens: University of Georgia Press, 1983); Carl N. Degler, "Thesis, Antithesis, Synthesis: The South and North and the Nation," *Journal of Southern History* 53 (February 1987), 5; James C. Cobb, "Why the New South Never Became the North," in *Industrialization and Southern Society, 1877–1984* (Lexington: University Press of Kentucky, 1984), 126–64.

2. C. Vann Woodward, "The Irony of Southern History," in *The Burden of Southern History*, 187–212. For examples of the more comparative approach to studying southern history see James C. Cobb, "An Epitaph for the North: Reflections on the Politics of Regional and National Identity at the Millennium," *Journal of Southern History* 56 (February 2000): 3–24; Cobb, "Southern Writers and the Challenge of Regional Convergence," *Georgia Historical Quarterly* 63 (Spring 1989): 1–25; Don H. Doyle, *Nations Divided: America, Italy, and the Southern Question* (Athens: University of Georgia Press, 2002); Dwight B. Billings Jr., *Planters and the Making of A New South: Class Politics and Development in North Carolina, 1865–1900* (Chapel Hill: University of North Carolina Press, 1979); John W. Cell, *The Highest Stage of White Supremacy: The Origins of Segregation in South Africa and the American South* (Cambridge, Mass.: Cambridge University Press, 1982). On European interest in the South, see James C. Cobb, "Europeans Can't Get Enough of the South," *Georgia Magazine* 82 (June 2003): 30–37; Michael O'Brien, "The Apprehension of the South in Modern Culture," *Southern Cultures* 4 (Winter 1998): 3–18.

3. On the South and globalization, see also James Peacock, "The South in a Global World," *Virginia Quarterly Review* 78 (Autumn 2002): 581–94; David Goldfield, "The Impact of Globalization on the American South: Culture, Ecology, and Economy," in *Which "Global Village"? Societies, Cultures, and Political-Economic Systems in a Euro-Atlantic Perspective*, ed. Valeria Gennaro Lerda (Westport, Conn.: Praeger, 2002), 145–54.

Globalization and the American South

Beyond the "Y'all Wall":
The American South Goes Global

James C. Cobb

In 1953, with Americans at large increasingly intent on understanding how such a progressive and enlightened nation could have produced such an abhorrent regional aberration, C. Vann Woodward first suggested that its history of cruelty, poverty, tragedy, defeat, and disillusionment gave the South more in common with the rest of the world than with the rest of the United States. Although many Americans, including southerners themselves, persist in emphasizing the distinctiveness of southern society and culture, events of the last half century clearly confirm Woodward's prescient observation that the South's uniqueness is, and always has been, a lot more universal than we thought. Through its struggle to throw off the burdens of racial and regional prejudices and break the stranglehold of widespread poverty while retaining a meaningful sense of its own identity, the American South has much to say to other regions and societies hoping to achieve similar objectives in an era of profound global economic and cultural transformation.[1]

From an industrial development perspective, the South may have become the nation's most globalized region. It attracted more than half the foreign businesses drawn to the United States in the 1990s, and one of eight manufacturing workers in the South now gets his or her paycheck from a foreign employer. Glamorous as this may sound, however, the South has become the apple of the international industrialist's eye primarily because of the continuing willingness of its political leaders to serve up the huge subsidies and the more than ample pool of relatively cheap, overwhelmingly nonunion labor that have long been the cornerstone of its industrial development strategy. In 1993, when Alabama gave Mercedes an announced subsidy of $253 million (some put the actual figure closer to $300 million) to open a vehicle assembly plant near Tuscaloosa, more than 63,000 applications were submitted for the 1,500 jobs that cost the state, depending on whose calculations you accepted, $167,000 to $200,000 each. In addition to the basic subsidy, the initial incentives package also included a promise to purchase some $75 million worth of Mercedes vehicles for use by state employees. At the time, although Mercedes' starting wage was well above the state average for manufacturing, it was still 30 percent lower than in

Germany even without the additional benefits, or as one Mercedes spokesman put it, "the social baggage we have in Germany." With BMW moving into South Carolina for essentially the same reasons, it is small wonder that some disgruntled German workers have taken to calling the South "our Mexico." Several southern states, especially Mississippi with its subsidy package of nearly $300 million for Nissan, have shown at least comparable generosity to the Japanese. To date, Alabama has invested an estimated total of $874 million in subsidizing Mercedes, Honda, and the Korean auto manufacturer Hyundai.[2]

Because these giveaways require the states to forego huge sums of badly needed tax revenue, development officials invariably turn to a group of economists-for-hire who crank out reams of politically pressure-cooked statistics projecting the hundred-megaton multiplier effect of these heavily subsidized new plants. Still, for all the economic benefits it may have brought, the courtship of foreign industry has so far done little to alter the traditional southern pattern of financing economic development at the expense of human development. Despite Alabama's dead last standing in spending for elementary and secondary education, only a threatened lawsuit by an Alabama teachers group prevented Governor Fob James from raiding the state's school fund to pay off a $43 million obligation to Mercedes in 1995, and the state cut $266 million from its education budget in 2001 before handing over $318 million in location and expansion incentives to Hyundai and Honda in 2002. Meanwhile, Mississippi's promise of $80 million for training Nissan's projected four thousand employees amounted to a contribution per worker that was more than four times the state's annual expenditures per pupil in grades K–12. International executives profess to factor the quality of local schools into their location decisions, but in 2002 South Carolina, North Carolina, and Tennessee, the southern states ranked in the top nine nationally for foreign direct investment, were in the bottom nine nationally in measures of educational achievement within the manufacturing workforce.[3]

As the size of the subsidies now being proffered would indicate, competition for foreign industrial investment is beyond intense. Although North Carolina developers suggested in 1993 that Alabama had gone too far in outbidding them for Mercedes, as they contemplated the heavy job losses to cheaper foreign labor markets that the state has suffered in the ensuing decade, one of them admitted that "if we had known in '93 how bad it would get across our economy, we may have been willing to put $200 million on the table." As it was, he could only hope "we have a chance of catching the next wave of vehicle plants."[4]

Like their native-born predecessors, foreign employers have not hesitated to leverage a state's investment in them in order to protect themselves from competition for their workers. After receiving a subsidy package worth nearly $300 million from Mississippi, a senior vice president for Nissan expressed dismay at

Governor Ronnie Musgrove's courtship of a new Hyundai plant, warning that if any such plant were "located within 80 miles of our Canton facility" Nissan might scrap plans for any future expansion in the state.[5]

Extravagance and indulgence toward industrial investors, domestic or foreign, has long since ceased to be a regional phenomenon, of course. With the rise of a more mobile industrial economy, northern governors and legislators quickly mastered the fine points of what had once seemed a peculiarly southern hospitality to industry. For example, when Lafayette, Indiana, was chosen for a new Subaru facility, developers not only told the company execs precisely what they wanted to hear about subsidies and other incentives, but they suggested initially that the road in front of the new plant be renamed the "Subaru Highway," despite the fact that it had originally been christened the "Bataan Highway" to honor the thousands of American soldiers who died during the infamous death march after their capture by the Japanese in 1942.[6]

Because the interstate scramble to woo new manufacturers is now part of a larger global one as well, southern development officials find it more difficult than ever to abandon the promises of low taxes and dirt-cheap nonunion labor that gave the region the nation's balmiest business climate while depriving many of its communities of the educational and other institutional resources needed to make them attractive to better-paying, more socially conscious employers. The South's overall inability to use its post–World War II industrial expansion as a more effective springboard to human and societal progress was not, as some have suggested, simply a reflection of the political persistence of an ultra-conservative agricultural elite. Rather, the region's social and institutional sectors have remained recognizably "southern" in no small measure because of the emergence and rapid expansion of an intensely competitive global manufacturing economy. Dramatic and still accelerating increases in industrial mobility and equally rapid and remarkable improvements in communications and production technology have not only eliminated many of the low-skill jobs that were a regional mainstay but have also facilitated the transfer of thousands of others to distant concentrations of labor far cheaper and more docile than anything even the greediest of the old southern textile barons could ever have imagined. Feeling the brunt of NAFTA, between 1994 and 2000, North Carolina accounted for nearly 40 percent of textile job losses nationwide and lost more jobs in textiles and apparels combined than any other state.[7]

Because of their heavy concentration of textile and apparel employment, rural areas have suffered the most, accounting for roughly half of the region's job losses since 1979. In this sense, job globalization seems to exacerbate the South's economic unevenness, because it tends to benefit metropolitan economies while decimating rural ones. East Alabama gleams with new auto facilities as West Alabama hemorrhages apparel plants. A strikingly internationalized

Spartanburg flourishes, while nearby, what had once been single-industry, textile-mill towns are now effectively no-industry ghost towns. During the first generation or so after World War II, many of these communities whose industrial bases have now gone farther south or east had mortgaged their social and institutional futures by promising minimal taxation and protection from unions and high-wage competition to manufacturers who were then fleeing northern locations in order to reduce their operating costs. Now, however, the more competitive global economy that initially brokered these Faustian bargains is suddenly foreclosing on them with a vengeance as the employers who were at once the beneficiaries and presumed guarantors of these transactions hurriedly skip town, leaving forwarding addresses like Honduras or Bangladesh.[8]

Meanwhile, although its wages for production workers, which are well below the U.S. average, continue to look good to certain employers from Western Europe or Japan, in the broader global context the South has become a high-wage region that in all too many cases has developed neither the labor force nor the infrastructure to support high-wage industries. The fate of such southern communities surely suggests what may lie ahead for other areas whose integration into the global economy is now proceeding so rapidly that they may have considerably less time than did the South to achieve a semblance of infrastructural maturity before their industrial benefactors begin eyeing the proverbial greener pastures that await them just a few thousand miles farther on. If the South's experience shows that have-not regions may actually benefit in the short term from facilitating their own economic exploitation, it also warns those who assume this type of development is merely a means to an end that they may face difficulty in preventing it from becoming an end in itself, and a dead one at that.

Surely those who have agonized over the presumed cultural consequences of the South's hell-for-leather pursuit of new industry have much to say to contemporary critics of American cultural imperialism and globalization in general. The most instructive example would seem to be the Nashville Agrarians, whose essays assailing industrialism as a threat to southern cultural identity appeared in the 1930 volume *I'll Take My Stand*. The Agrarians seem to fit within a global model in which the intelligentsia generally participate in initial efforts to free their society from its backwardness, only to become critical of these efforts or even reject them altogether later on. As the well-educated, well-traveled beneficiaries of modernization, they enjoy "the ideological vocabulary to . . . defend their culture" and, ironically enough, as John Shelton Reed points out, "modernization itself is what they protest." "If we examine *I'll Take My Stand* in the light of (cultural) nationalist manifestoes from around the world, the similarities are obvious. . . .," Reed argues, noting that "when nationalists come from a nation that is economically 'peripheral' in the world economy, one like the South of the 1920s that produced raw materials and supplied unskilled labor for a more 'advanced' economy, they often adopt the same stance the Agrarians did, rejecting the western science and technology that, in any case, they do not have, and insisting that their very backwardness in 'western' terms has preserved a spiritual and cultural superiority."[9]

Reed's analysis of the Agrarians clearly suggests the fiercely anti-acculturative, anti-Western ideology of many contemporary Islamic nationalists, and he notes that "From the nineteenth-century Slavophils, to the Hindu nationalists of early-twentieth-century India, to the apostles of *negritude,* today, it is easy to find cases of westernized intellectuals assuring the masses of peripheral nations of their superiority to those who dominate them economically and threaten to do so culturally."[10]

Richard H. King has observed that "contemporary left-wing French intellectuals bellyaching about the American cultural invasion sound like nothing so much as conservative Agrarians taking their stand." Certainly, as the apparent advocates of a return to subsistence farming at a time when the South was locked in the grinding poverty of the Great Depression, the Agrarians sounded about as credible as the French newspaper *Le Monde*'s recent effort to convince residents of a nation with more than nine hundred McDonald's restaurants scattered from Normandy to the Riviera "that resistance to the hegemonic pretenses of the hamburger is a cultural imperative."[11]

As globalization threatens to undermine the significance of national boundaries and institutions, the ongoing efforts of the European Union to shape Europe into what is effectively a single nation (and, some think, a single culture) make the South's relative success in avoiding total immersion in the American mainstream seem particularly relevant, as the European academic community's burgeoning interest in southern literature and culture appears to suggest. In reality, of course, as in other societies facing the onslaught of economic and cultural imperialism, the southern intellectual response to economic modernization was typically not one of outright resistance so much as genuine ambivalence. During the post–World War I southern literary renaissance, the prospect of the imminent Americanization or northernization of the region's economy and society fueled southern self-analysis in much the same way that rapid incursions of external economic and cultural influences have forced writers and intellectuals in other "developing" regions to reexamine their own cultures in a desperate effort to separate what can or must be surrendered to the forces of change from what should be defended and preserved.[12]

Like many an intellectual facing Westernization of his society, William Faulkner appeared to be locked in a love-hate struggle with his native region when he wrote in 1933 that he and his southern literary contemporaries seemed "to try in the simple furious breathing (or writing) span of the individual to draw a savage indictment of the contemporary scene or to escape from it into a make-believe region of swords and magnolias and mocking birds which perhaps never existed anywhere." In some ways, Faulkner and other southern writers of his era resembled the "been to," a character in West African fiction, so named because he has "been to the West" only to return "suffering from psychic division," torn between his admiration for Western enlightenment and power and his anxiety about the cultural upheaval and destruction likely to accompany Western penetration of the world from which he came.[13]

Deborah N. Cohn has compared the southern renaissance to the "so-called Boom in Spanish American literature" that occurred in the 1960s and 1970s as authors such as Julio Cortázar and Gabriel García Márquez wrestled with "the social chaos" and "the rapid change and upheaval" that accompanied the "modernization of Spanish America following the Second World War." As they reexamined the past and assessed "local and international forces competing for economic control," many of the key writers of the "Boom" readily acknowledged Faulkner's influence. After all, as Joel Williamson observed, Faulkner was "born into and reared among an imperialized people, a people . . . much reduced in power from what had been the case within living memory. In writing about their plight, he met the plight of the imperialized people of the world, the people whose land had been raped and labor taken to supply raw materials for the factories of the industrial powers." Born in the banana-growing country of Colombia that had been ravaged by the United Fruit Company, García Márquez read Faulkner and discovered that "the world of the southern United States which he writes about—was very like my world, . . . it was created by the same people." In both settings, as Lois Parkinson Zamora notes, "belated and abrupt modernization . . . masked (and sometimes exacerbated) long histories of political and racial and economic inequity."[14]

In recent years, black southerners have wrestled with external forces that threaten not just their southernness but their sense of blackness as well. When writer Randall Kenan returned to his tiny hometown of Chinquapin, North Carolina, he found a place where he could still chow down on chopped barbecue and chitlins and afterward "go home and watch BET and check my e-mail after calling a friend in Japan." Kenan realized, however, that the same family, school, and church experiences that had shaped his southern identity had also taught him "those things that I had taken so for granted about being black." Now, however, the cultural information acquired by local children was not very different from that given to "black kids, in Seattle and Madison and Salt Lake City and New York." Not only was Chinquapin "becoming like the rest of America," but instead of being instilled by people like his grandfather, aunts, uncles, and his teachers and pastor, blackness was now being "dictated by The Martin Lawrence Show and Moesha and Snoop Doggy Dogg."[15]

No longer subject to regional and perhaps not even individual interpretation, contemporary black culture seemed to Kenan little more than a "postmodern amalgam of . . . borrowings and findings and newfangled creations like Kwanzaa and media manipulations of street lingo . . . only interested in style, newness, the expression of being other." Concerned that this globalized and deceptively coercive image of a homogenized African American identity leaves little room for expressions of individuality, he also acknowledged that in the ultraefficient but often devastatingly impersonal world of instantaneous global communication "blackness was not so easily beamed through a satellite or through an optic fiber," and he was left to wonder, "how could you be black on a computer screen?"[16]

In reality, the South's intellectual struggle with the forces of economic modernization may be less striking than the way in which southerners in general have simply adapted to them. Humorist Roy Blount Jr. once insisted that "They don't have live bait/video stores in the North." I am not so sure about that, although I do know that they have live-bait vending machines in Alabama. Certainly, frequent travelers to other parts of the world encounter such adaptations of ancient cultures to contemporary innovations everywhere whey turn. No people on earth have absorbed and subdued external influences over a longer period of time than the Chinese. When he visited China back in 1988, Pico Iyer discovered that the Super Bowl had already captured more viewers in China than in the United States, and he found a buffet restaurant in Guangzhou where customers were enjoying such dishes as "'Bacon Your Pardon,' and 'Ike and Tuna Turner.'" Meanwhile, government slogans simultaneously urged the citizenry to "sacrifice for socialism" while assuring them that "to get rich is glorious." Struck by such omnipresent juxtapositions of traditional Maoism with western "Meism," Iyer wondered, "With Marxism like this, who needed capitalism?"[17]

Not only have the Chinese imported capitalism, but they have proven quite adept at exporting it as well. Blessed with rich local deposits, the northeast Georgia town of Elberton has long billed itself as the "granite capital of the world." However, Elberton's producers now face stiff competition from China, which has already snatched away the lucrative Japanese market for cemetery monuments. To make matters worse, Elberton's granite companies must now do battle with a local outlet for Sinostone, a China-based company that, despite its shipping costs, can capitalize on its 98 percent labor cost advantage and freedom from costly environmental and worker health and safety requirements to offer its tombstones at prices significantly below the going rate in Elberton itself.[18]

Adaptation to new economic strategies and technological advances is hardly confined to China, of course. Throughout Europe, sixteenth-century inns sport satellite dishes on their roofs or miniature golf courses in their courtyards. In tiny Italian towns, the funeral processional from the ancient church to the ancient cemetery features priests using wireless microphones to broadcast their recitations through speakers mounted on the hearse or carried by members of the cortege. As John Reed has pointed out: "We often see, elsewhere in the world, that economic development simply provides new ways to do old things, or ways to do what would have been old things if they hadn't been impossible."[19]

In some cases, what seem initially to be intrusive and intimidating technologies can not only be absorbed but employed to project certain aspects of the indigenous culture back onto the larger national or global scene. Such a story unfolds with the automobile, which definitely helped to break down the isolation and provincialism and accelerate the tempo of southern rural life. Yet, although his ministers warned him that it was far better "to be late at the pearly gate than to get to hell on time," the white male southerner's affinity for fast cars figured prominently in the meteoric rise to national and increasing international popularity of the once almost exclusively rednecks-racing-on-red-dirt phenomenon that we now know as NASCAR. Today's NASCAR circuit includes races in thirty-eight states, and the fabled Darlington, South Carolina, "500" will be moved to a track near Los Angeles in 2004. Meanwhile, the worldwide television presence of the sport suggests that not only are more drivers like Hideo Fukyama on the way but an international NASCAR circuit might soon be a reality as well.[20]

In a similar vein the radio not only made the rest of the world a part of southern life but provided opportunities for southerners, black and white, to hear their own music more frequently, and it also took this music to the rest of the world. Armed forces broadcasts of the Grand Ole Opry during World War II apparently did not appeal to some of the Japanese troops, who occasionally abandoned "Banzai" in favor of "To Hell with Roy Acuff." Although the Japanese have surely avenged themselves many times over by unleashing the insidious contagion of karaoke, its near-global ubiquity all but obscures its national origins. Likewise, anyone who sees Willie Nelson play to a packed house in Amsterdam or hears that a relatively low-profile performer like Don Williams is considered a megastar in Zimbabwe or hears the Russian country band Bering Straits understands that country music is no longer a southern or even American phenomenon.[21]

Clearly, the more globalized a cultural or commercial export becomes, the weaker its affiliations with the specific regional or national locale where it originated. A decade ago, despite its record of destroying many of the South's long-established small-town mercantile economies, Wal-Mart was identified as a significantly "southern" institution by nearly three-fourths of the respondents to a 1995 Southern FOCUS poll. In reality, of course, this perception is comparable to that of nearly half of the Chinese children who, in a recent survey, identified McDonald's as a Chinese company.[22]

Wal-Mart has long since ceased to be either southern or American but is now a truly global retail colossus, the world's largest private employer, with some twelve hundred stores in nine international locations stretching from Argentina to Europe to China and South Korea. To its multitude of critics, Wal-Mart seems to represent a corporate embodiment of Faulkner's soulless supercapitalist, Flem Snopes, who, as Joel Williamson put it, stands as a "symbol for the corruption of community, clan, and family in the modern world." Certainly, the Wal-Mart strategy entails the destruction of the econo-social nexus of community life by seducing consumers away from homegrown enterprises owned by people who are often their friends and neighbors. With its relentless shoot-the-wounded war of extermination against its smaller local competitors, and its determination, as CEO Lee Scott admitted, "to be where we're not," Wal-Mart seems to share not just Flem Snopes's fixation with turning a profit, but what one critic called his "ruthless drive for possession and control."[23]

On a recent visit to Shenzhen, just north of Hong Kong, a *Newsweek* correspondent described a Wal-Mart dotted with posters and photos of a kindly old man and liberally sprinkled with employees clad in red polos and eager to tell of that man's long journey from his humble rural roots to a position of great power and influence. The old man in question was not the late Mao Tse Tung, however, but the late Sam Walton, who, in China at least, has shed his down-home image as "Mr. Sam," the folksy founder of Wal-Mart, to become the equivalent of Chairman Sam, "the Mao of retailing." In keeping with the mass psychology of Maoism, the store even has its own fight song in which associates assure customers, "My heart is filled with pride . . . I long to tell you how deep my love for Wal-Mart is." Wal-Mart's omnipresent postings of Mr. Sam's business principles also strike an eerily Maoesque tone, as does the admission of its CEO that when some of the managers of its German stores balked at doing things the Wal-Mart way, they were summarily dispatched to the company's remote headquarters in Bentonville, Arkansas, to be "culturalized."[24]

After acquiring Britain's ASDA supermarket chain, Wal-Mart opened its first English superstore in Bristol in the year 2000. On a visit to this establishment, one encounters the company's familiar initial market penetration strategy of taking direct aim on its local rivals, which in this case means relatively high-end supermarket chains like Sainsburys and Safeway. Accordingly, Wal-Mart's Bristol store is a well-lit, wide-aisled affair that offers several rows of gourmet groceries, a wine section well stocked with quite respectable international labels, and a large, attractive cafeteria that spurns the rotating red-dyed hot dogs, Velveeta and jalapeno nachos, and tuna-melt sandwiches fancied by so many

Wal-Mart shoppers in these parts. Wal-Mart has also dramatically reduced the prices of some ASDA products, especially its jeans. By buying in lots of several million (as opposed to fifty thousand) yards, the new bosses were able to cut the cost of the jeans fabric by nearly 60 percent, allowing ASDA to slice its jeans prices in half and thereby increase its jeans sales sixfold. All of this seemed well and good to the gentleman who gave us directions to the store, but he did complain that, unlike its ASDA predecessor, the new Wal-Mart offered neither key making or shoe repair.[25]

As Wal-Mart moves to eliminate or neutralize its competition, it also fine-tunes its inventories with a precise, calculating coldness worthy of Flem Snopes himself, through a cutting-edge computer network that insures close and constant global oversight by the corporate braintrust back in Arkansas. Shoppers in China are not entirely at the mercy of the bean counters in Bentonville, however. The Shenzhen store offers tanks of live crabs, frogs, fish, and shrimp, selections from which may be taken home as is or gutted and/or skinned on the spot. At this point, Wal-Mart and hundreds of other major players in the global economy are actually pursuing a strategy that some have called "glocalism" by accommodating both local markets and local cultures in order to achieve the optimal balance between cost effectiveness and consumer satisfaction. This strategy has been adopted as well by a number of fast food chains such as Kentucky Fried Chicken, another ostensibly southern enterprise that has outgrown both its regional and national origins. With well over half of its eleven thousand restaurants in more than eighty foreign countries, KFC offers a huge variety of locally attuned alternatives and complements to its original recipe chicken, ranging from tempura crispy strips for the Japanese to potato and onion croquettes for the Dutch.[26]

China now boasts six hundred KFC outlets whose chicken gets progressively spicier as one moves inland. Such specialized global adaptation also requires an awareness of local languages and dialects. KFC's entry into China was a little bumpy until its executives realized that the Chinese translation of "finger lickin' good" was "eat your fingers off." In this, KFC's experience mirrored that of the mother of all southern corporations gone global, Coca-Cola, whose first choice as a pronunciation of its name apparently came through in Chinese as "bite the wax tadpole!" and had to be scrapped in favor of something very loosely translated as "happiness in the mouth."[27]

For all this corporate attentiveness to local peculiarities, the process of global adaptation is both mutual and incremental, involving considerable give-and-take over time; we should keep in mind that what we see now is not necessarily what we will ultimately get. The ideal long-term outcome for any internationalized retailer is the most homogeneous global inventory and marketing strategy attainable. In the final analysis, it will be the location, not of a retailer's corporate headquarters, but of its largest and most profitable markets that will carry the most weight in decisions about whose particularities will be universalized. Wal-Mart, for example, is already marketing ASDA's popular "George" line of clothing in the United States.[28]

The ability of southerners not only to adapt to the effort to Americanize their culture but in some cases to effectively southernize the culture of America at large and then export the result as its own product should be instructive, both to overproud Americans bragging about the unrivalled superiority of their products and institutions and to the vast array of critics who find it a bit too convenient to demonize the United States as the ubiquitous Great Satan of cultural imperialism. Owing primarily to the near-global feasibility of communication in English and the exceedingly marketable materialism that our currently perceived lifestyle seems to convey, globalization's primary distinguishing features at this moment do seem so indisputably American that many of us traveling abroad may wonder whether, contrary to Thomas Wolfe, it will soon be impossible for us to *leave* home again. Yet, Chinese president Jian Zemin has predicted that his country can quadruple its gross domestic product by 2020, and he seems to have torn a page from the southern governor's handbook when he insists that China must "do away with all notions which hinder development, change all practices and regulations which impede it, and get rid of the drawbacks of the system which adversely affect it." Some economists scoff at Jian's optimism, but with its shoppers spending like never before, China is poised to become the world's largest consumer market and has already moved ahead of the United States in value of annual foreign direct investment. If these trends continue, corporate rightists may yet follow the example of campus leftists by chanting, "Hey, hey, ho, ho, Western culture's got to go," and the face of globalization will quickly begin to look less like the Marlboro Man and more like Jackie Chan.[29]

We liberals seem quick to conclude that the critics of globalization's cultural ravages are simply expressing the views of those who can't speak for themselves. Before we do so, perhaps we should step back and consider the preservationists-versus-developers disputes that we are constantly witnessing in the faster growing communities of the contemporary South. Many of these essentially boil down to members of a local elite either protecting themselves from economic competition or reaffirming their social supremacy by insisting that it is more important to preserve certain architectural symbols of the elite-defined ambience of a previous century than it is to have a Pizza Hut or a strip mall where the less affluent members of the community can get a cheap meal or perhaps find a job. Monsieur José Bové became an international symbol of resistance to globalization when he presented a different take on French deconstructionism by leading an attack on a partially completed McDonald's restaurant in southern France. Although he was often described as a simple sheep grower turned heroic defender of France's cultural identity, Bové's storming of the Mickey-D's also reflected his anger at American restrictions on the importation of French Roquefort cheese made from milk produced by his sheep.[30]

Elsewhere, *New York Times* correspondent Thomas Friedman was shocked to find a two-story-high portrait of Colonel Sanders in downtown Kuala Lumpur, much less to hear of people in small towns all over Malaysia "queuing up" at local KFCs because, as the owner of all of the nation's franchises explained, "Anything Western, especially American, people here love. . . . They want to eat it and be it." As a Malaysian human rights activist observed, "Elites here say, 'You should not have McDonald's, but for the little people who don't get to travel to America, they have America come to them.'" The patrons who invest a week's wages in a meal at the gargantuan three-thousand-seat KFC in Beijing record this very special occasion in copious photographs and gaze wonderingly at its pictures of seductive but unreachable locales such as Los Angeles and Disneyland. "The Americans here are selling not just products but a culture," a Beijing marketing expert observed, "and it's a culture that many Chinese want." Though he was dismayed by the Coca-Colonization of Asia, Pico Iyer realized that "a kind of imperial arrogance underlies the very assumption that the people of the third world should be happier without the TVs and motorbikes that we find so indispensable ourselves."[31]

Paradoxically enough, by threatening to take our national, regional, or ethnic identities away from us, the global economy first stimulates our desire to preserve them, and then through a combination of commodification and clever marketing, it proceeds to sell them back to us. David Rieff scoffs at the insistence of many academics that multiculturalism represents a radical assault on the capitalist-imperialist establishment. On the contrary, he sees it as "perhaps the most salient epiphenomenon of an increasingly globalized capitalist system." Because "everything is commodifiable" at some level, Rieff insists, the global economy is actually "multiculturalism's silent partner."[32]

As a case in point, white southerners seeking to affirm a distinctive cultural identity can simply purchase it in a variety of formats. Acquired by New York–based Time Warner in 1985, *Southern Living* magazine became, as Diane Roberts put it, "a cash cow for the media leviathan of corporate Yankeedom" by serving up an uncomplicated and unblemished Bloody Mary and buffet brunch vision of southern life to those whose relative affluence or pretensions thereto make it seem almost plausible.[33]

As the pages of *Southern Living* quickly demonstrate, of course, the marketing process ultimately reduces the complex, uneven, often historically unwieldy concept of identity to a mere matter of a fashionable and appealing lifestyle. In this regard, *Southern Living*'s emphasis on good eating, good drinking, and gracious entertaining seems very much in tune with the aims of the International

Slow Food Movement, which now claims more than sixty thousand members in forty-five countries. This movement actually began in Italy in 1986 as a protest against the proliferation of McDonald's and other fast-food establishments in a nation traditionally known for the leisurely enjoyment of the dining experience. Inspired by the Slow Food Movement and grounded firmly in his native Tuscan tradition of the "long lunch" that often stretched over several hours, Paolo Saturnini, the mayor of Greve-in-Chianti, just south of Florence, has made his little town the anchor of the International Network of Slow Cities. As a certified "Slow City," Greve now offers tourists all sorts of opportunities to kick back and learn how to savor a commodified version of the local Chianti culture. This includes the prodigious consumption not only of local wines, olive oils, and cheeses, but pork from a once-indigenous breed of wild boar recently reintroduced to the local area and now allowed, so we are told, to roam "happy and free" in the local forests until it is ready to become the featured entree in somebody's slow lunch. Ironically, Greve's success in becoming a symbol of life in the slow lane has turned the once-sleepy market town into a bustling little burg so jammed with tourists that Mayor Saturnini and many local shopkeepers have not only forsaken the slow lunch but are hard pressed to find time for lunch at all. This paradox is best symbolized by the "Chianti Slow Travel Agency," which, without apparent recognition of the irony, offers tourists discount rates on high-speed Internet connections.[34]

Closer to home, the folks at southernness.com are heavily into "slow food" themselves, and near the top of their list of "50 Ways Y'all Can Help Save the South" is a call to boycott any McDonald's restaurant that refuses to use southern ingredients or to inculcate southern-style manners among their employees. Such a boycott would contribute to the construction of a symbolic "Y'all Wall" along the Mason-Dixon line "to retard or halt the aggressive cultural globalization troops." "Protest much," we are admonished. "Start a petition. Write a congressperson. Picket. Act now, y'all."[35]

Quite coincidentally, of course, southernness.com also urges those who truly want to save "the Southern life we love" to purchase only genuinely "southern" products ranging from country ham to dog biscuits, from a list of authentically southern establishments linked to the Web site. Its feature attraction, however, for those who want to be sure that they even smell "southern" is "The Southern Fragrance Library," which includes "Parfum Mist," the only world-class fragrance created to honor "The Southern Woman and her American South." This scent features "alluring hyper-romantic floral with notes of jasmine and a base of amber," and customers are cautioned that it is "best worn by a woman beyond the early teen years." There is also a cologne for the southern gentleman that "captures the great pleasures of the Southern out-of-doors . . . the classic fragrance with the celebrated Southern 'sense of place.'"[36]

Although the concept of a distinctive identity seems exclusionary by definition, from the commercial standpoint, the more claimants and aspirants to a particular identity, the better. For example, the megamarketing of St. Patrick's Day has caused so many Americans to feel "Irish" that Dublin's tourism officials actually visited New York City to get some pointers on how to transform what had been a relatively low-key religious observance on the Emerald Isle itself into a rip-roaring opportunity for Irish-American tourists to get in touch with their real or imagined Irish roots. Meanwhile, a panel of British experts warned of the dire economic consequences of "an unmanaged" national reputation and urged their fellow marketers to learn how to "leverage the brand values of their country." Pursuing just such a strategy as part of an effort to target both national and ethnic identities, an ad for Tetley tea urged American Jews to "think Yiddish" but "drink British."[37]

As a matter of fact, southernness is a big hit in the international identity market as well. "Mississippi Mud" is manufactured in Germany for a company based in Scotland and marketed throughout Europe as an "American" breakfast spread, although it tastes more like cake icing than anything I ever smeared on one of my mama's biscuits. Elsewhere, London offers many opportunities for fine southern dining, including a restaurant called "Arkansas Barbeque" and a huge cantina, "The Texas Embassy," just off Trafalgar Square. Texas is marketable as both West and South, of course, and on a recent Saturday night the Italian town of Bellagio turned out in force for a "Texas Party," where a Gucci-scooting good time was had by all. Meanwhile, just across Lake Como at Tremezzo, dancers moved to a different but still decidedly southern beat at the "Jook Joint Café."[38]

All of this role playing may seem no more harmful than attending a costume ball dressed as Scarlett O'Hara or Gomer Pyle, but as both the history of the South and the contemporary global scene demonstrate all too well, what Eric Hobsbawm calls "the politics of identity" can easily become a deadly serious, even bloody, matter. Headquartered in Tuscaloosa, Alabama, the League of the South is dedicated to saving southern whites from "cultural genocide." Although it is now demanding reparations for the depredations visited on white southerners during the recent unpleasantness of 1861–65, the league has announced its readiness to give secession another try in order to "protect the historic Anglo-Celtic core culture of the South" that has "given Dixie its unique institutions and civilization." In their move to promote southern independence, league representatives have likened themselves to cultural nationalists from Scotland to Quebec who have called for ethnic and cultural home rule, insisting that "American Southerners have much in common with the Scot and the Welsh in Britain, the Lombards and Sicilians in Italy and the Ukrainians in the defunct Soviet Union. All have made enormous economic, military and cultural contributions to their imperial rulers, who rewarded their loyalty with exploitation and contempt."[39]

The South absorbed 1.3 million foreign immigrants between 1990 and 1998 alone and currently boasts the nation's six fastest growing counties in terms of Hispanic population. Like many contemporary right-wing movements around the world, the League of the South blames globalization for the growth of the region's immigrant population. On April 24, 2002, league president Michael Hill congratulated anti-immigration National Front candidate Jean-Marie Le Pen on his stronger-than-expected showing in the first round of the French presidential elections. A league press release noted that over the past decade, "there has been a huge influx of nonwhite immigrants into both Europe and America that threatens to engulf our historic populations and culture." "Should the Christian, Anglo-Celtic core be displaced," league spokesmen warn, "the South would cease to be recognizable to us and our progeny." Citing the success of other rightist, anti-immigration candidates throughout Europe, Hill called for "others like Le Pen to arise in America and from every corner of Christendom in defense of the common folks who work, pay taxes and otherwise provide society's backbone. . . . [I]t's time for the deracinated globalists everywhere to be sent packing."[40]

The academics who do most of the talking for the League of the South consistently deny the racist and xenophobic subtext that their statements often seem to convey. Still, the language they employ is too redolent of the rhetoric that fueled disfranchisement, Jim Crow, and a wave of racial violence in the post-Reconstruction South and turned Europe inside out in the 1930s for the group to be dismissed as just another bunch of professors behaving foolishly. Reporting from the Alabama state capitol, a Scottish journalist heard the aforementioned Dr. Hill speak "on the very steps" where Jefferson Davis was sworn in as president of the Confederacy and where George Wallace gave his infamous "segregation now, segregation tomorrow, segregation forever" speech. Yet, when Hill described white southerners as a "demonized" people "at war" with those who believe they should be "eradicated," the reporter heard chilling echoes not of Davis or Wallace but of the terminology employed more recently by Serbia's ruthless proponent of ethnic purity, Radovan Karadzic. Appropriately enough, the League of the South Web site now urges visitors to "stop ethnic cleansing of true southerners."[41]

By appearing to diminish national distinctions, globalization seems to have fostered a divisive and ultimately dangerous kind of identity politics in which other sorts of group distinctions are blown way out of proportion. If the South's more distant history underscores the potentially tragic consequences of this trend, the recent struggle by southerners to preserve, recover, or reconfigure their regional identity even as marketers move rapidly to commodify it, is in many ways an international and intercultural phenomenon writ small. By the same token, the at best uneven results of the South's self-exploitive approach to industrial recruitment should warn leaders of other nations and regions who pursue a developed economy at the expense of a developed society that they may wind up achieving neither. Yet, as with all of the rich, globally relevant experiences that the South's history offers, the crucial question is not simply whether people elsewhere in the nation or the world can benefit from them, but whether southerners themselves will finally prove capable of learning from them as well.[42]

Notes

1. C. Vann Woodward, "The Irony of Southern History," in *The Burden of Southern History*, 3rd ed. (Baton Rouge: Louisiana State University Press, 1993), 187–212.

2. Kris Kromm, "Southerners Should Remember Seattle, State of the South," The Institute for Southern Studies, http://*www.southernstudies.org/records/seattle.html*; *Independent* (London), July 22, 1995; *New York Times*, September 1, 1996, June 22, 2002; *Omaha World-Herald*, September 8, 1996.

3. Pronita Gupta, "The Art of the Deal," *Southern Exposure* 26 (Summer/Fall 1998): 31; for state rankings see Progressive Policy Institute, http://www.neweconomyindex .org.

4. *Birmingham News*, June 16, 2002.

5. *New York Times*, January 28, 2002.

6. Thomas L. Friedman, *The Lexus and the Olive Tree: Understanding Globalization* (New York: Farrar, Straus and Giroux, 1999), 283.

7. Michael Steinberg, "North Carolina Among Hardest Hit by NAFTA Job Loss," *Asheville Global Report*, June 14–20, 2001, www.agrnews.org/issues/126/localnews.html.

8. *Washington Post*, March 28, 1999.

9. Twelve Southerners, *I'll Take My Stand: The South and the Agrarian Tradition* (New York: Harper Brothers Publishing, 1930); John Shelton Reed, *Surveying the South: Studies in Regional Sociology* (Columbia: University of Missouri Press, 1993), 31, 41.

10. John Shelton Reed, *One South: An Ethnic Approach to Regional Culture* (Baton Rouge: Louisiana State University Press, 1982), 41.

11. Richard H. King, review of *Not Like Us: How Europeans Have Loved, Hated, and Transformed American Culture Since World War II*, by Richard Pells, *Southern Cultures* 4 (Winter 1988): 81; Sophie Meunier, "The French Exception," *Foreign Affairs* (July/August 2000): 107.

12. James C. Cobb, "European Scholars Can't Get Enough of the American South," *Georgia Magazine* 82 (June 2003): 33–37; Cobb, "Southern Writers and the Challenge of Regional Convergence: A Comparative Perspective," *Georgia Historical Quarterly* 73 (Spring 1989): 1–25.

13. William Faulkner, "An Introduction to *The Sound and the Fury*," *Mississippi Quarterly* 16 (Summer 1973): 412; William Lawson, *The Western Scar: The Theme of the Been-To in West African Fiction* (Athens: Ohio University Press, 1982), 3.

14. Deborah N. Cohn, *History and Memory in the Two Souths: Recent Southern and Spanish American Fiction* (Nashville: Vanderbilt University Press, 1999), 10, 21–22; Joel

Williamson, *William Faulkner and Southern History* (New York: Oxford University Press, 1993), 363.

15. Randall Kenan, *Walking on Water: Black America Lives at the Turn of the Twentieth Century* (New York: Little, Brown, 1999), 612.

16. Kenan, *Walking on Water,* 625, 613, 623.

17. Pico Iyer, *Video Night in Katmandu and Other Reports from the Not-So-Far East* (New York: Bloomsbury Publishing, 1988), 145, 137.

18. *Athens (Ga.) Banner-Herald and Daily News,* April 13, 2002.

19. Reed, *One South,* 186.

20. Joe Souza, "NASCAR Popularity Drives Racing into Big Market," *Laconia (N.H.) Citizen,* July 17, 2003, http://www4.citizen.com/news2003/july%202003; Dan Huntley and John Frank, "Darlington, Rockingham Fans Left Reeling and Railing," http://www.thatsracin.com/mld/thatsracin/directory/6075861.htm.

21. *Billboard,* June 2, 2001; CDI *Russia Weekly,* no. 257, http://www.cdi.org/Russia/257–15.cfm.

22. Elizabeth Rosenthal, "Buicks, Starbucks, and Fried Chicken: Still China?" *New York Times,* February 25, 2002, http://egi.irss.unc.edu/tempdocs/14:20:35:1.htm.

23. Rosenthal, "Buicks, Starbucks, and Fried Chicken"; Williamson, *William Faulkner,* 423; Bill Saporito, "Can Wal-Mart Get Any Bigger?" *Time,* January 13, 2003, 38+, http://gateway.proquest.com/openurl?ctx_ver=z39.88–2003&res_id=xri:pqd&rft_val_fmt=ori:fmt:kev:mtx:journal&genre=article&rft_id=xri:pqd:did=000000274989811&svc_dat=xri:pqil:fmt=text&req_dat=xri:pqil:pq_clntid=30345

24. Saporito, "Can Wal-Mart . . . ?"

25. Ibid. The author visited this store in July 2001.

26. Brian O'Keefe, "The New Future: Global Brands," *Fortune,* November 11, 2001, http//www.fortune.com/fortune/articles/0,15114,374152,00.html.

27. "Globalization and Cultural Competency: The Untold Stories," California State University, Stanislaus, http://www.csustan.edu/social-work/mchu/globe.htm.

28. Saporito, "Can Wal-Mart . . . ?"

29. *Financial Times,* November 9, 2002; David Rieff, "Multiculturalism's Silent Partner," *Harper's,* August 1993, 69; Drew Wilson, "The Long Takeoff," *Electronic Business* 24 (February 1998): 56; *Strait Times* (Singapore), January 3, 2003.

30. *Independent* (London), February 20, 2000; Meunier, "The French Exception," *Foreign Affairs* (July/August 2000): 107.

31. Friedman, *The Lexus and the Olive Tree,* 233, 235; Iyer, *Video Night,* 14; Jazmine Ponce, "Iyer Shares Global Travel Experiences," *Campus Times* (University of Laverne), May 4, 2001; Rosenthal, "Buicks, Starbucks, and Fried Chicken."

32. Rieff, "Multiculturalism's Silent Partner," 63, 72.

33. Diane Roberts, "Living Southern in *Southern Living,*" in *Dixie Debates: Perspectives on Southern Cultures,* eds. Richard H. King and Helen Taylor (New York: New York University Press, 1996), 86.

34. *International Herald Tribune,* June 8–9, 2002. See also http://www.slowfood.com.

35. http://www.southernness.com. The author visited Greve-in-Chianti in June 2002.

36. http://www.southernness.com/pages/giftshop.html.

37. *Atlanta Journal-Constitution,* July 30, 2000; Mark Klugman, "Defining Britain's Brand Values," *Marketing* (November 23, 2002): 28; review of *Shopping for Identity: The Marketing of Ethnicity, Publisher's Weekly,* July 24, 2000, 76.

38. The author visited Bellagio and Tremezzo in May 2002.

39. Michael Hill and Thomas Fleming, "The New Dixie Manifesto: States' Rights Will Rise Again," "Frequently Asked Questions," Compiled for Dixienet by James C. Languster, The Southern League of Alabama, copy in possession of the author.

40. "Alarm over Immigration Effects French Presidential Election," April 24, 2002, www.dixienet.org//s-press-release; "Freedom of Association and Preserving the South's Core Anglo-Celtic Culture," www.dixienet.org/positions/free-ac-htm.

41. *Scotsman,* June 8, 2000.

42. Ibid.; www.dixienet.org.

Globalization before Globalization: The South and the World to 1950

Peter A. Coclanis

In a recent essay on the manner in which globalization has affected the South over the past few decades, James L. Peacock, the distinguished anthropologist at the University of North Carolina, Chapel Hill, whose principal scholarly work is on Java, used a bit of autobiography to drive home a point.[1] During his 1962–63 fieldwork in a slum in Surabaya, a gritty industrial port town in eastern Java, Peacock and his wife lived with a poor Indonesian family. The family had twelve children, two of whom died from tuberculosis during the Peacocks' stay. According to Peacock, the place "really did seem like the other side of the world then," totally insular, totally out of the loop. When they left, they were sure that they would never see this family again. Cut to 2002. One of the children from the Peacocks' Surabayan family now lives in Durham, North Carolina, and works for Mitsubishi. His Javanese-Tarheel son went to high school at the North Carolina School of Science and Math and is now getting his MBA at UNC.[2] Can you spell *globalization?*

A few vignettes or, better yet, riffs on the South and globalization, demonstrate that the relationship that, in my view at least, goes way back. Let's start with Captain John Smith. How can his life be seen as anything other than "global"? In the interval between his birth in 1580 and the time he reached Virginia in May 1607, Smith had already labored as a merchant seaman in the Mediterranean and a mercenary soldier in France, Hungary, and Transylvania. Enslaved by the Turks and sent to Istanbul, Smith escaped, ultimately returning to Transylvania via a circuitous route through Russia and Poland. Before signing on with the Virginia Company, Smith also found time to travel throughout Europe and North Africa.[3]

Then there's the famous story of Olaudah Equiano (Gustavus Vassa), who, we have long been told, was enslaved in the 1760s in what is now Nigeria in West Africa and shipped to the West Indies and later to Virginia, before being sold to a British naval officer and toiling as a slave seaman on the "Black Atlantic." After buying his freedom, Equiano gained world renown for an autobiography he published in London in 1789. A wonderful story, to be sure, one that suggests nothing if not transnational flows into and out of the South. Nonetheless, this story, too, has a twist, for if the literary scholar Vincent Carretta of the University of Maryland is correct, Equiano wasn't born in an Igbo village in northeast Nigeria at all but in the rapidly expanding plantation colony of South Carolina in the mid-1740s.[4] Talk about wheels within wheels.

And at about the same time that "South Carolinian" Olaudah Equiano was writing, Christophe Poulain DuBignon (1739–1825), the son of an impoverished Bréton aristocrat, arrived in Georgia. As a young man DuBignon, a seaman–ship captain–privateer, had plied the Indian Ocean and then returned to France a "bourgeois noble," making his way materially from moneylending and manufacturing, as well as from the land. Dislocated by the French Revolution, he found a haven on Jekyll Island, Georgia, in 1790, where he set up a slave plantation to produce cotton, which provided a platform for a variety of economic activities all across the Atlantic world for the rest of his life.[5]

I could push ahead in time and discuss European émigrés (Germans in particular) from the class of 1848, influential New South industrialists and editors such as Englishmen James Bowron and Francis W. Dawson, and Italian agricultural workers and Chinese shopkeepers in the Mississippi Delta in the early twentieth century.[6] The point, though, is hardly to establish an identity between individuals and region, much less to equate immigration with globalization. Rather, what I aim to do is merely begin complicating and imbricating our analysis of the nature and timing of the relationship between globalization and the American South.

Given no honorable alternative, this entails, first of all, that we take a shot at defining *globalization*. No subject has been bandied about, toyed with, as much in recent years. While writing the paper on which this essay is based, I did a quick Google search, which took 0.05 seconds and resulted in 1,050,000 references. If much of this stuff can be characterized as "globalony," to use Clare Booth Luce's punchy term, which has recently been recycled by economist Paul Krugman, some of it isn't, for there is surely *something* identifiable and analytically valuable about the concept *globalization*.[7]

In a very broad way, we all instinctively know or at least *think* we know what globalization is. The problem is pinning down the concept in analytical terms. Rather than look to Louis Armstrong for inspiration here—when asked about the definition of jazz, the great trumpeter famously responded that "if you gotta ask, you'll never know"—let's take a shot at specification. Despite much vaporous blather, there has in fact been some very useful writing on globalization and/or its effects. According to one, the globalizers have "given a cosmopolitan character to production and consumption in every country." As a result:

[a]ll old-established national industries have been destroyed or are daily being destroyed. They are dislodged by new industries, whose introduction becomes a life and death question for all civilized nations, by industries that no longer work up indige-

nous raw material, but raw material drawn from the remotest zones; industries whose products are consumed, not only at home, but in every quarter of the globe. In place of the old wants, satisfied by the productions of the country, we find new wants, requiring for their satisfaction the products of distant lands and climes. In place of the old local and national seclusion and self-sufficiency, we have intercourse in every direction, universal interdependence of nations. And as in material, so also in intellectual production. The intellectual creations of individual nations become common property.

Moreover, the globalizers "by the rapid improvement of all instruments of production, by the immensely facilitated means of communication, [draw] all, even the most barbarian nations into civilization. The cheap prices of [their] commodities are the heavy artillery with which [they batter] down all . . . walls."

The quotes come not from William Greider or Edward Luttwak or Tariq Ali, much less Naomi Klein, but from Marx and Engels's *Communist Manifesto*, published more than one hundred fifty years ago.[8] These two "scientific socialists" certainly captured something of the spirit of globalization, even if they employed different lingo; the group I refer to above as globalizers, they prefer to call the bourgeoisie.

However powerful Marx and Engels's descriptive language, other, more rigorous or at least testable and thus falsifiable approaches are possible. For example, in defining globalization, one can emphasize change and process, and, in so doing, stress increases in the absolute size of transnational flows of labor, capital, services, and the like, or, more fruitfully, increases in the relative importance of these flows. Krugman for one looks to the relationship between the rate of growth of world trade and the rate of growth of world production as a proxy measure of globalization, that is, if the former is consistently higher than the latter, the process called globalization is occurring.[9] Far be it from me to criticize definitional concision—in principle, I'm all for parsimony—but reducing globalization to a quantifiable ratio of one sort or another is a bit exiguous even for my tastes. Rather, I prefer to interpret long-term growth in the relative importance of world trade, for example, as a manifestation and expression of deeper, more complex, and ultimately more meaningful qualitative changes in the structure, organization, and operation of economic life.

Moving to the qualitative level also entails difficulties, of course, most notably, analytical imprecision, even among the best scholarly and popular writers on the subject. In this regard, social theorist Manuel Castells emphasizes interdependence, scale, scope, and simultaneity, defining the global economy as "an economy that works as a unit in real time on a planetary basis," while journalist Thomas Friedman contends that globalization came into existence when "everyone" felt the pressures, constraints, and opportunities attending the relative increase in importance in world trade, and the "democratizations" of technology, finance, and information associated with the same.[10] To each of these writers—and I could cite dozens more to the same effect—globalization is a fairly new thing, a creature of the last fifteen or twenty years or so. Here's where our problems begin, or, from another perspective, where they begin to get interesting.

We can start this section by quoting another prominent authority, although I promise you that this one is not a Marxist or even vaguely *Marxisant* in orientation.

> Now up to this time the world's history had been, so to speak, a series of disconnected transactions, as widely separated in their origins and results as in their localities. But from this time forth History becomes a connected whole: the affairs of Italy and Libya are involved with those of Asia and Greece, and the tendency of all is to unity.

The quote is from Polybius, who died in 118 BCE, speaking not about capitalism but the rise of Rome.[11] A great quote, but, even I admit, a bit arch and a wee bit old.

More to the point, though, Friedman's approach to globalization is not all that different in a formal sense from Fernand Braudel's approach to the emergence of capitalism in the sixteenth century: both stress the qualitative impact of a particular economic regime on the behaviors and *mentalités* of everyday people and everyday life, although Braudel's terrain is obviously more limited.[12] Still, it is not only plausible but also readily demonstrable that world trade was growing in the sixteenth century and that technology, finance, and information were being democratized. To be sure, not "everyone" was affected by capitalism's rise, but then it is unlikely that "everyone" is being affected by globalization even today. Picky, picky, you say. It is foolhardy to equate capitalism and globalization.

OK, fair enough, but other writers have taken the reins from the great French historian and ridden much further, as it were, arguing that a truly global economy, marked by powerfully significant transnational economic flows of one sort or another and a clear international division of labor, was emerging in the sixteenth century, whether under European suzerainty or not. Another constellation of scholars doesn't go quite that far but is nonetheless convinced and quite insistent that a global economy had clearly come into existence by the nineteenth century. Indeed, writers such as Krugman, Williamson, and O'Rourke have focused on transnational flows of products, capital, and people and employed both quantitative and qualitative evidence—regarding the latter, they often draw analogies between the telegraph and the Internet—in arguing that the world was by many measures more "global" in economic terms between roughly 1850 and 1914 than it ever was before or ever has been since.[13] Geographer David Harvey focuses on the same period but emphasizes qualitative factors, particularly the radical compression of space and time that occurred during the period.[14] These are just a few of the concerns with which we must deal in taking on the Herculean task of considering globalization and the American South over the course of 350 years.[15] That is to say, roughly from the time of our aforementioned friend Captain John Smith to 1950, the year after another famous southerner with a fancy title, one William Faulkner, Count No 'Count, won the Nobel Prize in Literature.

What then to do? Where do we go (hide)? Obviously we're not going to solve the globalization puzzle here. All I shall try to do in this piece is to lay out an approach to the question of globalization insofar as it relates to the history of the American South by considering transnational flows of one type or another and certain qualitative dimensions of the puzzle. The hope is to marshal sufficient evidence to support the case that the degree of integration between the global economy and the American South was generally close (though hardly complete) right from the start.

One of the few things we know for sure is that the South—or, more properly, Britain's southernmost colonies on the North American mainland—was an expression of the outward expansion of the European economy during the early modern period. Whether one would call this outward thrust a manifestation of capitalism, of precapitalism, of the transition to capitalism, or of the so-called primitive accumulation seems at this late date anachronistic, if not immaterial. Whatever term one prefers, one finds in the seventeenth and eighteenth centuries sizable transnational, indeed, intercontinental flows of labor, capital, and entrepreneurship into the region and, with the establishment by Europeans and European Americans of institutions and production platforms conducive to plantation slavery, impressive product flows out.[16] In many ways, Britain's southern colonies, with the partial exception of North Carolina, by and large could be considered exemplary mercantilist entities, whose valuable agricultural and forest products—tobacco, rice, indigo, deerskins, and naval stores most notably—and high export/output ratios made both merchants and political authorities in the metropolis perk up and take notice.[17]

Data from shortly before the American Revolution demonstrates this point. In the five-year period 1768–72, combined commodity exports from the Upper South (Chesapeake colonies) and the Lower South (the Carolinas and Georgia) totaled almost nine million pounds sterling, which came to over 63 percent of the total value of commodity exports from the thirteen colonies during this period.[18] The South's export performance becomes more impressive still in light of the fact that the combined white and black population in the region constituted less than 47 percent of the population of the colonies.[19] As economist Robert Lipsey, among others, has pointed out, moreover, export/output ratios in the colonies were considerably higher at the time of the Revolution than such ratios ever would be again in U.S. history. Nowhere in colonial America were such ratios higher than in the South.[20]

Despite the fact that slaves constituted a large proportion (roughly 40 percent) of the region's population, the South also imported impressive quantities of goods on the eve of the Revolution. During the five-year period 1768–72 (legal) commodity imports into the South amounted to well over seven million pounds sterling, almost 48 percent of total commodity imports into the colonies as a whole during this period. Clearly, "[b]aubles of Britain"—T. H. Breen's phrase—and imported goods and commodities from other places were flowing freely to consumers in the region.[21]

To be sure, product flows are not the sole nor necessarily the best measures of globalization. However, population flows to the South from Europe and Africa were also extremely impressive in the seventeenth and eighteenth centuries, as were flows of physical, financial, and human capital. Lifting our gaze briefly from the material to the cultural realm, we find other powerful evidence of globalization as well. According to linguist Patricia Nichols, at least fifty languages were spoken in South Carolina during the colonial period, most of them of African or European origin.[22]

This basic pattern was recapitulated, albeit with some variations, in the period between the Revolution and the Civil War. As the region's plantation economy spread westward—scholars now view the plantation complex as a versatile and portable organizational form conducive to simple "knockoff-like" iterations—the South's early developmental pattern held true.[23] In a general sense, the South developed through space rather than through time, to appropriate a phrase from Drew McCoy, and, as a result, the region retained its export orientation throughout the period between 1775 and 1860. We long have known that cotton was the nation's leading export in the antebellum period, but the South's export dominance becomes more apparent still when one includes two other leading southern staples—tobacco and rice—in the export equation.[24] These three crops alone—southern crops but for a tiny amount of exported tobacco originating from Ohio—accounted for fully 55 percent of the total value of U.S. exports in the period between 1815 and 1860. During the last decade of the antebellum period—a decade in which just over a third of the nation's population, white and black, lived in the South—this percentage increased a bit to more than 56 percent of the total value of U.S. exports.[25] Imports continued to pour into the region as well, albeit often "indirectly" after a stopover in a northeastern port, particularly New York City.[26] For better or worse, the region's economy, or at least the commercial expressions of this economy, remained oriented largely toward the outside world, to which thousands of plantation records and merchants' accounts attest.

But how does the South stack up if we employ other proxy measures of globalization? Here the record is more mixed. Inflows of people from other parts of the United States and other parts of the world declined in importance during the days of the early republic and the antebellum decades. This is not surprising, of course, as slavery limited opportunities for free migrants and the (legal) closing of the external slave trade placed great constraints on the importation of more slaves. At the same time, capital continued to flow into the South: bankers and capitalists from both the North and from Europe included southern state bonds in their portfolios, and offerings of southern railroad securities generally sold well in the same places. Regarding the latter, investors typically preferred to finance railroads via bonds—rails and rolling stock could readily be seized and, thus, served as good security—while equity investment was more common in the preparation of roadbeds.[27]

Moreover, contrary to older notions, the South was not closed to outside ideas in the period between the Revolution and the Civil War. As a result, or, rather, manifestation of this, intellectual currents circulating throughout the Atlantic world—Ricardian economics and Romanticism, to cite but two examples—received wide play in the region, and technological transfers of one kind or another into and out of the region were commonplace.[28] If the South was not southern New England or Philadelphia in terms of innovation and inventive activity, the region compared well with most areas in other "advanced" parts of the world during the period in question.

Similar complications emerge if one looks closely at the region's political economy. What seems from afar a region committed to export agriculture, minimal government, and free trade on closer inspection seems quite diverse— there clearly were important urban, industrial, and Whiggish dimensions to the region—and rather conditional about its attachment to free trade. Regarding opposition to free trade, one thinks immediately of the sugar protectionists in the Old Southwest, of course, but by the 1840s we see similar calls for protection from the rice grandees in the South Atlantic states.[29] In both cases, such calls were successful, which doesn't mean that the South qua South should not be considered a "free trade" zone, but that its commitment, such as it was, was situational, arising from what might today be called "positionality" rather than first principles.

As everyone knows, the structure of economic opportunity in the South changed significantly after and partially as a result of the Civil War. War-related destruction to physical property, the emancipation of human property, and the traumas and dislocations attending the reorganization of the southern economy (particularly the agricultural sector) all played a part.[30] At the same time, however, other, largely exogenous, forces were also working to reshape the South's prospects. An integrated national economy, centered in the Industrial Belt of the Northeast and Midwest, was gradually emerging, a development that would have major consequences, often negative, for less developed regions adjacent to it, such as the South, northern New England, and the Plains states.[31] This is not the time or place for full elaboration, but think here of the problems arising from what Gunnar Myrdal long ago called "backwash effects," that is to say, the problems faced by indigenous industries in a less developed area when that area is integrated into a more developed region.[32] Sometimes such problems are short term, sometimes not, but doubtless there is considerable economic pain involved whatever the length of the integration process.

Alas, in the case of agriculture, we find another similar but even more momentous (ominous?) integration process occurring virtually simultaneously. Between roughly 1850 and 1914, the emergence of a truly global market in many agricultural products led to increased competition among farmers worldwide: wheat producers from the United States versus producers from Canada, Russia, and Argentina; U.S. rice producers versus producers from northwestern Italy, Lower Burma, Siam, and Cochinchina; U.S. cotton producers versus Indian and Egyptian producers; Caribbean cane sugar producers versus producers from the United States, East and Southeast Asia, and beet sugar producers from Europe; cattlemen from the Great Plains of North America versus cattlemen from the Argentine Pampas. Such heightened competition, during a period in which Ernst Engel's law (which in simple terms posits that the proportion of income spent on food rises less rapidly than income, once past a basic level of subsistence) was operative in many parts of the West, meant that both food prices and farmgate prices for many products dropped dramatically.[33] Even in a period of deflation such as that existing through most of the last three decades of the nineteenth century, one finds that farm prices fell much more than did the general price level. In brief, this is the troubling new economic world the South confronted after Appomattox.

The region's response to this world—and, more broadly, to *the* world—once again was mixed. Nowhere is this truer than in the agricultural sector, obviously the key sector in the southern economy until relatively recent times. Briefly put, we find that the region's two key export staples, cotton and tobacco, continued to hold their own in world markets, with rice, the third staple, falling by the wayside until well into the twentieth century when new production technologies and production sites, particularly in east central Arkansas (and the Sacramento Valley of California) helped the South/United States reclaim a place among the world's leading exporters.[34] Exports of cotton and tobacco were impressive during the entire period from the Civil War right through World War II. For much of this period, these two commodities alone comprised a large share of the total value of American merchandise exports: 30 percent of the total between 1861 and 1910 and about 21.5 percent from 1861 to 1940.[35] Although cotton production/exports in the West—again, particularly in California—

had begun to emerge by the late 1920s, the South completely dominated both production and exports of cotton throughout the period covered in this essay.[36] Clearly, despite the huge problems afflicting southern agriculture for much of the period, the region was still successfully exporting its two bellwether staples.

Moreover, net exports, export/output ratios, and the like—however telling—hardly capture the full story of the southern agricultural sector's degree of engagement with the world. At a conceptual level, as markets become integrated, it doesn't much matter if commodity A is actually exported or sold domestically: the price in each market is *set* in the *global* market. This is particularly true of fairly homogeneous commodities such as wheat and rice but applies to a considerable degree to other most agricultural staples as well.

Although we properly privilege agriculture in our quick run through the global economic history of the South between the Civil War and 1950, the region's manufacturing sector deserves attention as well. With all due respect both to the numerous manufacturing initiatives in the South during the antebellum period and to the surprisingly successful efforts at hothouse industrialization during the Civil War, the region's modern manufacturing history really begins with the creation of the cotton textiles complex in the South Atlantic states in the 1880s. Over time, the South developed a sizeable manufacturing sector, comprised of various and sundry industries other than textiles: furniture, tobacco products, food processing, and so-called forest industries, not to mention coal, iron, and steel.[37] Most of these industries did some exporting, and, at times (especially in the late nineteenth century), considerable quantities of naval stores and even iron were shipped abroad. Similarly, both American Tobacco and some of the independents demonstrated an early interest in export markets, though by the turn of the century—particularly after the creation of British American Tobacco in 1902—the proportion of U.S. manufactured tobacco that was exported dropped sharply, and American manufacturers increasingly focused their attention on domestic markets.[38]

By and large, only textiles were consistently exported throughout the entire period in question, though the "internationalism" of even this industry can be (and often is) overstated. Indeed, despite an interest in exports, significant exports at times, and some mills and commission houses specializing in exports—one thinks immediately of the Loray Mill in Gastonia and the house of Woodward, Baldwin in Baltimore in this regard—the southern textile industry as a whole, pace Patrick Hearden, was never fixated by, nor primarily dependent upon exports.[39] For example, in 1900—purportedly at the height of the southern textile industry's export "campaign"—only about fifteen percent of the total value of the region's cotton manufactures was destined for foreign markets.[40] This is not to say that the southern textile industry was not influenced, conditioned, shaped, and disciplined by world markets, only that such influence, conditioning, shaping, and discipline were reflected as much in domestic prices and in calls for protectionism as in exports per se.

All in all, the South continued to export a far greater proportion of its output than did the nation as a whole in this period. As marketing channels in the region transformed in the wake of the Civil War and emancipation, however, the value of "direct" imports into the South remained relatively small, and goods made in the industrial North increasingly pushed aside even "indirect" imports.[41]

Enough of product markets for the time being. What about markets for labor and capital? In both we find significant flows: labor out of and capital into the American South. Few processes were so dramatic or so important to the history of the modern South than the massive migration of population out of the region in the period from 1870 to 1960. If we use 1950 as our cutoff date, we find that during this period the South experienced a net outflow of population totaling just under four million (3,873,800), with the vast majority of the outflow coming after 1910.[42]

Not surprisingly, blacks constituted the vast majority of this total—3,258,600. Still, the nonblack population of the region experienced a net outflow totaling 615,200 over this eighty-year period. If we disaggregate a bit further, this time by subperiods, we find a net outflow of 860,200 nonblacks between 1930 and 1950, which means that there was actually a small inflow of nonblacks—245,000—to the South between 1870 and 1930.[43] Most of the black and nonblack migrants from the South remained in the United States, heading north and west, where they often found themselves competing for jobs against immigrants and children of immigrants from southern and eastern Europe, ethnic populations that largely forsook the South. What is clear, though, is that southern migrants and European immigrants were responding to similar global forces during the 1870–1950 period, forces that created greater economic and social opportunities in the North and West than in the areas they left behind.

And what of capital? Anecdotal evidence certainly suggests that outside capital was exceptionally important in the rise of the modern South. Luminaries ranging from Henry Grady to Vann Woodward to present-day neo-Woodwardians have stressed that outside capital came in aplenty, if only to establish economic platforms that would enable their owners, executors, and legatees to proceed with the main business at hand: exploitation, accumulation, expropriation, expatriation. What's wrong with this picture? Aplenty, in my view, for there is little hard evidence to support the "colonial economy" hypothesis associated with Woodward and others, that is, that outside capital and personnel, primarily from the North, intentionally distorted the southern economy in rebuilding it after the Civil War, reducing the region to a status analogous to a satellite or colony of the northern metropolis.[44]

To be sure, a good deal of northern and European (primarily British and Dutch) capital flowed into the South over the course of the 1870–1950 period, either directly or as portfolio investment. A considerable amount of southern land fell into the hands of outside individuals and corporations (particularly insurance companies); outsiders invested in southern state bonds; and transportation facilities, utilities, and mills in the region enjoyed access to a greater or lesser degree to outside capital. But there is little evidence that outside investors ceteris paribus treated their southern investments any differently than they treated their investments elsewhere. Conversely, much evidence demonstrates that indigenous capital—drawn largely from small, scattered, risk-averse individuals and intermediaries—was of greater importance to southern economic development and attests to the structural and entrepreneurial problems the employment of such capital imposed.[45] Indeed, if we assume that colonies are entities closely tied to parental units, the principal problem for the South—or at least for southern capital markets—may have been that the region was not colonial enough!

In terms of regional political economy—assuming one can legitimately generalize in this way—the South, or southern Democrats in any case, remained fairly consistent free traders throughout the period. To be sure, there were always individuals, individual industries, and individual subregions in the South seeking some type of protection—think sugar growers, rice producers, and textile executives here, for example—but, by and large, the South remained far less protectionistic than many other parts of the United States, particularly the Industrial Belt in the Midwest and Northeast. However closed, however "backward," the South may have seemed in other ways—in race relations, for example—the region, because of "positionality" again, was generally in the vanguard of trade reform, supporting Underwood-Simmons and, later, trade reciprocity, anticipating in many ways the world ushered in by Bretton Woods. The South certainly was to become much more protectionistic in the period after 1950, perhaps a sign that the region was, as locals might put it, "gittin' above its raisin'," but perhaps that damned "positionality" thing was to blame yet again.[46]

And what about socially and culturally? The South's retrograde racial policies, alluded to above, are well known, and we've long been told about the hold of antievolutionary thought in many parts of the region. That said, it is abundantly clear that such policies and ideas don't capture everything about the South's social and cultural development in this period. Indeed, broader currents sweeping the rest of the Western world—social reform, modernism, radicalism, and the like—had southern manifestations and expressions as well.[47]

How, then, do we conclude this breakneck pass at the question of the South and the world? We could go for cleverness and square the circle, as it were, by coming back to the South and Surabaya, the conceit with which we began: In the 1830s and 1840s Javan rice shipped from Surabaya competed with rice from the American South in the principal European markets. For that matter, we could go further back and link Java to the American Revolution—the British seized the island from the Dutch during the war and instituted some important, if short-lived, trade reforms there that hastened the development of Java in the nineteenth century—but I think you get my drift.[48]

Simply put, the South was born of global forces, and, if we think hard enough and look deep enough, we come to understand that the region, economically speaking, has remained in and of the world ever since. Prior to 1950, the economy of this world obviously didn't work "as a unit in real time on a planetary basis," so it wouldn't meet Manuel Castells's exacting criteria. But certainly substantial transnational flows of one sort or another came into and out of the South as far back as the colonial period, and, since the late nineteenth century, space and time in the region have been subject to radical compression. As a result, people the world over—from Igbo villages to Manchester mills and from Javan rice paddies to London bourses—have been affected by events, activities, and processes occurring over what Faulkner (to beckon Count No 'Count again) referred to as miles and miles of afternoon in the American South. Although the record is mixed in many ways, the South was global long before 1950. This being the case, we could do worse than to close by paraphrasing the great southern country-and-western icon Barbara Mandrell: The South was global, so to speak, when global wasn't cool.[49]

Notes

1. James L. Peacock, "The South in a Global World," *Virginia Quarterly Review* 78 (Autumn 2002): 582–94.

2. Peacock, "The South in a Global World," 586.

3. On Smith's early career, see Alden T. Vaughan, *American Genesis: Captain John Smith and the Founding of Virginia* (Boston: Little, Brown and Company, 1975), 1–21.

4. Vincent Carretta, "Olaudah Equiano or Gustavus Vassa? New Light on an Eighteenth-Century Question of Identity," *Slavery and Abolition* 20 (December 1999): 96–105.

5. Martha L. Keber, *Seas of Gold, Seas of Cotton: Christophe Poulain DuBignon of Jekyll Island* (Athens: University of Georgia Press, 2002).

6. See, for example, James W. Hagy, *This Happy Land: The Jews of Colonial and Antebellum Charleston* (Tuscaloosa: The University of Alabama Press, 1993), 15–27; Leo E. Turitz and Evelyn Turitz, *Jews in Early Mississippi* (Jackson: University Press of Mississippi, 1983); Robert J. Norrell, *James Bowron: The Autobiography of a New South Industrialist* (Chapel Hill: University of North Carolina Press, 1991); E. Culpepper Clark, *Francis Warrington Dawson and the Politics of Restoration: South Carolina, 1874–89* (University: University of Alabama Press, 1980); J. William Harris, *Deep Souths: Delta, Piedmont, and Sea Island Society in the Age of Segregation* (Baltimore: The Johns Hop-

kins University Press, 2001), 134–35; James W. Loewen, *The Mississippi Chinese: Between Black and White* (Cambridge: Harvard University Press, 1971), 9–72 especially; Robert Seto Quan, *Lotus among the Magnolias: The Mississippi Chinese* (Jackson: University Press of Mississippi, 1982), 3–11.

7. Paul Krugman, *The Accidental Theorist and Other Dispatches from the Dismal Science* (New York: W.W. Norton and Company, 1998), 73.

8. Karl Marx and Frederick Engels, *The Communist Manifesto: A Modern Edition* (London: Verso, 1998), 39–40. *The Communist Manifesto* was originally published in 1848.

9. Krugman, *The Accidental Theorist*, 73.

10. Manuel Castells, "European Cities, the Informational Society, and the Global Economy," *New Left Review* 204 (March/April 1994): 18–32, especially 21; Thomas L. Friedman, *The Lexus and the Olive Tree: Understanding Globalization* (New York: Farrar, Straus and Giroux, 1999), 59.

11. Polybius, *The Histories,* translated from the text of F. Hultsch by Evelyn S. Shuckburgh (Bloomington: Indiana University Press, 1962), 1:3.

12. Friedman, *The Lexus and the Olive Tree;* Fernand Braudel, *Capitalism and Material Life, 1400–1800,* trans. Miriam Kochan (New York: Harper and Row, 1973), xiv–xv and passim.

13. See Krugman, "The Localization of the World Economy," in *Pop Internationalism,* ed. Krugman (Cambridge: The MIT Press, 1996), 205–14; Jeffrey G. Williamson and Kevin H. O'Rourke, *Globalization and History: The Evolution of a Nineteenth-Century Atlantic Economy* (Cambridge: The MIT Press, 1999). On the telegraph and the Internet, see, for example, Tom Standage, *The Victorian Internet: The Remarkable Story of the Telegraph and the Nineteenth Century's On-line Pioneers* (New York: Walker and Company, 1998).

14. David Harvey, *The Condition of Postmodernity* (Oxford: Blackwell, 1989).

15. For an elaboration of my views on globalization, see Peter A. Coclanis and Tilak Doshi, "Globalization in Southeast Asia," *The Annals of the American Academy of Political and Social Science* 570 (July 2000): 49–64.

16. For a much more detailed account of this process, see Coclanis, *The Shadow of a Dream: Economic Life and Death in the South Carolina Low Country, 1670–1920* (New York: Oxford University Press, 1989), 13–110 especially.

17. Coclanis, "Tracking the Economic Divergence of the North and the South," *Southern Cultures* 6 (Winter 2000): 82–103.

18. The figures in the text were calculated from data in James F. Shepherd and Gary M. Walton, *Shipping, Maritime Trade, and the Economic Development of Colonial North America* (Cambridge: Cambridge University Press, 1972), 94–95, table 6.1.

19. The percentage figure for the South's white and black population is derived from data in John J. McCusker and Russell R. Menard, *The Economy of British America, 1607–1789* (Chapel Hill: Published for the Institute of Early American History and Culture by the University of North Carolina Press, 1985), 103, 136, 172, 203.

20. Robert E. Lipsey, "Foreign Trade," in *American Economic Growth: An Economist's History of the United States,* ed. Lance E. Davis et al. (New York: Harper and Row, 1972), 548–81, especially 554, table 14.1.

21. The data on imports were calculated from Shepherd and Walton, *Shipping, Maritime Trade, and the Economic Development of Colonial North America,* 113, table 6.3. On the eighteenth-century "consumer revolution" in America, see T. H. Breen, "'Baubles of Britain': The American and Consumer Revolutions of the Eighteenth Century," *Past and Present* 119 (May 1988): 73–104. For an examination of the way this "revolution" expressed itself in one part of the South, see Edward Pearson, "'Planters Full of Money': The Self-Fashioning of the Eighteenth-Century South Carolina Elite," in *Money, Trade, and Power: The Evolution of Colonial South Carolina's Plantation Society,* ed. Jack P. Greene, Rosemary Brana-Shute, and Randy J. Sparks (Columbia: University of South Carolina Press, 2001), 299–321.

22. See Peacock, "The South in a Global World"; Patricia C. Nichols, "Storytelling in Carolina: Continuities and Contrasts," *Anthropology and Education Quarterly* 20 (September 1989): 232–45, especially 233.

23. On the portability of southern plantations in the antebellum period, see David F. Weiman, "Staple Crops and Slave Plantations: Alternative Perspectives on Regional Development in the Antebellum Cotton South," in *Agriculture and National Development: Views on the Nineteenth Century,* ed. Lou Ferleger (Ames: Iowa State University Press, 1990), 119–61, especially 132–37.

24. On the place of cotton in the U.S. export trade during the antebellum period, see, for example, Douglass C. North, *The Economic Growth of the United States, 1790–1860* (New York: W. W. Norton and Company, 1966; originally published 1961), 66–100, 122–34, 233.

25. The percentage figures for both the 1815–60 period and the 1851–60 period were derived from data assembled in U.S. Department of Commerce, Bureau of the Census, *Historical Statistics of the United States: Colonial Times to 1970* (Washington, D.C.: U. S. Government Printing Office, 1975), 2:898–99; Lewis C. Gray, *History of Agriculture in the Southern United States to 1860* (Gloucester, Mass.: Peter Smith, 1958; originally published in 1933), 2:1030. Note that the data on cotton, tobacco, and total U.S. exports are from the former source; the data on rice exports from the latter.

26. For data on imports into various southern states in the antebellum period, see J. Smith Homans, *An Historical and Statistical Account of the Foreign Commerce of the United States . . .* (New York: G. P. Putnam and Company, 1857), 28–45, 51–53; Robert G. Albion, *The Rise of New York Port* (New York: Charles Scribner's Sons, 1939), 391. In the antebellum period, the only southern states to register sizable direct imports were Maryland and (especially) Louisiana. Note that the issue of "direct trade" often surfaced in antebellum southern politics, particularly in the Southeast.

27. On "external" investment in southern railroads, see, for example, Leland H. Jenks, *The Migration of British Capital to 1875* (New York: A. A. Knopf, 1927), passim; John F. Stover, *The Railroads of the South: A Study in Finance and Control* (Chapel Hill: University of North Carolina Press, 1955), passim; Dorothy Adler, *British Investment in American Railways, 1834–98,* ed. Muriel E. Hidy (Charlottesville: Published by the University Press of Virginia for the Eleutherian Mills-Hagley Foundation, 1970), 123–25, 192–93, 198, 203–13, and passim; Scott R. Nelson, *Iron Confederacies: Southern Railways, Klan Violence, and Reconstruction* (Chapel Hill: University of North Carolina Press, 1999), 20–22, 147–48; Augustus J. Veenendaal Jr., *Slow Train to Paradise: How Dutch In-*

vestment Helped Build American Railroads (Stanford: Stanford University Press, 1996), 201–75 especially.

28. See Paul K. Conkin, *Prophets of Prosperity: America's First Political Economists* (Bloomington: Indiana University Press, 1980), 135–67 especially; John K. Whitaker, "Early Flowering in the Old Dominion: Political Economy at the College of William and Mary and the University of Virginia," in *Breaking the Academic Mould: Economists and American Higher Learning in the Nineteenth Century*, ed. William J. Barber (Middletown, Conn.: Wesleyan University Press, 1988), 15–41; Michael D. Bordo and William Phillips, "Faithful Index to the Ambitions and Fortunes of the State: The Development of Political Economy at South Carolina College," in *Breaking the Mould*, 42–71; Michael O'Brien and David Moltke-Hansen, "The Expansion of Intellectual Life: A Prospectus," in *Intellectual Life in Antebellum Charleston*, ed. O'Brien and Moltke-Hansen (Knoxville: University of Tennessee Press, 1986), 3–44; O'Brien, "Politics, Romanticism, and Hugh Legaré: 'The Fondness of Disappointed Love,'" in *Intellectual Life in Antebellum Charleston*, 123–51. O'Brien's forthcoming intellectual history of the antebellum South demonstrates the degree to which southern intellectual currents fit into broader Western developments. On the economic "modernity" of the antebellum South, see, for example, Robert William Fogel and Stanley L. Engerman, *Time on the Cross: The Economics of American Negro Slavery* (Boston: Little, Brown, 1974), 1:247–57 especially; Coclanis, *The Shadow of a Dream*, chap. 4.

29. Coclanis, *The Shadow of a Dream*, 136–37.

30. On the relative weight of these factors in the restructuring (and relative decline) of the southern economy, see, for example, Peter Temin, "The Post-Bellum Recovery of the South and the Cost of the Civil War," *Journal of Economic History* 36 (December 1976): 898–907.

31. See David L. Carlton, "The Revolution from Above: The National Market and the Beginnings of Industrialization in North Carolina," *Journal of American History* 77 (September 1990): 445–75; Carlton and Coclanis, "The Uninventive South? A Quantitative Look at Region and American Inventiveness," *Technology and Culture* 36 (April 1995): 302–26.

32. Gunnar Myrdal, *Rich Lands and Poor: The Road to World Prosperity* (New York: Harper and Row, 1957). Note that Albert O. Hirschman refers to the same phenomenon as "polarization." See Hirschman, *The Strategy of Economic Development* (New Haven: Yale University Press, 1958).

33. See Coclanis, "Southeast Asia's Incorporation into the World Rice Market: A Revisionist View," *Journal of Southeast Asian Studies* 24 (September 1993): 251–67; Coclanis, "Distant Thunder: The Creation of a World Market in Rice and the Transformations It Wrought," *American Historical Review* 98 (October 1993): 1050–78; Gavin Wright, *The Political Economy of the Cotton South: Households, Markets, and Wealth in the Nineteenth Century* (New York: W. W. Norton and Company, 1978), 158–84. Also see Wright, "Cotton Competition and the Post-Bellum Recovery of the American South," *Journal of Economic History* 34 (September 1974): 610–35.

34. On the shifting fortunes of the U.S. rice industry, see Coclanis, "Distant Thunder"; Coclanis, "The Poetics of American Agriculture: The U.S. Rice Industry in International Perspective," *Agricultural History* 69 (June 1995): 140–62.

35. The percentage figure in the text was calculated from data assembled in U.S. Department of Commerce, Bureau of the Census, *Historical Statistics of the United States: Colonial Times to 1970*, 2:898–99.

36. For data on cotton production and the value of cotton production by state, see U.S. Department of Commerce, Bureau of the Census, *Sixteenth Census of the United States: 1940, Agriculture, Special Cotton Report* (Washington, D.C.: U.S. Government Printing Office, 1943), xiv–xv.

37. For a concise overview of the South's modern industrialization, see James C. Cobb, *Industrialization and Southern Society, 1877–1984* (Lexington: University Press of Kentucky, 1984).

38. See Joseph A. Fry, *Dixie Looks Abroad: The South and U.S. Foreign Relations, 1789–1973* (Baton Rouge: Louisiana State University Press, 2002), 110–11; Nannie May Tilley, *The Bright-Tobacco Industry, 1860–1929* (Chapel Hill: University of North Carolina Press, 1948), 331–45, 543–44.

39. Patrick J. Hearden, *Independence and Empire: The New South's Cotton Mill Campaign, 1865–1901* (DeKalb: Northern Illinois University Press, 1982). On Woodward, Baldwin and Company's success in exporting cotton textiles, particularly to China, see Mary Baldwin Baer and John Wilbur Baer, *A History of Woodward, Baldwin & Co.* (Baltimore: n.p., 1977), 36–38.

40. The percentage figure cited above was calculated from data assembled in U.S. Census Office, *Twelfth Census of the United States, 1900, Census Reports, Vol. IX: Manufactures, Part III: Special Reports on Selected Industries* (Washington: U.S. Census Office, 1902), 19–72, especially 25, 56–57, 65.

41. Fry, *Dixie Looks Abroad*, 110; Harold D. Woodman, *King Cotton and His Retainers: Financing and Marketing the Cotton Crop of the South, 1800–1925* (Lexington: University of Kentucky Press, 1968), 269–359; Edward L. Ayers, *The Promise of the New South: Life After Reconstruction* (New York: Oxford University Press, 1992), 3–33, 81–103; Ted Ownby, *American Dreams in Mississippi: Consumers, Poverty, and Culture, 1830–1998* (Chapel Hill: University of North Carolina Press, 1999), 82–97.

42. See David F. Sly, "Migration," in *The Population of the South: Structure and Change in Social Demographic Context*, ed. Dudley L. Poston Jr. and Robert H. Weller (Austin: University of Texas Press, 1981), 109–36, especially 124–5, table 4.5. On southern labor markets and population flows in the late nineteenth century and early twentieth century, see Joshua L. Rosenbloom, *Looking for Work, Searching for Workers: American Labor Markets During Industrialization* (New York: Cambridge University Press, 2002), passim.

43. Sly, "Migration," 124–5, table 4.5.

44. For an excellent critique of the "colonial economy" hypothesis, see Carlton, "The Revolution from Above." Also see George B. Tindall, *The Emergence of the New South, 1913–45*, A History of the South (Baton Rouge: Louisiana University Press, 1967), 10:594–606.

45. David L. Carlton, "'Builders of a New State': The Town Classes and Early Industrialization of South Carolina, 1880–1907," in *From the Old South to the New: Essays on the Transitional South*, ed. Walter J. Fraser and Winfred B. Moore Jr. (Westport, Conn.:

Greenwood Press, 1981), 43–62.; Carlton and Coclanis, "Capital Mobilization and Southern Industry, 1880–1905: The Case of the Carolina Piedmont," *Journal of Economic History* 49 (March 1989): 73–94. On "external" capital flows into the South, see the works cited in endnote 28. Also see Reginald C. McGrane, *Foreign Bondholders and American State Debts* (New York: The Macmillan Company, 1935), 282–389; B. U. Ratchford, *American State Debts* (Durham, N.C.: Duke University Press, 1941), 178–80; B. Michael Pritchett, *Financing Growth: A Financial History of American Life Insurance through 1900*, S.S. Huebner Foundation Monograph Series, no. 13 (Homewood, Ill.: Richard D. Irwin, Inc., for the S.S. Huebner Foundation, Wharton School, University of Pennsylvania, 1985), 20–71, especially 65, table 29. Note that data on interregional capital flows within the United States during this period are very difficult to get. One must often proceed indirectly to obtain even rough estimates. For example, many years ago Everett S. Lee et al. compiled data showing a sharp discrepancy between the proportion of U.S. wealth located in various southern states in 1880, 1900, and 1919–21 and the proportion of U.S. wealth owned by residents of those states during the same years. In almost every case, more wealth was located in individual southern states than was owned by residents in these states. The situation was precisely the opposite in some of the northern states, particularly in New York. Residents of New York owned a far greater proportion of U.S. wealth in these years than the proportion of U.S. wealth located in that state. See Everett S. Lee et al., *Population Redistribution and Economic Growth: United States, 1870–1950* (Philadelphia: The American Philosophical Society, 1957), 1:727–37. See especially table 4.6.

46. On the South's historical commitment to low tariffs and free trade, and its shift in the 1950s towards protectionism, see, for example, Alfred O. Hero Jr., *The Southerner and World Affairs* (Baton Rouge: Louisiana State University Press, 1965), 139–82; Fry, *Dixie Looks Abroad*, passim.

47. See, for example, William A. Link, *The Paradox of Southern Progressivism, 1880–1930* (Chapel Hill: University of North Carolina Press, 1992); Daniel Joseph Singal, *The War Within: From Victorianism to Modernist Thought in the South, 1919–45* (Chapel Hill: University of North Carolina Press, 1982); Jacquelyn Dowd Hall, "Women Writers, the 'Southern Front,' and the Dialectical Imagination," *Journal of Southern History* 69 (February 2003): 3–38.

48. On these developments, see Coclanis, "Distant Thunder."

49. The reference, of course, is to the song "I Was Country When Country Wasn't Cool," written by K. Fleming and D. Morgan. Singer Barbara Mandrell recorded the song as a solo and as a duet with George Jones.

The South and Economic Globalization, 1950 to the Future

Alfred E. Eckes

A variety of social, economic, political, and cultural forces have transformed the South, and indeed the American nation, over the last half century. None has been more significant than a new wave of globalization driven by pathbreaking technological innovations, expanding markets, and probusiness public policies.[1] They combined synergistically to compress barriers of time and distance and to accelerate flows of information, capital, and goods so that once-isolated communities and regions integrated into national and world markets. As these flows brought convergence and harmonization, the South became less distinctive. Gradually, it lost the competitive advantage of cheap and productive labor that had spurred regional economic development for much of the twentieth century. As a result, the South, like other high-income areas in the United States and Western Europe, now faces the challenge of adapting to a rapid and revolutionary turn in world competitive conditions. In the globalized economy of the new millennium, China and India, with millions of inexpensive but motivated workers, offer cost advantages even greater than the ones that once lured industry to the American South.

Futurist John Naisbitt was apparently the first to use the term *globalization* in a 1982 book focusing on the economic and social "megatrends" restructuring America. The following year Theodore Levitt, a Harvard University marketing professor, published an important article on marketing aspects of *globalization* that resonated with business leaders and gave oxygen to the word. While the word is new, the underlying process is at least as old as Marco Polo, Christopher Columbus, and other early traders and explorers.[2] British imperial historian A. G. Hopkins has observed that globalization has exhibited different historical forms and characteristics. He suggests four different categories of globalization for analysis: archaic (before industrialization and the nation-state), proto (between 1600 and 1800), modern (between 1800 and 1950), and postcolonial (from the 1950s).[3] Indeed, many of the features of pre-1950 southern globalization discussed in Peter A. Coclanis's chapter in this volume appear consistent with Hopkins's characterization of world globalization trends in the proto and modern phases, extending from 1600 to 1950. In particular, this applies to the growth of the Atlantic economy based on the exchange of raw materials and foodstuffs, like tobacco, cotton, and rice, for manufactures from Western Europe and slaves from Africa.

In a sense, as Coclanis observes, the South has always been globalized. But it is important to emphasize that contemporary globalization involves far more than economic interdependence resulting from trade and investments among nations. In the opinion of business strategists, globalization brings a fundamental shift in outlook—one that requires a global perspective rather than an emphasis on national markets—and it is synergistic. Changes in technology—particularly in transportation and communications—have dynamic and disproportionate impacts on other variables, or to state it differently, the result is more than the sum of its individual parts. In the late twentieth century, the jet plane, container ship, and satellite communications not only accelerated flows of people, goods, and information but enabled large businesses to run global supply chains efficiently. They learned to source inputs from a variety of suppliers in different regions, assemble products in other areas, and distribute the goods globally so as to satisfy customers eager to maintain limited inventories. Increasingly, business began to think of a world without boundaries, and Japanese strategist Kenichi Ohmae even suggested that the nation-state was a dinosaur preparing to die. Contemporary globalization also permits ordinary individuals to network and communicate cheaply, rapidly, and regularly, widening and deepening personal and cultural relationships.[4]

The South in 1950

Like many others of my generation, I have observed firsthand some of the important changes in the southern economy as it transformed and became integrated into the modern global economy. My father was a Yankee from New York, my mother from Confederate Virginia—the relatives considered it a mixed marriage. Even in the mid–twentieth century, sectional differences still stirred discussion among some of my relatives. In the early 1950s my parents moved to Marion, a small town in Smyth County in southwest Virginia that achieved some fame as the home of Mountain Dew and the last resting place of Ohio author Sherwood Anderson. That Appalachian region was renowned for moonshine, burley tobacco, one-room shacks with outdoor plumbing, coal, country music, radio evangelists, and blue laws. One of my most vivid memories is of the local Piggly Wiggly where we shopped. Piggly Wiggly is the Memphis chain that pioneered the self-service grocery store, but despite this innovation and an imaginative name, it came to epitomize the unchanging face of life in small-town America. Unlike Wal-Mart, Piggly Wiggly never succeeded in breaking with the region and establishing a national retail presence.

Aside from the main line of the Norfolk and Western, which still used steam engines to move coal to eastern ports, there was little evidence of economic globalization in Marion in 1953. In the decade before interstate highways arrived, I often stood on the street corner and counted the eighteen-wheelers that rumbled slowly up the main street of town—old U.S. Route 11—linking Tennessee with the mid-Atlantic region. The Greyhound bus provided our detailed information about the outside world—even delivering the Sunday *New York Times* the following Wednesday, three days late. Marion had a Burlington apparel plant, and textile jobs provided good wages for low-skilled Appalachian workers—at least far better than one could earn farming, and perhaps making moonshine. The generation of high-school educated workers who returned from World War II found jobs in the apparel industry and soon bought homes, new cars, appliances, and of course television sets. In retrospect, these workers were fortunate. They entered the work force during the post–World War II consumer boom and enjoyed relative job security. They did not face competition from low-cost foreign labor that today produces quality goods for the American consumer at discount prices. The devastation of World War II, high tariffs on many imports, and the costs of time and distance effectively segmented national markets and insulated the U.S. economy from serious competition.

The South: 1950 and 2000

To understand how the South has changed, how it has globalized, since 1950, one must compare and contrast the Dixie of 1950 with that of today, making use of census and other government data. The South of the 1950s relied on one-party politics, racial segregation, commodity agriculture (cotton, tobacco, peanuts), textile mills, and of course the Piggly Wigglies. In this decade before mass television harmonized common tastes, the South remained isolated and culturally separate. The eleven states of the old Confederacy (Alabama, Arkansas, Georgia, Florida, Louisiana, Mississippi, North Carolina, South Carolina, Tennessee, Texas, and Virginia) had roughly a quarter (24.2 percent) of the nation's resident population, then 150.7 million, and occupied 25 percent of the nation's area. A half century later, Dixie had about 84 million people, or 30 percent, of the nation's population of 281 million. With the addition of Alaska and Hawaii, its share of total land area declined to 20.5 percent. Out-migration was a problem until the mid–twentieth century. Between 1910 and 1950, an estimated ten million people left the South, a pattern that would reverse itself in the last half of the century. Between 1970 and 1978 the

South had a net gain of 3.5 million people. Obviously, with its abundant waterfront property and retirement communities, Florida was a major beneficiary of internal migration, growing nearly 470 percent, but Texas, Georgia, and Virginia more than doubled during the period.[5]

Per Capita Income

Economically, the South of 1950 was relatively disadvantaged and economically depressed. Before the Civil War the southern states had per capita incomes about 70 percent of the national average. In the postwar period and indeed in 1900, the comparable figure was about 45 percent of the national average. In the next half century, the Confederacy's per capita personal income returned to pre–Civil War levels, reaching some 69 percent of the national average by 1950. Heavy World War II defense spending in the South for equipment and training facilities had given the regional economy a shot in the arm. Nonetheless, in 1950 some states lagged far behind. Mississippi's per capita personal income was 50 percent of the national average, while Arkansas, Alabama, and South Carolina each stood under 60 percent.[6]

During the next half century the Sun Belt soared economically, increasing its per capita income significantly in comparison to the nation as a whole. By 2001, Dixie had reached 87.1 percent of the national average. Per capita incomes averaged $30,472 in the United States; in the South, $26,531. Virginia, the only southern state with average per capita incomes above the national average, was 6.4 percent higher. Perhaps this reflected the dynamism and urbanism of Fairfax County and northern Virginia. Not surprisingly, the more rural Deep South remained off the pace, particularly Alabama, Arkansas, Louisiana, and Mississippi. The latter, which had the lowest state per capita income ranking in the nation, was only 71.4 percent of the national average. Of course, poverty was not confined to the South. My county in southeast Ohio—Athens County, where President Lyndon Johnson announced his war on poverty—ranked even lower than Mississippi. This rural county had an average per capita income only 63.3 percent of the national average in the 2000 census, a reminder that pockets of poverty, which once characterized the Deep South, remain in Appalachia.[7] (See table 1.)

From Farms to Factories

In 1950 the South was a rural and agricultural region, heavily dependent on commodities like tobacco, cotton, and peanuts. It had a farm population of 9.74 million, 42 percent of the nation's, but these farms produced only

TABLE 1

Per Capita Personal Income by States: United States and Confederate States, 1929–2001

United States/State	1929	1940	1950	1970	2001
United States	$705	$592	$1,496	$3,943	$30,472
	100%	100%	100%	100%	100%
Confederacy	$372	$345	$1,036	$3,117	$26,531
	52.8%	58.3%	69.3%	79.1%	87.1%
Confederacy + Ky., Okla.	$380	$344.5	$1,040	$3,134	$26,295
	53.9%	58.2%	69.5%	79.5%	86.3%
Alabama	$322	$278	$880	$2,913	$24,589
Arkansas	$306	$254	$825	$2,869	$22,887
Florida	$525	$507	$1,281	$3,692	$28,947
Georgia	$349	$336	$1,034	$3,318	$28,733
Kentucky	$394	$317	$981	$3,104	$24,923
Louisiana	$414	$360	$1,120	$3,068	$24,535
Mississippi	$287	$216	$755	$2,596	$21,750
North Carolina	$333	$323	$1,037	$3,218	$27,514
Oklahoma	$454	$366	$1,143	$3,350	$25,071
South Carolina	$269	$301	$893	$2,963	$24,886
Tennessee	$375	$334	$994	$3,082	$26,988
Texas	$480	$430	$1,349	$3,576	$28,581
Virginia	$434	$458	$1,228	$3,653	$32,431

Source: Survey of Current Business 82, no. 10 (October 2002): 128; Survey of Current Business 82, no. 5 (May 2002): 45; Historical Statistics, vol. 1, 243–45.

23 percent of total national farm income.[8] A half century later the South had fewer farms, but its share of farm income had risen to 26.9 percent of the national total. Part of the story was the mechanization of cotton picking, which drove African Americans off the land and into the cities, and the industrialization of Dixie in the quarter century before 1975. In 1950 the South had only 15.7 percent of the nation's manufacturing workers. This rose to 23.6 percent in 1975 and to 28.3 percent in 2000. The South had created some 2.9 million manufacturing jobs net, or 81 percent of the nation's growth in manufacturing employment. In 2000 Dixie could claim nearly 30 percent of all U.S. production workers, and it accounted for 28 percent of manufacturing value added. (See table 2.)

While manufacturing was important to the South's economic boom in the 1960s and 1970s, the southern region, like the nation more generally, was diversifying away from factories and smokestacks. During the last half of the twentieth century the United States generated 87.3 million nonfarm jobs, and the South created 35 percent of them (30.5 million). The decade from January 1992 to January 2002 was an important period of transition during which the South created 4.3 million service jobs—health care, tourism, and the like—while it lost some 400,000 manufacturing jobs net. (See table 3.) Thirty-five percent of

TABLE 2
All Manufacturing Employment by States

State / Region	Manufacturing Jobs (data in 000s)		
	1950	1975	2000
United States	14,884	18,347	18,437
	100%	100%	100%
Confederacy	2,332.1	4,330	5,216
	15.7%	23.6%	28.3%
Alabama	213.5	320	361
Arkansas	74.2	176	251
Florida	95.0	328	487
Georgia	281.8	433	587
Louisiana	135.9	182	184
Mississippi	84.9	198	234
North Carolina	414.8	737	782
South Carolina	208.3	336	347
Tennessee	245.9	454	508
Texas	351.6	800	1,086
Virginia	226.2	366	389

Source: Statistical Abstract: 1951, 175–76; Statistical Abstract: 1976, 367; Statistical Abstract: 2001, 392.

the new service jobs (12.3 million) created in the United States during this ten-year period were located in Dixie. By January 2002, every southern state was more reliant on services than manufacturing. Alabama, Arkansas, Mississippi, and the Carolinas, which had more manufacturing than service jobs in 1992, had made that transition during the preceding decade.[9]

Labor, Immigration, and Student Exchanges

Undoubtedly, low labor costs and the relative weakness of labor unions contributed to the phenomenal growth of southern manufacturing, as scholars and business analysts have observed. In 1964, the first year in our data chain, 29.3 percent of nonagricultural workers were unionized across the nation, but in the South the figure was about half (14.75 percent) that. Unions were conspicuously weak in the Carolinas (North Carolina, 8.4 percent; South Carolina, 7.0 percent), where the textile and apparel industries had successfully resisted unionization. By 2002, the comparable national figure of union membership had fallen sharply to 13.2 percent. In Dixie the same occurred; Dixie averaged 6.3 percent, but in North and South Carolina unionization was only 3.2 and 4.9 percent respectively. The sharp decline of labor unions in the South, and across the nation, is partly attributable to globalization. In highly organized manufacturing industries, such as automobiles, steel, and machine tools, surg-

TABLE 3
Job Growth in the Old South, Jan. 1992–Jan. 2002 (data in 000s)

Unit	Jan. 1992			Jan. 2002		
	Non-Farm	Manu-facturing	Services	Non-Farm	Manu-facturing	Services
U.S.	108,084	18,151	28,670	130,871	16,947	40,908
	100%	100%	100%	100%	100%	100%
Confed.	30,278.1	5,166.7	7,434.2	38,567.2	4,747.1	11,757.4
	28.0%	28.5%	25.9%	29.5%	28.0%	28.7%
Confed. + Ky., Okla.	32,989.9	5,615.3	8,067.3	41,905.2	5,222.3	12,686.4
Alabama	1,657.6	380.9	338.3	1,900.5	332.8	480.1
Arkansas	951.9	236.0	206.0	1,154.1	232.0	280.0
Florida	5,301.1	485.5	1,662.4	7,176.9	452.3	2,869.4
Georgia	2,945.8	542.2	657.0	3,876.5	464.1	1,122.8
Kentucky	1,494.5	283.4	345.7	1,828.1	301.2	492.5
Louisiana	1,619.7	185.4	391.1	1,933.2	176.8	547.7
Mississippi	948.6	251.2	170.2	1,130.4	207.2	271.0
North Carolina	3,096.2	827.9	623.5	3,885.3	709.9	1,049.7
Oklahoma	1,217.3	165.2	287.4	1,509.9	174.0	436.5
South Carolina	1,517.3	371.0	303.7	1,829.4	320.0	464.1
Tennessee	2,210.0	509.6	524.4	2,720.1	468.6	773.4
Texas	7,198.1	967.3	1,808.2	9,452.5	1,022.8	2,745.0
Virginia	2,831.8	409.7	749.4	3,508.3	360.6	1,154.2

Source: U.S. Bureau of Labor Statistics, http://data.bls.gov/servlet/SurveyOutputServlet (August 21, 2002).

ing import competition in the 1970s and 1980s brought restructuring, plant closings, and layoffs. Labor unions succeeded in expanding membership in sectors such as retail and state governments, where foreign competition had little direct impact.[10] (See table 4.)

As students of globalization know, the process tends to accelerate flows of workers and migrants. At mid–twentieth century there were few signs of this mobility in the South. The South of 1950 was divided along racial lines between American-born descendants of European stock and American-born descendants of African stock. African Americans comprised about 22 percent of the South's population. Many of them had lived outside Dixie, having taken jobs in northern industry during World War II. In 1950, New York had more African Americans than all but four southern states. But the 2000 census showed the impact of the globalization process. While African Americans comprised 19.5 percent of the once Confederate states, Hispanics now accounted for 13.1 percent. Indeed, they were the leading minority group in Florida and Texas.

In 1950 only a small percentage of southerners were foreign born. While the percentage for the United States was 6.9 percent and reached 13.4 percent in the northeast, the South's foreign-born population was only 1.6 percent—and

TABLE 4
Labor Union Membership as a Percentage of Nonagricultural Workers

State/Region	1964	1984	2002
All States	29.3%	19.1%	13.2%
Confederacy	14.75	10.0	6.3
Alabama	21.1	15.2	8.9
Arkansas	15.0	10.0	5.9
Florida	14.0	9.6	5.7
Georgia	11.9	10.3	6.0
Kentucky	25.0	17.3	10.0
Louisiana	18.1	11.1	8.1
Mississippi	15.4	9.7	6.1
North Carolina	8.4	7.5	3.2
Oklahoma	15.8	10.4	8.9
South Carolina	7.0	4.2	4.9
Tennessee	22.1	13.5	9.0
Texas	13.5	8.0	5.1
Virginia	15.8	10.8	5.9

Source: Barry T. Hirsch, David A. Macpherson, and Wayne G. Vroman, "Estimates of Union Density by State," *Monthly Labor Review* 124, no. 7 (July 2001): 51–52; 2002 data from Bureau of Labor Statistics, http://www.bls.gov/news.release/union2.t05.htm.

three states had less than one percent: South Carolina (0.3 percent), North Carolina (0.4 percent), and Georgia (0.5 percent). Tennessee, Alabama, Mississippi, and Arkansas were not much different, although Florida had 4.7 percent foreign-born population and Texas 3.6 percent—all well below the national average. No wonder Mexican and Chinese restaurants, or pizza parlors for that matter, were few and far between in the South of 1950. That would change, as new immigrants introduced new tastes.

By the end of the twentieth century the South was becoming more of a melting pot, like the nation, attracting immigrants from many areas of the world. According to the 2000 census, nearly 2 percent of southerners had arrived from Asia, and Texas had more Asians (562,000) than any state but California and New York. Foreign-born people comprised 7.9 percent of population in the South, compared to 10.4 percent for the nation. But Florida (18.4 percent) and Texas (12.2 percent) ranked third and fourth among the fifty states, behind California and New York. Except for Mississippi, each of the states in the old Confederacy had more than 1 percent foreign-born population. Virginia had 7.7 percent, while both Georgia and North Carolina had 4.4 percent. By contrast, Pennsylvania and Ohio, often considered multiethnic industrial states, had only 2.9 and 2.5 percent foreign-born population, respectively. In the South and across the nation, foreign-born people concentrated in large urban areas such as Miami and Dallas, and rural areas had lower percentages. Nonetheless, Mississippi (0.9 percent) had slightly more than Montana (0.8 percent), while Alabama, Arkansas, and South Carolina all had larger percentages than North and South Dakota.[11]

Another important aspect of globalization involves the flow of visitors—such as tourists, businesspeople, and students—across borders. Because many major southern cities had no direct air links with foreign nations until recently, it is difficult to estimate the numbers of foreign tourists or business travelers who may have visited the region. Some airplane passengers arriving from Europe may have disembarked in New York and traveled to the South via connecting flights. Similarly, many visitors from Latin America entered through Miami, Houston, or Dallas and then took domestic transportation to other destinations. Good data does exist on the number of foreign students studying in the United States and their host institutions. These show that southern universities failed to attract foreign students proportionate to the region's population. In 1959–60 there were 48,486 foreign students studying in the United States, but only 11.6 percent of these attended southern universities. That pattern would change somewhat in the next forty years. In 2000 some 22 percent of foreign students studying in the United States attended southern universities; more than half of these attended institutions of higher learning in Texas and Florida. For a variety of reasons—including inadequate financial resources and the concentration of prestigious universities in other regions—the Deep South continued to lag on this standard.[12] (See table 5.)

Information and Communications

The spread of information is another critical aspect of globalization. Alfred Chandler Jr. and James Cortada have written a stimulating book about how Americans entered the "information highway" in colonial times and gradually developed technologies that expanded the reach of information across a continent and to the whole world. In the case of the South the postal service and railroads helped integrate Dixie into the larger union. This trend accelerated in the late 1950s with interstate highways, facilitating the flow of both goods and information, and new communications technologies. But until the mid-1950s, individual Americans could not communicate quickly and easily across the Atlantic and the Pacific Oceans. Submarine cables, dating to the 1850s, did permit exchange of coded messages, but ordinary people could not communicate cheaply except by surface mail, which took at least a week to go one way. Nor did early telephone service bring major changes. In 1927, commercial telephone service using high-frequency radio opened between New York and London. But this interactive advance was not designed for mass communications. Radio telephones were noisy, unreliable, and costly—forty-five dollars for the first three minutes.

TABLE 5
Foreign Students Studying in the United States

Location	1959–60	1979–80	2000–2001	2001/1960
U.S. Total	48,486	286,343	547,867	1,130%
Confederacy	5,621	65,671	121,072	
	11.6%	22.9%	22.1%	2,154%
Confed. w/o Tex.	4,047	41,255	83,337	
	8.3%	14.4%	15.2%	2,059%
Confed. w/o Tex., Fla.	3,317	29,336	57,971	
	6.8%	10.2%	10.6%	1,748%
Alabama	311	3,220	5,600	1,801%
Arkansas	107	1,328	2,649	2,476%
Florida	730	11,919	25,366	3,475%
Georgia	416	4,472	10,844	2,607%
Louisiana	815	5,546	6,400	785%
Mississippi	130	1,704	2,331	1,793%
North Carolina	628	3,709	7,957	1,267%
South Carolina	185	1,484	3,573	1,931%
Tennessee	450	4,499	5,835	1,297%
Texas	1,574	24,416	37,735	2,397%
Virginia	275	3,374	12,782	4,648%

Source: Open Doors International Web site, http://www.opendoorsweb.org.

The most significant improvement in communications in over a century occurred in September 1956 when AT&T opened the first transatlantic telephone
cable (TAT-1), using coaxial cables and microwave amplification techniques.
The number of transatlantic telephone calls soared—climbing slowly from
10,000 calls in 1927 to 250,000 in 1957 and then jumping in four years to 4.3 million in 1961. Soon large corporations such as Ford began using the telephone
cable to exchange information and coordinate their overseas operations from
the U.S. headquarters. Nonetheless, while telephone cables improved business
communications among metropolitan centers, large areas of the world did not
have access to the telephone.[13]

Satellite communications finally ended regional isolation and made the
emerging global village truly interactive. AT&T's Telstar, launched in 1962, carried the first live television scenes across the Atlantic, and in 1964 U.S. television viewers watched portions of the Tokyo Olympics. The real triumph for
global television came on July 20, 1969, shortly after the launching of Intelsat III,
which provided coverage to the Indian Ocean. A half-billion people watched
the Apollo 11 moon landing, which reestablished American leadership in the
space race. Communications satellites facilitated a surge in telephone communications. Intelsat 1 (Early Bird), built by Hughes and launched in 1965, had
240 two-way voice channels or one two-way television channel. But Intelsat IV,
launched in 1971, carried twelve color television channels or four thousand

to six thousand voice channels and had a capacity greater than all the submarine cables combined. The proliferation of cable and satellite capacity brought a sharp reduction in costs, which benefited business and individual consumers.[14]

One individual sensitive to these trends, and to the commercial potential, was Ted Turner, a flamboyant Atlanta entrepreneur. A former racing sailor and advertiser and then owner of professional baseball and basketball teams as well as a television station in Atlanta, Turner had a vision for global news. Seizing opportunities presented by satellite technology, he transformed a small UHF channel into a "super station" in the 1970s. Turner chose Atlanta because it was home and because costs were lower than in established media centers like New York. He turned to cable and the idea of a twenty-four-hour all-news station. By 1989, ten years after the network was born, CNN had a large audience in America and abroad, with satellites feeding viewers in 140 nations.[15]

Undoubtedly the new communications technologies facilitated the South's integration into the national and global economies. Yet available data on computer ownership and Internet access suggest that the South lagged behind the nation somewhat. In the South newspaper readership per capita is considerably lower than the national average, except in Florida and Virginia. Similarly, except in the same two states, the South apparently has been slower to adapt to home computer use and Internet access.[16]

Transportation

The impact of the globalization process on shipping was visible relatively early. For geographical reasons, southern ports have long connected a vast interior region, including farms of the Mississippi Valley, with European markets. Dixie's ports accounted for about 39 percent of total shipping tonnage in the late 1950s, with perhaps half of that going to foreign markets. That figure rose to 57.4 percent in 1999, reflecting the growing importance of the Mississippi River as a link to ocean shipping and the role of railroads connecting interior states to southern ports. At the end of the twentieth century, Dixie has twenty-one of the fifty largest ports, and thirteen of the top twenty. Four of the twelve largest are in one state, Louisiana: the ports of southern Louisiana, New Orleans, Plaquemine, and Lake Charles.

In aviation the South seems to have lagged behind the nation in the 1950s but advanced to a leading position at the end of the twentieth century. In 1950, New York's LaGuardia and Chicago's Midway were the largest airports, and among southern airports only Miami, a point of departure for Cuba and Latin America, was one of the most active, but it ranked far behind Midway or LaGuardia. But the arrival of jet air travel in the late 1950s made the South increasingly accessible to the global marketplace. At the beginning of the twenty-first century, the South had six of the nation's twenty busiest airports: Atlanta's Hartsfield Airport (1), Dallas-Fort Worth (3), Houston (13), Miami (15), Orlando (16), and Charlotte (20).[17]

Air-Conditioning Revolution

Until the 1950s a fundamental barrier to southern economic development was the hot and humid climate. In 1950 air-conditioning was a novelty in most southern residences, although many textile and tobacco mills obtained climate control systems before World War I. But air-conditioning began to proliferate after the development of inexpensive window units in 1951. By 1955 an estimated one in ten southern homes had some form of air-conditioning. This would transform the South, economically and culturally. It has been written that General Electric (the maker of window air units) did more to reshape the South than General Sherman. By the mid-1970s, wrote one historian, "air conditioning had made its way into more than 90 percent of the South's high-rise office buildings, banks, apartments, and railroad passenger coaches; more than 80 percent of its automobiles, government buildings, and hotels; approximately two-thirds of its homes, stores, trucks, and hospital rooms; roughly half of its classrooms; and at least a third of its tractors."[18]

Business Expansion and Relocation

Another way to find evidence of the globalization of the South is to focus on private-sector activities. In the mid-1950s when the Fortune 500 list of America's largest industrial corporations first appeared, only eighteen firms were headquartered in the old Confederacy. Five were in Dallas, and two in Richmond. Among the largest southern firms were Continental Oil (67) in Houston; Burlington Mills (70) in Greensboro, N.C.; Reynolds Metals (88) in Richmond; Cannon Mills (184) in Kannapolis, N.C.; and General Shoe (200) in Nashville. A large number of southern corporations were labor-intensive firms making textiles and apparel or shoes. But at that time the largest corporations operated from America's largest cities, such as New York, which had 134 of the 500 (27 percent).[19] (See table 6.)

Time would slowly erode New York's advantage. Twenty years later, another *Fortune* survey (1975) showed forty-two top-five-hundred corporations resident in the South. Of these, sixteen were located in Texas (nine in Houston), seven in North Carolina, six in Georgia, three each in Florida, Tennessee, and Virginia, and one each in Alabama and Louisiana. Mississippi and Arkansas had no businesses on the Fortune 500.[20]

TABLE 6
Five Hundred Largest Corporations

This table shows the ten largest corporations, according to *Fortune* magazine, in the years 1955, 1975, and 2002. It also shows the six largest Southern companies in the Fortune 500, not among the top ten, and lists their rankings.

1955	1975	2002
1. General Motors (Detroit)	Exxon (New York)	Wal-Mart (Bentonville, Ark.)
2. Standard Oil (New York)	General Motors (Detroit)	Exxon-Mobil (Irving, Tex.)
3. Ford (Dearborn, Mich.)	Texaco (New York)	General Motors (Detroit)
4. U.S. Steel (New York)	Ford (Dearborn, Mich.)	Ford (Dearborn, Mich.)
5. Chrysler (Detroit)	Mobil (New York)	Enron (Houston)
6. General Electric (Fairfield, Conn.)	Standard Oil (San Francisco)	General Electric (Fairfield, Conn.)
7. Swift (Chicago)	IBM (Armonk, N.Y.)	Citigroup (New York)
8. Beth Steel (Bethlehem, Pa.)	Gulf Oil (Pittsburgh)	Chevron / Texaco (San Francisco)
9. Armour (Chicago)	General Electric (Conn.)	IBM (Armonk, N.Y.)
10. DuPont (Wilmington, Del.)	Chrysler (Michigan)	Philip Morris (New York)
67. Continental Oil (Houston)	14. Shell Oil (Houston)	14. Duke Energy (Charlotte)
70. Burlington (Greensboro, N.C.)	22. Tenneco (Houston)	17. El Paso (Houston)
88. Reynolds Metals (Richmond)	37. LTV (Dallas)	18. Home Depot (Atlanta)
184. Cannon Mills (Kannapolis, N.C.)	48. R. J. Reynolds (N.C.)	19. Bank of America (Charlotte)
200. General Shoe (Nashville)	64. Coca-Cola (Atlanta)	26. Reliant Energy (Houston)
205. Dresser (Dallas)	104. Burlington (Greensboro, N.C.)	27. SBC Corp. (San Antonio)
	123. Reynolds Metals (Richmond)	30. Dynegy (Houston)

Source: Fortune Magazine, July 1955, 2–10; May 1976, 318–37; April 15, 2002, F-68.

The 2002 *Fortune* listing of the five hundred largest corporations demonstrates the degree to which southern business has joined the globalization rush and reveals the sweeping scale of corporate realignment over the last half century. Fully 123 of the 500 (24 percent) big corporations now have their headquarters in the old Confederacy, and these include two of the largest transnational corporations. Retailing giant Wal-Mart (1) in Bentonville, Arkansas, tops the list, ahead of oil-industry behemoth Exxon-Mobil (2) in Irving, Texas. Wal-Mart, the first service company to head the Fortune 500, a list once dominated by oil and auto companies, has nearly $220 billion in revenues, and its four thousand stores around the world take in as much as $1 billion a day. Wal-Mart's revenues exceed the combined revenues of the next nine largest merchandisers—Sears, Target, Kmart, J.C. Penney, Federated, May, Dillard's, Kohl's, and Saks. Two of these—J.C. Penney and Dillard's—also consider the South home. In recent years Wal-Mart has become the world's largest corporate employer, with 1.3 million workers at stores around the world, and it is the largest employer in all but two southern states. Interestingly, in 1955 when *Fortune* began its rankings, Wal-Mart did not exist.[21]

Who would have expected the world's largest private employer to emerge from the heart of the Ozarks, Bentonville, Arkansas, population 19,736? Founded in 1962, along with Kmart, Target, and Woolco, Wal-Mart concentrated on expanding in small towns and county seats rather than in the cutthroat retail environment of large markets. As late as 1970 Wal-Mart was not even on the list of the seventy-one largest retailers. But in the 1980s founder Sam Walton inspired many consumers with his pledge to sell American-made goods, and his patriotism appealed to small-town America. In recent years Walton's successors shifted the basic plan to one that relies on the sale of low-cost, high-quality imported goods (which typically have higher markups than domestic goods) to American consumers and the exportation of a retail revolution to the world's consumer markets. Last year Wal-Mart purchased more than $12 billion of Chinese goods for its stores through a "global procurement center," located not in Bentonville, Arkansas, but in Shenzhen, China. Wal-Mart continues to expand abroad, with twenty-six outlets in nine Chinese cities. Company officials plan to increase the number of outlets to forty-four in 2003.[22]

Retailing and petroleum are not the only areas that southern firms dominate. In commercial banking the South has three of the ten largest—Bank of America (1) and Wachovia (5), both based in Charlotte, and SunTrust Banks (10) in Atlanta. A comparison of the various states on the 2002 list further demonstrates the rise of southern-based business. While California stands first with fifty-six big corporations, and New York second with fifty-one, Texas follows in third place with forty-six. Virginia has sixteen, Georgia and North Carolina fourteen, Florida eleven, Alabama seven, Tennessee seven, Arkansas five, Louisiana one, Mississippi one, and South Carolina one. In the city rankings, New York City continues to lead (but with only forty firms), followed by two southern cities, Houston (twenty firms) and Atlanta (twelve), both of them ahead of Chicago (eleven) and San Francisco (ten). Charlotte is tied with Cleveland (seven each), and Birmingham and Dallas (six firms each) are tied with Pittsburgh, Cincinnati, and Boston. After years of being ostracized and ignored as a backwater, the South has established a presence high on the corporate hierarchy. With the arrival of corporate America, the South has gained an infusion of new talents and people with diverse backgrounds, and executives and their families have pressed for better schools, improved cultural opportunities, and of course the construction of golf courses. Business activity also brings a steady flow of visitors to this region—including customers, vendors, and legal and financial professionals—as well as tourists.

Foreign investors also rediscovered the South and contributed to its economic boom. In the nineteenth century European investors were primarily interested in minerals, railroads, ranches, and banking, and the bulk of investments were portfolio investments, such as the purchase of railroad bonds. Two world wars and the Great Depression interrupted these flows and shattered private investors' enthusiasm for portfolio investment. But after Europe and Japan recovered from World War II, their large corporations boosted export sales to the United States and then sought to establish a permanent presence in the U.S. market through direct investments. Foreign companies were motivated to locate plants in the United States by a variety of factors: fear of U.S. protectionism and other import restrictions, uncertain exchange rates, a favorable labor climate, easier access to technology, and a desire to locate facilities closer to North American customers.[23] Over the last quarter century the inflow of foreign capital became a flood as European and Japanese firms took over existing firms and constructed greenfield manufacturing facilities. European and Japanese automakers opted for the latter approach and focused many of their investments on the Southeast and border states like Tennessee and Kentucky. The last published data for foreign direct investment (that is, foreign companies having management rights or owning plants) in the United States concerns activity in 1998. At that time foreign companies had $923 billion invested here, and they employed 5.6 million workers. Interestingly, the eleven-state southern region obtained 31.3 percent of this direct investment (gross book value) and had 30.5 percent of the employment. With some 84.3 million people now resident in Dixie, 30 percent of the total U.S. population, the region has attracted a share of foreign investment and jobs approximately equal to its share of the nation's population.[24] (See table 7.)

Harmonization and Convergence

The data considered in this paper, gathered from the Census Bureau, the Bureau of Labor Statistics, and other official sources, generally show a pattern consistent with the globalization process. Over the last half century, as technology has continued to improve and as neoliberal policies to deregulate markets and borders have opened the vast American market to global competition, the South has become better integrated into national and world markets.

TABLE 7
Foreign Direct Investment by States, 1998

Unit	Gross Book Value (data in millions)		Total Employment (data in 000s)		% of All Business Employment
	1981	1998	1981	1998	
United States	$178,003	$922,951	2,416.6	5,608.9	5.1%
Confederacy	$64,605	$288,432	695.5	1,713.4	
	36.3%	31.3%	28.8%	30.5%	
Confed. w/o Tex., Fla.	$34,927	$162,233	442.6	1,068.2	
	19.6%	17.6%	18.3%	19.0%	
Confed. + Ky., Okla.	$69,213	$318,448	746.5	1,847.4	
	38.9%	34.5%	30.9%	32.9%	
Alabama	$2,776	$15,025	27.0	74.8	4.7%
Arkansas	$636	$4,188	17.5	37.2	3.9%
Florida	$6,295	$33,899	73.9	264.0	4.5%
Georgia	$4,558	$26,953	78.5	200.7	6.2%
Kentucky	$1,848	$21,083	26.0	93.4	6.2%
Louisiana	$7,872	$28,422	47.0	59.7	3.8%
Mississippi	$1,431	$3,694	11.3	24.0	2.5%
North Carolina	$5,543	$25,603	89.0	238.8	7.3%
Oklahoma	$2,760	$8,933	25.0	40.6	3.4%
South Carolina	$5,318	$19,958	65.1	125.4	8.2%
Tennessee	$3,747	$18,413	57.4	155.4	6.7%
Texas	$23,383	$92,300	179.0	381.2	5.0%
Virginia	$3,046	$19,977	49.8	152.2	5.5%

Source: Statistical Abstract: 1993, 799; Statistical Abstract: 2001, 792.

Within the United States this process has brought about a significant increase in average per capita incomes, as increasingly integrated markets produce a convergence and harmonization of earnings.[25]

A review of the major events of the last fifty years reveals that the most important technical innovations supporting globalization in the South include air-conditioning, jet travel, and satellite communications. But other significant factors are state and local support for economic development, particularly as demonstrated by improved roads, water, and sewers; tax abatements; and better educational systems. As other scholars have noted, southern states aggressively use local resources to recruit domestic and foreign industry.[26] Given the South's long-term and persistent commitment to economic development, it is not surprising that in 2002 six southern states ranked among the ten with the most attractive business climates, according to *Site Selection Magazine*. North Carolina was in first place, followed by Texas (3), Florida (4), Georgia (5), South Carolina (6), and Alabama (9). Kentucky, a border state, was in tenth place. Virginia, Tennessee, Mississippi, and Louisiana were among the top twenty-five. Only Arkansas, among the eleven members of the Confederacy, failed to rank among the top twenty-five states.[27]

The federal government also played a major role in globalizing the South, and not simply through pork-barrel projects and military expenditures. While the United States has been a giant free-trade area, at least in a legal sense, since the Constitution took effect in 1789, a host of structural barriers and impediments long discouraged firms and workers from taking advantage of opportunities. These factors included the absence of modern transportation infrastructure, segregation and racial strife, a poorly educated workforce, and protective tariffs, which sheltered domestic manufacturers from low-cost foreign labor.[28]

All that would change in the last half of the twentieth century. The Eisenhower administration successfully launched a program of interstate highway construction, which not only served U.S. military needs but facilitated the growth of commerce and tourism. The administration also modernized the nation's air traffic control system with new radars and airport expansions to accommodate jet travel. That age arrived in 1957 with the Boeing 707–120, a plane originally designed as a jet tanker, and in January 1959 American Airlines started transcontinental service from New York to Los Angeles. Improved transportation undoubtedly played an important role in the development of the South and its integration into the nation and the international community. With the arrival of the wide-bodied Boeing 747 in 1969, it became possible to move containers of air freight between major world airports in twenty-four hours or less.[29]

Along with improvements in infrastructure, the federal government provided leadership—particularly in the Kennedy and Johnson administrations—in striking down vestiges of segregation and promoting racial integration. Historian Gavin Wright has observed that turmoil over school desegregation handicapped the South's industrial development efforts in the mid-1950s and thus persuaded business leaders, however grudgingly, to embrace integration and racial justice. Much more remains to be written about the relationship between the globalization process and racial issues. Some foreign direct investors may have sought to avoid recruiting African American workers, thinking them less productive than others of Scotch-Irish or German extraction. Honda admitted to this in Ohio. But over time the civil rights revolution, and the willingness of the federal government and the federal courts to implement laws, ushered in a new era of racial tranquility that appealed to business investors—domestic and foreign.[30]

On the trade front, a series of presidents—Republicans and Democrats—from Harry Truman to Ronald Reagan and Bill Clinton pressed import liberalization under the auspices of the General Agreement on Tariffs and Trade

(GATT). While Congress, which was more skeptical of trade liberalization than the executive branch, declined to approve U.S. membership in GATT, the White House took a strategic view of trade policy as part of its overall effort to prosecute the cold war. Washington encouraged allies and former adversaries to abandon their reliance on foreign aid and earn a living from trade—and therefore moved systematically to open the vast American market to foreign competition.

A turning point for American business came at the end of the Kennedy Round in 1967, when the United States sharply reduced remaining tariffs. Commerce Secretary Alexander Trowbridge warned American business: The "Kennedy Round . . . represents a very large step toward the thing we've heard so much about in the postwar years: the truly one-world market." He added: "The American domestic market—the greatest and most lucrative market in the world—is no longer the private preserve of the American businessman." Over time, as inexpensive foreign goods gained market share in the United States, consumers did benefit from lower prices and greater variety, but imports hammered labor-intensive domestic industries such as footwear, apparel, and textiles. Unable to compete with cheap foreign labor (such as shoe and apparel workers in some Asian countries who earned as little as thirty dollars per month), thousands of domestic facilities closed plants, laid off workers, and reluctantly became importers themselves.[31]

Until the Uruguay Round (1986–94), in which the United States agreed to phase out remaining textile and apparel duties by 2005, southern politicians succeeded in protecting textile and apparel producers from low-cost foreign competition. In particular, they persuaded Presidents John Kennedy, Lyndon Johnson, and Richard Nixon to craft a complex multifiber accord to limit access to the U.S. market with quantitative restraints.

For many low-skilled workers and their communities, the new foreign competition had devastating effects—lost wages, joblessness, declining tax revenues, and psychological distress. To cushion these effects, proponents of trade liberalization have long advocated trade adjustment assistance to workers and communities. Unfortunately, such programs generally have not worked well. Labor Department data show that dislocated textile and other low-skilled workers often have considerable difficulty obtaining new jobs in a timely manner at wages comparable to those earned in the lost jobs. Many have less than a high-school diploma and frequently have difficulty reading and calculating. Only 61.5 percent of dislocated workers reporting to the government indicated that new jobs paid at least 80 percent of the former job's wages. Those living in small communities had particularly difficult adjustments.[32]

Many of the textile and apparel job losses have severely impacted rural communities with large numbers of poor, often African Americans. In South Carolina, for example, rural counties host 47 percent of the manufacturing workforce but absorbed 72 percent of the job cuts from December 2000 to March 2002, as plants closed doors and shifted to offshore locations, often in China. In my former home, Smyth County in southwest Virginia, ten factories employing 2,075 workers have closed since 1988. Five of these, with a total of 1,430 jobs, were in Chilhowie, population 1,827. The growth of service jobs has had limited impact on rural counties in the South, and as a result, many of the unemployed move to cities and urban areas where there are more opportunities. Government retraining programs offer little advantage in rural counties where few job opportunities exist and few entrepreneurs are eager to take risks.[33]

Globalization and the South's Future

Clearly the globalization process has had a major impact on the South over the last half of the twentieth century. Per capita incomes have risen relative to the nation, and flows of goods, people, information, and capital have markedly expanded. The South has become increasingly integrated into national and international markets. And this has created dislocations, especially for less skilled factory workers and their families and communities, and anxieties about future developments.

Rejuvenation of Southern Manufacturing

One can envisage two quite different scenarios for the future.

The first should appeal to chambers of commerce and to state-based economic development agencies. According to this vision, the South continues to globalize as foreign manufacturing and service-oriented firms relocate plants to the region — away from high-cost workers and rigid regulatory requirements in Europe — to serve the huge North American market. Meanwhile, a steady stream of technological innovations from American research institutions and universities generates new products and erases remaining barriers of time, distance, and lack of information. Science, technology, and education keep the South, and America generally, on the leading edge. Certainly, the success of the South in luring foreign investors into high-productivity manufacturing such as automobiles, pharmaceuticals, industrial machinery, and chemicals (including old-economy European and Japanese automakers—BMW in South Carolina, Mercedes Benz in Alabama, and Nissan in Tennessee) suggests some future possibilities. The growth of manufacturing inevitably creates the need for a variety of business services — ranging from computer software design to security and custodial services — and generates many other new jobs among suppliers, some of whom follow European and Asian automakers to America. As one state development report asserted, "manufacturing remains the prize sought by every entity engaged in economic development throughout the world. Manufacturing is a catalyst for economic growth." Manufacturing generally pays well, far better than retail service jobs, and supports additional jobs in services, construction, and agriculture.[34]

According to this logic, the South must continue to upgrade its educational systems, providing the knowledge, technical, and scientific workers necessary to support business needs. Moreover, if the South retains its "business-friendly" environment (including low taxes and state-based support for technical education) and right-to-work laws that discourage union organization, the region should remain attractive to transnational corporations desiring a presence in the world's largest and most dynamic high-income market. And, of course, executives from Western Europe and Japan may find appealing the South's mild climate and its varied recreational facilities, such as sailing and golf, accessible to urban areas.

Exponents of this scenario are not oblivious to troublesome global trends. They recognize the enormous labor-cost advantage of Chinese and other Asian countries and understand the challenge this poses to low-end manufacturing growth in the South. But they believe that specialty manufacturing, including technology-driven processes, will "survive and grow" in North America. The key is continued public and private investment in research and development, and in the education of the workforce. Also, the South may be able to build on its many Hispanic connections—especially in Texas and Florida—and benefit from the proposed hemispheric free-trade arrangement. Of course, some in import-ravaged industries, such as shrimp and catfish, think government should protect domestic producers, but they are in the minority. At present, protectionism offers little but stopgap remedies for a few minor industries. Unless there is a seismic shift in elite opinion, which supports free trade, or a grassroots rebellion in a presidential election, the nation seems committed to policies that will encourage economic globalization.[35]

Race to the Bottom: Part I

The alternative scenario is much more pessimistic. It hypothesizes a race to the bottom for skilled and unskilled workers in high-income countries, as the market-driven globalization process forces business to continue cutting costs so as to generate profits and stockholder value. This doomsday scenario has several distinct phases, involving manufacturing, back-office processes, and research and technological innovation.

The first phase is already far advanced in labor-intensive, low-skilled manufacturing, particularly apparel and footwear. These American industries have been hollowed out as domestic companies abandon domestic manufacturing and either set up foreign operations or outsource to subcontractors in Asian countries. Many of the firms that attempt this strategy become "virtual" corporations—designing and marketing imported merchandise. Beginning in the late 1950s and accelerating in the 1980s and 1990s, particularly after approval of the North American Free Trade Agreement (NAFTA), domestic producers found they could not compete with cheap foreign production. As globalization and trade liberalization opened the American market to foreign competition, plants began to close and firms declared bankruptcy. The survivors, or their successors, became importers. Robert Scott, an economist with the Economic Policy Institute, has estimated that trade-related job losses cost over three million jobs in the period 1994–2000. Of these, 954,218 (31.3 percent) were lost in Dixie. Separately, Washington economist Charles McMillion has analyzed government data and concluded that in the 86 months from December 1994 to February 2002, NAFTA cost 444,000 U.S. apparel jobs and 243,000 textile jobs (687,000 total), far more than the 158,000 textile and apparel jobs lost in the 108 months after December 1985. Seven southern states—Alabama, Georgia, Mississippi, North Carolina, South Carolina, Tennessee, and Texas—lost 385,000 of these positions. Interestingly, many of the factory jobs that moved first to Mexico in search of lower labor costs are now moving on to destinations in Southeast and East Asia—Indonesia, Vietnam, Bangladesh, and interior China—where monthly wages approach thirty dollars per month.[36] (See table 8.)

To what extent will the transplant automobile industry that established itself in Alabama, Kentucky, South Carolina, and Tennessee follow the textile and apparel industry in pursuit of the cheapest labor? Obviously, the industries are very different. Apparel plants can move virtually overnight, while the automobile industry is capital intensive and requires a complex network of suppliers. Suppliers to foreign automakers continue to invest in U.S. plants and facilities in order to maintain traditional supplier-customer relationships. But if the example of Honda in Ohio is any guide, the suppliers will be under constant pressure to cut costs and inevitably will search for the cheapest labor compatible with their customer's requirements. Honda supplier T. S. Trim, which makes seat covers for Honda vehicles, does sewing in both Appalachia and in Mexico. Over time it is likely that the subcontractors will hollow out their operations and extend their supply chains in efforts to access the world's cheapest labor—in China, Vietnam, and elsewhere. As the automakers gain experience in China, they too may choose to assemble cheaper lines there and supply the North American market from Asia.

Educated elites are tempted to explain the decline of manufacturing and the shift to services as part of the inevitable "creative destruction" process associated with capitalism. Until recently, conventional wisdom held that expanding

TABLE 8
Textile and Apparel Industry Employment, Jan. 1994–Jan. 2002 (data in 000s)

Unit	January 1994			January 2002		
	Textiles	Apparel	Total	Textiles	Apparel	Total
United States	673.0	971.0	1,644.0	440.0	534.0	974.0 (−674)
Alabama	42.9	52.5	95.4	33.9	21.2	55.1 (−40.3)
Georgia	111.2	56.1	167.3	89.4	17.3	106.7 (−60.6)
Mississippi	6.6	33.4	40.0	2.8	11.1	13.9 (−26.1)
North Carolina	204.6	70.1	274.7	120.6	28.7	149.3 (−125.4)
South Carolina	91.5	34.8	126.3	60.3	13.3	73.6 (−52.7)
Tennessee	22.2	57.4	79.6	13.0	17.8	30.8 (−48.8)
Texas	—	65.2	65.2	—	34.1	34.1 (−31.1)

Source: U.S. Bureau of Labor Statistics, State and Area Employment, Hours, and Earnings, Series ID SAS0100004230021, http://data.bls.gov/serlet/SurveyOUtputServlet?jrunsessionid=1020459978212343925 (data was extracted from these online series on May 2, 2002: SAS1300004220021 and SAS1300004230021). See also U.S. Bureau of Labor Statistics, "Textile Plant Employment in the Southeast: First Quarter 2002," news Release, no. 9305, July 18, 2002.

service industries would take up the employment slack from manufacturing's decline. Workers only needed to upgrade skills and improve education levels to change jobs successfully, while global competitive forces continued to restructure the marketplace. As table 7 indicates, the South has generated millions of new service jobs at a time when it was losing manufacturing jobs.

But recent developments suggest that better-educated residents of the South and nation have little reason for complacency in the age of globalization. Already some of them have received pink slips and face job dislocations as their positions move overseas. In efforts to remain competitive, many large transnational firms have begun to move research and backroom operations (non-customer-related) offshore in search of well-trained, English-speaking professionals prepared to work for a fraction of American wages. Foreign engineers, scientists, accountants, software designers, and even lawyers are benefiting from global cost cutting. General Electric, one of the largest transnational corporations, is a leader in this type of outsourcing. Company officials have promised to cut ten billion dollars in backroom costs over the next three years by moving substantial scientific, engineering, and backroom activities to cheap labor countries such as India that have large quantities of college-educated, English-speaking professionals. Indian centers process some 60 percent of GE accounts, involving six million invoices annually, at a savings estimated at $275 million.[37]

Another country benefiting from the globalization of services is the Philippines. In December 2002, this writer toured a call center in suburban Manila where seven hundred highly motivated Philippine college graduates responded to calls and electronic messages from customers in North America. They provided technical assistance to owners of Minolta digital cameras and Black and Decker appliances, as well as to customers of Dannon yogurt, JVC electronics, and a major oil company credit card. In a modern office building, equipped with a cafeteria and a health-care center, the Philippine workers worked a night shift that corresponded to daytime in North America. They earned the equivalent of two hundred dollars per month and had low worker turnover because of the general scarcity of white-collar and professional jobs. The center afforded clients a substantial cost savings over similar call centers in the United States.

Race to the Bottom: Part II

How will the emergence of a global market for such white-collar and professional jobs impact the South? Because U.S. compensation costs are higher than in low-income countries, factor-price equalization theory suggests that many service jobs not tied to location may move overseas. And growing competition from foreign professionals could undercut efforts of U.S. service workers to boost incomes. According to Forrester Research, a Cambridge, Massachusetts, consulting firm, U.S. employers may transfer 3.3 million white-collar service jobs and $136 billion in wages overseas in the next fifteen years, and in the process achieve substantial cost savings. Of 700 service-job categories, Forrester anticipates that 550 will experience offshore outsourcing. These include not only backroom and customer call centers, but also many professional positions in technology, law, art, architecture, life sciences, and business management.[38]

Already some major corporations headquartered in the South—such as Wal-Mart, Bank of America, Dell Computer, and Delta Airlines—are experimenting with or engaged in overseas outsourcing. Wal-Mart, a retailer that once took pride in selling American-made merchandise, now concentrates on selling low-cost imported merchandise, much of it from China. Last year, Wal-Mart imported some twelve billion dollars worth of Chinese goods, an expenditure estimated to have created—directly and indirectly—twelve million Chinese job opportunities. The retail giant also makes use of foreign call centers to serve U.S. customers. Bank of America, headquartered in Charlotte, is outsourcing technology operations to India, where technical workers earn up to ten thousand dollars, about one-tenth of comparable U.S. salaries. According to a *BusinessWeek* cover story, Bank of America has slashed some 4,700 of its tech and backroom jobs. One-third of these will go to India, others perhaps to Eastern Europe and other locations.[39]

In Texas a number of large technology-related firms, such as Dell Computer, Intel, and Computer Sciences Corporation, have been cutting back professional employment while expanding in China, India, and Russia. *India Today* reports that "more than a quarter of the Fortune 500 companies"—including General Electric, American Express, Citibank and AT&T—are "shifting their back-office operations to India." With wages about one-tenth of those in the United States, the decision to relocate a call center to India translates into savings of about thirty thousand dollars per year for every call center employee. Delta Airlines has contracted with Sykes Enterprises, of Tampa, and Wipro Ltd. to open airline call centers in the Philippines and India with some six thousand employees. The airline estimates it would save twelve million to fifteen million dollars annually, and even greater savings and productivity gains could occur if Delta closes its high-cost U.S. and European call centers.[40]

The Sykes story suggests another way that globalization is negatively impacting the rural South. A Tampa-based company, Sykes has roots in rural America where it established call centers for a variety of domestic clients, including credit card and high-tech companies. At facilities in Palatka and Marianna, Florida, for example, Sykes found cheap labor; workers were prepared to accept starting wages of $7.25 per hour because they had few job alternatives. In such circumstances, Sykes frequently obtained five million dollars worth of incentives from local communities for bringing jobs to rural areas. But with technological advances and competitors moving abroad to access even cheaper labor, Sykes shifted its strategy. It has begun to shutter rural call centers in the United States and to open new customer centers in the Philippines, Costa Rica, and India, where workers earn 60 percent less than U.S. employees.[41]

Convergys, the international leader in call centers and integrated bill and employee care facilities, which began as a spin-off of Cincinnati Bell in 1998, is on an aggressive expansion plan in India. It runs the biggest call center in India, employing 2,600, and plans to open five other facilities in the next three years. Meanwhile, it is closing high-cost facilities in Western Europe, and employees in rural southern towns, such as Jacksonville, N.C., fear their jobs may be eliminated as expansion overseas proceeds. In February 2003, Office Depot, the world's leading seller of office products, based in Delray Beach, Florida, signed a contract with Convergys to outsource health and welfare benefits and leave of absence administration services for approximately thirty-seven thousand U.S. employees. A news release did not disclose which facility would service the

Office Depot account, but overseas customer service centers are equipped to handle such activities.[42]

Nor is the outsourcing of service and back-office activities limited to U.S.-based firms. Siemens Energy of Alpharetta, Georgia, an affiliate of a German transnational corporation, contracts with Infosys Technologies Ltd., India's second-largest software company, for order entry, sales, and marketing systems. Infosys also offers U.S. corporations "low-margin, high-volume services including accounting, finance, and call centers." A service that might cost twenty-seven dollars per hour in Georgia is done for a fraction of that in India.[43]

The anecdotal evidence suggests that a new pattern is emerging—one that some critics may label an upscale version of the race to the bottom. In the earlier phase, which involved manufacturing, low-skilled jobs first moved from the old manufacturing belt in the northeast and Midwest of the United States to Dixie to avoid labor unions and cut costs. In the process this migration of manufacturing helped raise per capita state incomes in southern states close to the national average by end the end of the twentieth century. But as recent events suggest, Dixie was not the final destination. Because low-skilled labor is a fungible commodity, these jobs were destined to move on to Mexico, or China, as soon as technological innovations and trade liberalization made it feasible for business to access cheaper labor in developing countries. In the most recent phase, one that began near the opening of the twenty-first century, many highly skilled positions joined the global race to the bottom, moving to cheap labor countries with an abundance of English-speaking, college-educated professionals.

Is Globalization Sustainable?

In an increasingly integrated, open, and volatile global economy, there are few certainties. But the current pattern of globalization could prove unsustainable for a variety of reasons. One possibility is that dislocated and dissatisfied workers in high-income countries will successfully exert pressure through the democratic political process to reestablish border barriers and protect the jobs of high-income workers. Already some state legislators are moving to bar the outsourcing of public contracts, but such buy-America restrictions may prove incompatible with U.S. obligations under the World Trade Organization. The offshore movement of jobs also has become an issue in the 2004 presidential campaign. Many in the import-competing business community, as well as in labor unions, support measures to offset China's cheap labor advantage. Some manufacturers believe that China maintains an undervalued currency to promote exports, in effect subsidizing them. The Bush administration and the European Union have urged China to revalue its currency. Others in

Congress say currency adjustment would do too little to counter cheap Chinese labor, and they favor tariff increases on Chinese goods to offset social and environmental costs.

Epidemics, terrorism, and asymmetrical warfare may also play a role in discouraging the current pattern of globalization by so disrupting the global supply chain and fragmenting markets that corporations give less weight to cost advantages in sourcing work. Domestic manufacturers point out that they have several advantages over cheap imports. For example, domestic firms respond more quickly to orders in the textile and apparel industry, a time-sensitive fashion business. Moreover, U.S. producers need not worry about costly delays as authorities employ intrusive and time-consuming examinations of containers to protect against terrorism. The domestic automobile industry, which relies heavily on imported components, might also benefit from a shorter supply chain. Service providers, however, because they rely on electronic communications and do not depend on the clearance of cargoes at ports, may be less vulnerable to the transportation disruptions associated with terrorism and its countermeasures. But they may be more vulnerable to theft, sabotage, hacking, and loss of confidential information if they outsource to cheap-labor countries like Pakistan, Russia, and the Philippines, which may have inadequate controls.[44]

A third problem also could prove serious. America's appetite for inexpensive but high-quality imports has fueled the contemporary age of globalization, but this pattern may not be sustainable financially. For more than twenty years the United States has run balance of trade and current account deficits, as imports of goods and services have exceeded exports and earnings. The merchandise deficit was $484.4 billion in 2002. To sustain the payments system the United States must attract some $500 billion annually in foreign capital merely to finance the accumulated $2 trillion in international indebtedness resulting from years of current account deficits (presently over $430 billion per annum). An overdue correction in the value of the dollar—perhaps as much as 50 percent—to restore balance in our international accounts could give new life to American-based industry and to export-driven growth. But the dollar must fall against the currencies of developing countries like China if exchange depreciation is to make production in North America more cost competitive and imports more expensive.

How might these changing circumstances impact the American South? It is difficult to tell. Over the last half century, the globalization process has slowly chipped away at the South's most enticing competitive advantage—relatively cheap and productive labor. Instead, the South has become more homogenized and risks losing its distinctive regional identity. With improvements in communications and transportation have come accelerated flows of people, goods, information, and capital. As the South has integrated into the global village, accents have faded, tastes changed (burritos and pizza now rival fried chicken in some areas), the quality of educational institutions improved, and racial tensions subsided. Twenty years ago, before the term globalization appeared, economist Mancur Olson predicted that the South would "fall again . . . . With a per capita income similar to the rest of the country," the South would lose its "regional peculiarities." The American South has become more diverse, more prosperous, and more like the larger American nation—vulnerable to the changing winds and fashions of the global marketplace. Ironically, the economic advantages that the South once enjoyed, and that fueled the remarkable growth of the post–World War II era, have now fueled the growth of China in manufacturing and India in software and backroom services.[45]

Notes

1. In this paper I refer to the South, and Dixie, as the eleven states of the Confederacy. Many of the tables also include data for Kentucky and Oklahoma, sometimes considered part of the South.

2. John Naisbitt, *Megatrends: Ten New Directions Transforming Our Lives* (New York: Warner, 1982), 65, 76; Theodore Levitt, "The Globalization of Markets," *Harvard Business Review* 61, no. 3 (1983): 92–102; Daniel J. Boorstin, *The Republic of Technology: Reflections on Our Future Community* (New York: Harper and Row, 1978), 5.

3. A. G. Hopkins, ed., *Globalization in World History* (New York: W. W. Norton, 2002), 3–11.

4. For additional discussion relating to the concept of globalization, see Alfred Eckes and Thomas Zeiler, *Globalization and the American Century* (New York: Cambridge University Press, 2003), 1–7. On the South and its recent economic history, see James C. Cobb, *The Selling of the South: The Southern Crusade for Industrial Development 1936–80* (Baton Rouge: Louisiana State University Press, 1982); Cobb, *Industrialization and Southern Society, 1877–1984* (Lexington: University Press of Kentucky, 1984); John Egerton, *The Americanization of Dixie: The Southernization of America* (New York: Harper and Row, 1974); Gavin Wright, *The Old South, New South: Revolutions in the Southern Economy Since the Civil War* (New York: Basic Books, 1986); and Wright, "The Persistence of the South as an Economic Region," *Atlanta History* 44, no. 4 (Winter 2001): 69–80. I also benefitted from Peter Applebome, *Dixie Rising: How the South Is Shaping American Values, Politics, and Culture* (New York: Random House, 1996), and Philip Scranton, ed., *The Second Wave: Southern Industrialization from the 1940s to the 1970s* (Athens: University of Georgia Press, 2001). For another helpful discussion of globalization and the South from a development point of view, see MDC, *The State of the South 2000* (Chapel Hill, N.C.: MDC Inc., September 2000), http://www.mdcinc.org.

5. Statistics on population and land area from U.S. Bureau of the Census, *Historical Statistics of the United States: Colonial Times to 1970* (Washington, D.C.: GPO, 1975), 1:24–38; U.S. Bureau of the Census, *Statistical Abstract of the United States: 2001* (Washington, D.C.: 2001), 208.

6. U.S. Bureau of Economic Analysis, Department of Commerce, *Survey of Current Business* 81, no. 5 (May 2001), D-66. On the impact of federal and defense spending, see Gregory Hooks, "Guns and Butter, North and South: The Federal Contribution to Manufacturing Growth, 1940–90," in *Second Wave,* 254–85.

7. *Survey of Current Business* 81, no. 5 (May 2001), D-66; *Survey of Current Business* 82, no. 5 (May 2002), 70–82; *Historical Statistics,* 1:243–45.

8. *Historical Statistics,* 1:458, 464; *Statistical Abstract: 1951,* 175–76; *Statistical Abstract: 1960,* 211, 786; *Statistical Abstract: 1976,* 367; *Statistical Abstract: 1978,* 812–13; Statistical *Abstract: 2001,* 292; U.S. Bureau of the Census, *Geographical Area Statistics: 2000* (Washington, D.C.: GPO, 2002), 3–5.

9. *Statistical Abstract: 2001,* 531. On the mechanization of cotton-picking, see Wright, *Old South, New South,* 241–47. Julie Hatch and Angela Clinton, "Job Growth in the 1990s: A Retrospect," *Monthly Labor Review* 123, no. 12 (December 2000): 3–18.

10. Wright, *Old South, New South,* 260–61.

11. *Historical Statistics,* 1:22–23; Diane A. Schmidley, U.S. Bureau of the Census, *Profile of the Foreign Born Population in the United States: 2000,* Current Population Reports, Series P23-206 (Washington: GPO, 2001), 15.

12. Open Doors International, http://www.opendoors.org.

13. John Brooks, *Telephone: The First Hundred Years* (New York: Harper, 1975), 245–47; Brian Winston, *Media, Technology and Society: History: From the Telegraph to the Internet* (London: Routledge, 1998), 293–94.

14. David J. Whalen, "Communications Satellites: Making the Global Village Possible," NASA Office of External Relations, History Office, http://www.hq.nasa.gov/office/pao/History/satcomhistory.html; Winston, *Media, Technology and Society,* 292–93.

15. Alfred D. Chandler Jr. and James W. Cortada, eds., *A Nation Transformed by Information: How Information Has Shaped the United States from Colonial Times to the Present* (New York: Oxford University Press, 2000). On CNN, see especially Reese Schonfeld, *Me and Ted Against the World* (New York: Harper Collins, 2001).

16. *Statistical Abstract: 2001,* 707, 720.

17. U.S. Federal Aviation Administration, *Statistical Handbook* (Washington, D.C.: GPO, 1959). On Delta Air Lines see W. David Lewis and Wesley Phillips Newton, *Delta: The History of an Airline* (Athens: University of Georgia Press, 1979); U.S. Bureau of Transportation Statistics, *National Transportation Statistics 2001,* http://www.bts.gov/publications/national_transportation_statistics/2001/index.html.

18. Raymond Arsenault, "The End of the Long Hot Summer: The Air Conditioner and Southern Culture," *The Journal of Southern History* 50, no. 4 (Nov. 1984): 609–18, 628. See also Gail Cooper, *Air-Conditioning America: Engineers and the Controlled Environment, 1900–1960* (Baltimore: Johns Hopkins University Press, 1998).

19. "The Fortune Directory," *Fortune,* July 1955, 2–10.

20. "The 500 Largest Industrial Corporations," *Fortune,* May 1976, 318–37.

21. "The Fortune 5 Hundred," *Fortune,* April 15, 2002, F-68; Jerry Useem, "One Nation under Wal-Mart," *Fortune,* March 3, 2003, 64.

22. Sandra S. Vance and Roy V. Scott, *Wal-Mart: A History of Sam Walton's Retail Phenomenon* (New York: Twayne, 1994), 45; Bayan Rahman and Mariko Sanchanta,

"Wal-Mart Develops a Taste for Japan," *Financial Times,* May 3, 2002, 13; "Chinese-Made Goods Seek Overseas Markets Through Chain Stores," *Asia Pulse,* April 22, 2002.

23. See generally Norman J. Glickman and Douglas P. Woodward, *The New Competitors: How Foreign Investors Are Changing the U.S. Economy* (New York: Basic Books, 1989), 96–118.

24. *Statistical Abstract: 2001,* 26, 792.

25. G. Andrew Bernat Jr., "Convergence in State Per Capita Personal Income, 1950–99," *Survey of Current Business* 81, vol. 6 (June 2001): 36–46. Bernat notes that much of the convergence in per capita earnings among the states occurred in the period 1950–79. Gavin Wright offers his own explanation for convergence in *Old South, New South,* 239–44. He emphasizes the development of the mechanical cotton picker and notes that the percentage of the cotton crop that was machine harvested rose from 5 percent in 1950 to nearly 100 percent by 1970.

26. Glickman and Woodward provide an insightful discussion of the state competition to lure foreign investors in *New Competitors,* 225–54. For an excellent discussion of earlier efforts to lure industry to the South, see generally Cobb, *The Selling of the South.*

27. Mark Arend, "North Carolina Retains the No. 1 Business Climate Ranking," *Site Selection Magazine,* November 2002, http://www.siteselection.com/issues/2002/nov/p741/.

28. On the federal contribution to manufacturing growth, see generally Hooks, "Guns and Butter . . ." in *Second Wave,* 255–85.

29. Eckes and Zeiler, *Globalization and the American Century,* 152, 157–58.

30. David Gelsanliter, *Jump Start: Japan Comes to the Heartland* (New York: Kodansha International, 1992), 92–96; Wright, "Persistence of the South," 75.

31. For discussion of tariff-related issues involving the footwear industry, see Alfred E. Eckes Jr., *Opening America's Market: U.S. Foreign Trade Policy since 1776* (Chapel Hill: University of North Carolina Press, 1995), 219–56; Trowbridge quote, 199.

32. For the problems with adjustment assistance, see U.S. General Accounting Office, *Trade Adjustment Assistance: Experiences of Six Trade-Impacted Communities,* August 2001, 11–12.

33. David Halbfinger, "Factory Jobs, Then Workers, Leaving Poorest Southern Areas," *New York Times,* May 10, 2002, 20; Warren Vieth, "A Town Traded Away," *Los Angeles Times,* April 19, 2002, sec. 3, 1.

34. Maryland Advisory Commission on Manufacturing Competitiveness, *Maryland Manufacturing: The Status, The Challenges, The Recommendations,* December 2002, 3, http://www.choosemaryland.org/assets/document/DBED%20MACMC%20Report%20Final%20Version.pdf

35. Dan Chapman, "A Sinking Shrimping Industry: Imports Eating Away at Georgians' Livelihood," *Atlanta Journal-Constitution,* February 26, 2003, F1.

36. Robert E. Scott, "Fast Track to Lost Jobs," Economic Policy Institute briefing paper, October 2001; Charles McMillion, e-mail to author, April 2002. McMillion assumes that it took nearly a year for NAFTA to have any significant effect. The agreement took effect legally in January 1994, but the consequences became evident in 1995. See also, Alan Tonelson, *The Race to the Bottom: Why a Worldwide Worker Surplus and Uncontrolled*

Free Trade Are Sinking American Living Standards (Boulder, Colo.: Westview Press, 2000). For a more theoretical discussion of the problem, see Adrian Wood, *North-South Trade Employment and Inequality: Changing Fortunes in a Skill-Driven World* (Oxford: Clarendon Press, 1994). On Mexican jobs moving to China, see Claire Serant, "Mexico Spins a New Orbit," *Electronic Buyer's News*, January 20, 2003, 27.

37. General Electric, *Annual Report 2001*, 4; "Is Your Job Next?" *BusinessWeek*, Feb. 3, 2003, 50; Raj Changappe, "Housekeepers to the World," *India Today*, November 18, 2002, 36.

38. Diane E. Lewis, "Shift of Tech Jobs Abroad Speeding Up, Report Says," *Boston Globe*, December 25, 2002, E1.

39. "Is Your Job Next?," *BusinessWeek*, February 3, 2003, 50; "Bank of America joins companies sending tech jobs overseas," Associated Press, March 6, 2002, online Lexis-Nexis Academic (accessed February 23, 2003).

40. Russell Grantham, "Delta Contracts for Reservation Work," *Atlanta Journal-Constitution*, October 8, 2002, D1; "Is Your Job Next?," *BusinessWeek*, February 3, 2003, 56; John Pietz, "Cheaper Labor Drawing High-Skilled Tech Jobs from U.S.," Cox News Service, October 21, 2002; Evelyn Iritani, "High-Paid Jobs Latest U.S. Export," *Los Angeles Times*, April 2, 2002; Raj Changappe, "Housekeepers to the World," *India Today*, November 18, 2002, 36.

41. Scott Barancik, "Hard Work: Unionizing Call Centers," *St. Petersburg Times*, September 17, 2001, E3; Scott Barancik, "Rival Grabs Sykes Account," *St. Petersburg Times*, April 04, 2002, E1; Scott Barancik, "India to Answer Sykes Phones," *St. Petersburg Times*, August 30, 2002, E1; Dan Morse, "Kentucky Answered Call of the Future—but Got Bad News; Outsourcer Set Up in Hazard, then Headed Overseas," *Wall Street Journal*, March 9, 2004, A1.

42. "Convergys Charts Expansion," *Financial Express* (India), May 16, 2002; Khozem Merchant, "Calling India for IT outsourcing growth," *Financial Times* (London), February 5, 2003; Matt Dees, "Call Center Firm with Jacksonville, N.C., Facility to Cut 950 Jobs Worldwide," *Jacksonville (N.C.) Daily News*, December 10, 2002; Convergys, "Office Depot Selects Convergys to Provide Outsourced Benefits Administration Services," news release, February 12, 2003, http://cygcorpdom.convergys.com/apps/.

43. Moni Basu, "Indian Tech Firm Seeks to Rebuild Ga. Business," *Atlanta Journal-Constitution*, July 24, 2002, E2.

44. John Schwartz, "Experts See Vulnerability as Outsiders Code Software," *New York Times*, January 6, 2003, 1.

45. Mancur Olson, "The South Will Fall Again," *Southern Economic Journal* 49 (1983): 932.

Globalization, Latinization, and the *Nuevo* New South

Raymond A. Mohl

In 1992 Fellipe Patino settled in Russellville, Alabama, along with his wife, Patricia, and their children, Juan and Alma. They were among a small handful of Hispanics living in Russellville at the time. During the previous four years, Fellipe had traveled back and forth from Mexico to Florida for work while his family remained behind in Mexico. Still earlier, he had made numerous annual migrations to work in California agriculture. Patino was drawn to heavily rural, mostly white, northwest Alabama by the opportunity to work in the Gold Kist poultry plant in Russellville, where, he was told by fellow Mexicans, he could almost double the wages he earned as a migrant farmworker in Florida. The Russellville poultry plant had opened in 1990, but Gold Kist managers had had trouble securing a stable labor force locally. Like other chicken processors in Alabama and elsewhere, Gold Kist found in Hispanic workers like Patino the reliable, low-cost labor pool they needed to maintain efficient production. By the end of the 1990s, population of the Russellville area had become more than one-third Hispanic, some thirty-five hundred of about ten thousand people. By that time, the Patino family had bought a home. The children enrolled in local schools and endured ethnic harassment from American schoolmates, but ultimately they became fluent in English and adjusted to life in small-town Alabama. The family missed the Mexican homeland to a degree, but by the end of the 1990s the Mexican community in Russellville was large enough to provide many homeland comforts: native foods such as flat tacos, hot peppers, and goat meat; Mexican movie videos; Spanish-language soap operas on satellite television; weekend soccer leagues; familiar church services on Sundays; Spanish-speaking workers in government agencies; and Hispanic clerks in local retail stores.[1]

The Patinos adapted to life in Russellville's "Little Mexico." But as the new residents came to feel more at home, the town's white population gradually became uneasy about the ethnic change that upset the stability of small-town southern life. Initially, newcomers from south of the South were received cautiously, but in generally positive ways. They worked hard and spent their money locally, boosting rental housing, retail stores, and the used-car market. They

provided about one-third of the labor force in the Gold Kist plant and contributed to the economic turnaround of the local economy. By the late 1990s,
however, as the Mexican population continued to grow, local reaction turned
less positive. Increasingly, Russellville locals complained about the newcomers' preference for the Spanish language and about the rising costs for health
care, social services, schooling, and police services. A few raised the disturbing
specter of a rejuvenated Ku Klux Klan that might scare off the Hispanics and restore the familiar whiteness of the past. Whatever their intentions, these dis-
contented whites had little appreciable effect in stemming the flow of new immigrants to the area. Despite rising ethnic tensions in Russellville and elsewhere
in Alabama, the Patino family seemed permanently settled in their new place.[2]

The scene is much the same in northeast Alabama, where tens of thousands
of additional Hispanics have settled. Near Gadsden, in the small town of Attalla,
Raul and Guadalupe Cantellano live in a small, ramshackle house with fifteen
other family members, including six children, three of them married with children of their own. Raul had worked as a migrant farm laborer in Florida and Alabama in the 1980s and early 1990s, leaving his family behind in Mexico. In 1994
he brought his family to live in Alabama, settling at first into agricultural labor
but eventually getting a job at the Cagle poultry plant in nearby Collinsville. After obtaining green cards permitting work in the United States, Cantellano's
three adult sons and their wives all found jobs at the Cagle plant, where Hispanics comprised 63 percent of the work force by 1999. Guadalupe Cantellano
works at home, caring for younger children, cooking ten pounds of tortillas
a day, and raising chickens in the backyard. The Cantellanos have paid off the
mortgage on their fifteen thousand dollar home, own four used cars, and col-
lectively earn a good income at the Cagle plant. Raul speaks no English and remains illiterate in Spanish, and his adult sons never had much education in
Mexico. But like other Hispanic newcomers, they expect that educational opportunity in the United States will enable their younger family members to
break the cycle of poverty and low-skill, low-pay work that characterizes Hispanic life in the American South.[3]

As these family stories suggest, Dixie is experiencing a dramatic demographic,
economic, and cultural transformation. These transformations have resulted
from two patterns of powerful change that are connected and that have coincided in the state of Alabama and in the South generally. Major shifts in the
global economy have produced new forms of both deindustrialization and economic investment. New free trade policies such as the 1994 North American
Free Trade Agreement (NAFTA) have encouraged the migration of capital and
labor. A restructuring of regional, national, and global economies has under-
mined older forms of production in the South, such as in agriculture, steel, textiles, and apparel. At the same time, new economic investment has poured into

the region as American and foreign capital seek cheap labor, new markets, and government incentives. The region's new economy features foreign-owned auto plants in Tennessee, Kentucky, Alabama, Mississippi, and South Carolina; high-tech research and manufacturing in Atlanta, Austin, Huntsville, and North Carolina's Research Triangle Park; biomedical research in Birmingham and other major medical centers; and the new food processing plants for poultry, hogs, and seafood that have sprung up all over the rural South. In the past decade, about half of all poultry processing has come to be concentrated in four low-wage, antiunion southern states—Alabama, Arkansas, Georgia, and North Carolina. In addition, rapid population growth in southern states and Sun Belt cities has created an immense service economy and a consequent demand for low-wage labor.[4]

Global economic change has also created new transnational labor migration patterns. Immigration scholars have noted the historic and deeply entrenched symbiotic relationship between Mexican immigrants and the American economy. Mexico's proximity to southwestern labor markets, immigration scholar Kitty Calavita has suggested, made it possible to easily "expand and contract" the migrant labor force over time in relation to demand. Indeed, throughout much of the twentieth century, Mexican labor migrants found willing employers in agriculture, manufacturing, and service work. During the 1920s, Mexican workers replaced European immigrants in midwestern steel and meatpacking plants, and they found railroad construction and maintenance jobs throughout the West. The immigration quota system established in the 1920s effectively shut off European immigration but did not apply to Mexico. When job losses nationwide mounted during the Great Depression, Mexican workers in the United States were "repatriated" in massive numbers. With new farm labor demands during and after World War II, the newly instituted bracero program legalized the temporary recruitment of as many as four million Mexican migrant farm workers annually. The bracero program officially ended in 1964, but Mexican farmworkers continued their migratory ways. As anthropologist Thomas Weaver has written, "the bracero movement institutionalized migrant networks for the flood of undocumented workers that followed its demise."[5]

During the bracero period and until the late 1980s, most Mexican border crossers sought agricultural and manufacturing jobs in California and the southwestern states, with a sizeable number also heading to the Chicago area. Economic crisis in Mexico in the early 1980s brought to power a new government that promoted free market economic policies. This new economic program encouraged global trade and investment in Mexico, especially American trade and investment, but it did little to improve the economic situation of most Mexicans. These changes coincided with new American immigration policy, primarily the 1986 Immigration Reform and Control Act (IRCA), which beefed up border controls and imposed tough new sanctions on employers who willfully hired undocumented immigrants. Because of worsening economic conditions in Mexico and despite the new American immigration law, Mexicans continued to seek work and higher wages in the United States. However, as sociologist Douglas S. Massey and colleagues have noted, the new border controls eventually "diverted the migratory flows away from traditional points of destination," such as California, thus transforming Mexican immigration "from a regional into a national phenomenon." The same forces encouraged undocumented workers to stay longer, or even permanently, to avoid the now more difficult border crossings that had been more easily managed in earlier years.[6]

IRCA influenced labor migration flows in other ways, as well. Under pressure from big agricultural interests and proimmigrant groups, Congress added an amnesty provision to IRCA, legalizing 2.3 million Mexicans who could document at least five years of work and residence in the United States. Those amnestied subsequently had full labor rights and the freedom to move within the country in search of better opportunities. They also gained the right to bring family members from Mexico, potentially as many as 9.2 million additional Mexican migrants. In addition, IRCA policies eventually encouraged amnestied Mexicans and their families to seek citizenship—an outcome speeded by Mexican legislation in the late 1990s permitting dual U.S.-Mexican citizenship. IRCA's amnesty provisions suggested the contradictions in American immigration policy, seeking to curb illegal Mexican migration while simultaneously granting permanent residency to millions. The surge of Hispanic migration to the South coincided with the new immigration provisions introduced by IRCA, as both illegal and amnestied Mexicans found new labor markets in the Southeast. By the end of the 1990s, the dispersal of Hispanic population from traditional areas of settlement had intensified dramatically. Documenting this new migration pattern, an Urban Institute study in 2001 demonstrated that "California's net population loss from internal migration of foreign-born households during the 1990s was 363,000," mostly Mexican-born immigrants. Amnesty provisions of IRCA encouraged internal migration from heavily Hispanic states such as California, while new job opportunities in the South determined new destinations. Labor recruitment played a role in the dispersal of Hispanic population, as well, as poultry companies and construction firms advertised for workers in Spanish-language newspapers in Mexico, California, and the Southwest.[7]

Taken together, the globalization of markets and capital *and* new American immigration policy diversified the migratory flows of Mexican labor. Within a few years of passage of IRCA, for example, hiring of legal and illegal Hispanic workers had become "a cornerstone of changing labor relations" in southern poultry processing plants. Hispanic labor flows to the South intensified in the wake of NAFTA, which failed to produce promised wage increases in Mexico and fostered further immigration. Large American companies recruited workers directly from Mexico, reflected in 2002 in the message conveyed on a huge billboard in Tijuana, Mexico, sponsored by Gold Kist: "Mucho Trabajo en Russellville, Alabama" [There's plenty of work in Russellville, Alabama]. Similar billboards elsewhere in Mexico advertised job opportunities in North Carolina. Consequently, newcomers from below the border, mostly amnestied or illegal Mexicans, have now become ubiquitously visible in isolated small towns and rural places, as well as in sprawling metropolitan regions such as Atlanta, Nashville, Memphis, Louisville, Birmingham, Charlotte, Greensboro, Raleigh-Durham, Greenville, South Carolina, and Arlington, Alexandria, Norfolk, Virginia Beach, and Fairfax County in Virginia. As labor researcher Hector Figueroa noted in 1996, "Latino labor in the United States is a product of the complex forces that have integrated Latin America into the orbit of U.S. capitalism." Nothing has changed since that time to alter Figueroa's conclusions.[8]

New immigration has fueled the South's changing economy, but it has had other consequences, too. Black and white once defined the racial landscape of the American South, but multicultural and multiethnic rather than biracial now describe society in many southern places. As one Alabama editorialist noted in 2000, "Life in the South used to be defined in shades of black and white. But a growing wave of Hispanic immigrants is adding brown to that color scheme." "A world of racial technicolor is exploding in the South," the *Christian Science Monitor* reported in 1999, "as the ethos of black and white that has defined the region for more than a century diminishes." "The future is brown," Richard Rodriguez has argued in a recent book, *Brown: The Last Discovery of America* (2002), which makes the case that Hispanic migrations to the United States over time have tended to blur racial distinctions and break down racial and ethnic barriers across generations, especially through intermarriage and sexual contact. The seemingly permanent Hispanic influx to the South, a *Washington Post* reporter suggested in 2000, has been "changing forever the old idea of what a southerner is." In northeast Atlanta, journalist Anne Hull wrote, the heavy concentration of Hispanic and Asian immigrants along a fifteen-mile stretch of Buford Highway "has come to symbolize the transformation of the white and black South." In Hull's opinion, with its multiple clusters of immigrant apartment complexes, shopping centers, churches, restaurants, and groceries, Atlanta "represents the two-tone world of the past that is now giving way to a new society." The silent wave of Latin migration that has transformed much of America is now working its way through the South.[9]

Hispanic migration to the Deep South was barely noticeable to most in the 1980s, but the migratory flow surged dramatically in the 1990s. Texas and Florida had long had heavy concentrations of Hispanics—Texas because of its proximity and historic connections to Mexico, and Florida because of the massive waves of Cubans, Nicaraguans, and other Latin exiles, immigrants, and internal migrants that began to arrive in the 1960s. In the 1990s, new and different migration streams deposited Latin newcomers all over the southern United States. Texas and Florida continued to attract Hispanics in substantial numbers, but in virtually every other southern state the Hispanic growth rate surpassed the national growth rate in Hispanic population by three, four, five, or six times. And unlike the 1980s, by the mid-1990s southerners in destination towns and cities found it difficult to ignore the sudden intensity of ethnic change. Verifying these patterns, a few social scientists by the mid-1990s had begun writing about the powerful surge of Hispanic migration to the South.[10]

U.S. Census Bureau statistics tell part of the story of this astonishing shift in population patterns. During the 1990s, for example, the Hispanic population surged nationally by a hefty 61.2 percent, rising from 22.4 million in 1990 to 35.3 million in 2000. By 2003, new census counts confirmed that Hispanics surpassed African Americans as the nation's largest minority, "a symbolic benchmark of some significance," asserted writer and policy analyst Robert Suro. Hispanic population gains nationally were impressive, but statistical evidence of recent Latino migration to the South has been even more dramatic. The most startling example is that of North Carolina, where the census recorded a sizzling 394 percent growth rate for Hispanics in the 1990s. The decennial growth rate was similarly very high in other southern states: 337 percent in Arkansas, 300 percent in Georgia, 278 percent in Tennessee, 212 percent in South Carolina, 208 percent in Alabama, and by lesser but still substantial amounts in other southern states (see table 1). Aside from Texas and Florida, the Hispanic population in southern states in 2000 ranged from a low of 39,500 in Mississippi to a high of 435,000 in Georgia. Virginia, with almost 330,000 Hispanics, and North Carolina, with 379,000, also ranked high on the list. Overall, the 2000 census revealed a decennial increase of almost 4.6 million Hispanics in the South, bringing the total Hispanic population of twelve southern states to a little over 11 million. Another census report in September 2003 revealed that between 2000 and 2002, Georgia had the fastest growing Hispanic population, rising an astonishing 17 percent over two years to 516,500. The same report documented that Atlanta had the highest Hispanic growth rate among the nation's twenty largest metropolitan areas. Interim census studies also showed that Hispanic populations continued to rise rapidly in other southern states. Alabama, for example, recorded a 12.7 percent Hispanic increase between 2000 and 2002.[11]

Many recent Hispanic migrants to the South have settled in small towns and rural areas for agricultural and poultry work. But large numbers of newcomers have chosen urban destinations as well. Metro Atlanta, with 269,000 Hispanics

TABLE 1
Hispanic Population Growth in Twelve Southern States, 1990–2000

State	1990 Hispanic Population	2000 Hispanic Population	Percent Growth 1990–2000	Percent of Total Population
North Carolina	76,745	378,963	393.8	4.7
Arkansas	19,876	86,866	337.0	3.2
Georgia	108,933	435,227	299.5	5.3
Tennessee	32,742	123,838	278.2	2.2
South Carolina	30,500	95,076	211.7	2.4
Alabama	24,629	75,830	207.9	1.7
Kentucky	22,005	59,939	172.4	1.5
Mississippi	15,998	39,569	147.3	1.4
Virginia	160,403	329,540	105.4	4.7
Florida	1,574,148	2,682,715	70.4	16.8
Texas	4,339,874	6,669,666	53.7	32.0
Louisiana	93,067	107,738	15.8	2.4
South	6,498,920	11,084,967	70.6	12.6

Source: U.S. Census, 1990, 2000.
Note: States ranked by percentage Hispanic growth, 1990–2000.

in 2000, provides the most startling example of this pattern of urban migration. According to the census, fully 62 percent of all Hispanics in Georgia reside in the twenty-county Atlanta metropolitan area. This new urban pattern is common throughout the South. North Carolina cities along the Interstate-85 corridor had huge increases in Hispanic migration during the 1990s. The newcomers are now heavily represented in the state's metro population, typified by the 77,000 Hispanics in metro Charlotte, 73,000 in Raleigh–Durham–Chapel Hill, and 62,000 in Greensboro–Winston-Salem. Virginia, too, has striking numbers of Hispanics, including 219,000 in the Virginia portion of the Washington, D.C., metro area. Suburban Fairfax County alone has almost half of that number, about 107,000 or more than 11 percent of Fairfax's total population. Similar urban concentrations of Hispanics can be found in most of the South's other metropolitan areas (see table 2).[12]

The 2000 census also provided a better sense of Hispanic diversity in the South. The census broke down the Hispanic population into four major categories: Mexican, Puerto Rican, Cuban, and "Other Hispanic or Latino," a reference to those from other Central American and South American nations. Generally, observers have tended to identify the South's new Hispanic immigrants and migrants as primarily or almost exclusively Mexican. This may actually be the case in selected small towns, but statewide census statistics demonstrate not only diversity of national origin but wide disparities among south-

TABLE 2
Hispanic Population Growth, Selected Southern Metropolitan Areas, 1990–2000

Metro Area	1990 Hispanic Population	2000 Hispanic Population	Percent Growth 1990–2000
Atlanta	57,169	268,851	370.3
Birmingham	3,989	16,598	316.1
Charleston	7,512	13,091	74.3
Charlotte	10,671	77,092	622.4
Fayetteville, Ark.	1,526	26,401	1,630.1
Greensboro–Winston-Salem	7,096	62,210	776.7
Greenville-Spartanburg, S.C.	5,120	26,167	411.1
Jackson, Miss.	1,944	4,240	118.1
Lexington, Ky.	3,117	11,880	281.1
Little Rock	4,164	12,337	196.3
Louisville	5,765	16,479	185.8
Memphis	7,986	27,520	244.6
Nashville	7,665	40,139	423.7
New Orleans	53,226	58,545	10.0
Norfolk–Newport News–Va. Beach	32,329	48,963	51.5
Raleigh–Durham–Chapel Hill	9,019	72,580	704.7
Virginia Part of Wash., D.C. Metro	102,489	218,778	113.5

Source: U.S. Census, 1990, 2000.

ern states. For example, with the exception of Texas and Arkansas, where the proportions of Mexicans surpass 70 percent of all Hispanics, in no southern state do Mexicans exceed about two-thirds of all Hispanics, and in some states the Mexican proportion is quite low: 30 percent in Louisiana, 22.4 percent in Virginia, and 13.6 percent in Florida. The statistics for the "Other Hispanic" category also suggest surprising ethnic differentials among southern states. For instance, the proportion of "Other Hispanic" ranges from a low of 22.5 percent in Texas to a high of 62.5 percent in Virginia, with most states in the 25 to 35 percent range. Even in Florida, generally thought of as dominated by Cubans, that group is surpassed numerically by Hispanics from Central and South America. Finally, excepting Florida, the proportions of Cubans and Puerto Ricans in the South tend to be much lower than the other two categories (see table 3). This Hispanic diversity, of course, can also be traced in the population statistics for individual southern cities, counties, and metropolitan areas.[13]

Census statistics reveal only part of the Hispanic migration story, however. Actual Hispanic population counts are much higher, perhaps as much as twice as high in many southern cities, counties, and states, according to local sources. For example, the 2000 census counted 39,500 Hispanics in Mississippi, but state economic planner Pete Walley conceded that the actual number "could be well over 100,000." Similarly, Memphis had 23,400 Hispanics according to the cen-

TABLE 3
Diversity of Hispanic Population, Twelve Southern States, 2000

State	Mexican	Puerto Rican	Cuban	Other	Total
Alabama					
Hispanic Pop.	44,522	6,322	2,354	22,632	75,830
% Hisp. Pop.	58.8	8.3	3.1	29.8	
Arkansas					
Hispanic Pop.	61,204	2,473	950	22,239	86,866
%Hisp. Pop.	70.5	2.8	1.1	25.6	
Florida					
Hispanic Pop.	363,925	482,027	833,120	1,003,643	2,682,715
% Hisp. Pop.	13.6	18.0	31.1	37.4	
Georgia					
Hispanic Pop.	275,288	35,532	12,536	111,871	435,227
% Hisp. Pop.	63.3	8.2	2.9	25.7	
Kentucky					
Hispanic Pop.	31,385	6,469	3,516	18,569	59,939
% Hisp. Pop.	52.4	10.8	5.9	31.0	
Louisiana					
Hispanic Pop.	32,267	7,670	8,448	59,353	107,738
% Hisp. Pop.	30.0	7.1	7.8	55.1	
Mississippi					
Hispanic Pop.	21,616	2,881	1,508	13,564	39,569
% Hisp. Pop.	54.6	7.3	3.8	34.3	
North Carolina					
Hispanic Pop.	246,545	31,117	7,389	93,912	378,963
% Hisp. Pop.	65.1	8.2	1.9	24.8	
South Carolina					
Hispanic Pop.	52,871	12,211	2,875	27,119	95,076
% Hisp. Pop.	55.6	12.8	3.0	28.5	
Tennessee					
Hispanic Pop.	77,372	10,303	3,695	32,468	123,838
% Hisp. Pop.	62.5	8.3	3.0	26.2	
Texas					
Hispanic Pop.	5,071,963	69,504	25,705	1,502,494	6,669,666
% Hisp. Pop.	76.0	1.0	0.4	22.5	
Virginia					
Hispanic Pop.	73,979	41,131	8,332	206,098	329,540
% Hisp. Pop.	22.4	12.5	2.5	62.5	

Source: U.S. Census, 2000.

sus, but local leaders contend that "the real population is probably closer to 100,000 in the metro area." The census reported 13,000 Hispanics in Charleston, South Carolina, but knowledgeable observers offer 50,000 as a more likely Hispanic population total for the city. Some 435,000 Hispanics resided in Georgia, according to the 2000 census, but at least one Georgia demographer suggests the actual number is closer to 800,000, or about 10 percent of the state's population. The Census Bureau, in fact, has routinely undercounted minorities, including new immigrants, many of whom are undocumented and thus avoid any contact with government agencies. As South Carolina journalist James Shannon of the *Greenville News* noted in 2002, "documentation issues make many members of this demographic group less inclined to sit still for official head counters." Indeed, the Census Bureau admitted early in 2001 that its national population count for 2000 could be off by as much as 2.7 to 3.9 million people, most of whom were Hispanics, African Americans, and Native Americans. Nevertheless, census statistics provide important evidence for tracking rapid demographic and ethnic change in the South.[14]

Case studies of several southern states and cities provide a more revealing snapshot of the recent Hispanic migration and its impact. Centrally located in the Deep South, Alabama became an important destination for Hispanic immigrants and migrants in the 1990s. The Census Bureau count for 2000 placed the number of Hispanics in the state at about 76,000. Those who work with the Hispanic communities—public health professionals, social workers, church people, school and police officials—place the actual Hispanic population of Alabama, mostly Mexicans, at considerably more than 100,000 at the turn of the twenty-first century. Hispanics are spread throughout the state, in both rural and urban areas. Metropolitan Birmingham has the largest concentration of newcomers, some 16,600 according to the 2000 census—an increase of more than 300 percent from 1990. Other major cities such as Montgomery, Mobile, and Huntsville have anywhere between 4,000 and 7,000 Hispanics each. Local estimates suggest that doubling the census numbers for Alabama's largest cities would be more accurate. In north Alabama, where the poultry and garment industries are concentrated, small cities and towns such as Gadsden, Anniston, Cullman, Decatur, Russellville, Albertville, Collinsville, Oneonta, and a few others have substantial numbers of Hispanics as well. "Little Mexicos" are sprouting up in north Alabama neighborhoods, trailer parks, and apartment complexes.[15]

Jobs and economic opportunity have provided the magnetic pull attracting Hispanics to Alabama, and to the rest of the South as well. As immigration scholar George J. Borjas has written, "the same economic incentives that drive global trade flows motivate workers to move across international borders." The booming American economy of the 1990s, with the lowest unemployment rates in decades, created a demand for cheap, reliable, nonunion labor. An ongoing economic crisis in Mexico through the 1980s and 1990s helped drive legal as well as undocumented newcomers to the United States. Many labor migrants came directly from rural and small-town Mexico, but many others, such as Fellipe Patino and Raul Cantellano, had already worked in Texas, Florida, California, or elsewhere before arriving in Alabama.[16]

This new immigrant labor force has become an essential ingredient in Alabama's rural and urban economies. In small north Alabama towns, Hispanics are heavily employed on chicken farms and in poultry processing plants; in hosiery, garment, textile, carpet, furniture, and plastics manufacturing; and in agriculture, where they pick and pack tomatoes, peaches, strawberries, potatoes, cucumbers, and watermelons. Notably, former migrant agricultural workers are settling down permanently in north Alabama towns, many moving into factory jobs and chicken plants. Hispanics are fewer in number but still very much in evidence in south Alabama, where they provide migrant agricultural labor, replant timberland, process seafood, and work dairy farms, truck farms, and sawmills. In metropolitan areas such as Birmingham, they work in restaurants, landscaping, roofing, building construction, and car washes. They clean rooms and make beds in Birmingham area hotels. A major portion of the janitorial work in Birmingham's downtown and edge-city office buildings is done by Hispanic service workers, under contract with large building-maintenance firms. The hotels, cleaning companies, construction and landscaping firms, and poultry processors all found in Hispanics a cheap, reliable, and nonunionized labor force at a time when national labor markets were very tight. The Hispanic immigrants, in turn, found numerous ethnic niches in the American economy.[17]

As with other immigrants in past eras, the initial Hispanic newcomers were primarily young, single men who shared cramped housing, worked in teams or crews, and sent earnings to families back home. News of job opportunities in Alabama spread quickly to their villages and towns in Mexico and elsewhere. Through a familiar process of chain migration, homeland relatives, neighbors, and friends joined compadres in specific Alabama towns and work places. In a style reminiscent of employment practices of the industrial era, Alabama plants and firms relied on their Hispanic workforce as a recruitment mechanism. Mexicans, especially, returned home often, eventually bringing wives, children, and even aging parents to the United States. They began putting down more permanent roots, sending children to American schools, and buying homes and property.[18]

The pattern of migration, work, and settlement is much the same elsewhere. For example, Gainesville, Georgia, claimed at one time to be the "Poultry Capital of the World." Gainesville lost its top poultry ranking in recent years, even as production increased and Hispanic migration surged. Low wages and difficult working conditions drove black and white American workers from the industry. But in the 1980s and 1990s, rising demand for processed chickens, or broilers, both nationally and globally, led to recruitment of primarily Mexican workers, who often shifted from migrant agricultural labor to poultry work. Kinship and community networks facilitated the recruitment of additional Hispanic workers for replacement jobs and for new poultry plants. Moreover, substantial numbers of Hispanic women found employment in the chicken industry. In 2000, over twenty-seven thousand Hispanics in Gainesville and Hall County made up 20 percent of the population, and they dominated the workforce in the county's chicken plants. They began arriving in Gainesville for poultry work in the 1980s, primarily from California. The numbers rose dramatically in the 1990s, with most coming directly from Mexico and a smaller number from other Central American countries. For the chicken processing companies, Hispanics represented an ideal low-pay, low-turnover, nonunion labor force, but the workers found benefits as well. They were able to bring families to the United States, send children to local schools, and look forward to upward mobility. By the end of 2002, for instance, Hispanic children accounted for 47 percent of the total enrollment in the Gainesville city schools. The new Hispanic immigrants have built dynamic ethnic communities, become a stable presence in the Gainesville area, and shown little inclination to return permanently to Mexico or other Latin homelands.[19]

In the far northwest corner of Georgia, signs proclaim Dalton to be the "Carpet Capital of the World." In the early 1990s, local carpet factories experienced strong demand, but production was hampered by high worker turnover and persistent labor shortages. Many of the area's 120 carpet factories turned to Hispanic workers, some of whom were already working in north Georgia poultry plants or in agriculture. Through chain migration, others came from California, Texas, and Mexico—mostly amnestied Mexicans and family members, but others were undocumented. By the official count of the census takers, Dalton and Whitfield County had 18,500 Hispanics in 2000, or 22 percent of county population, but unofficial estimates from the INS and university researchers proclaim as many as 40,000 to 45,000 Hispanics in the Dalton area. As in Gainesville, these newcomers have put down roots, built stable communities, and helped to revive dying and abandoned business sections of Dalton and other rural towns. At the same time, they have had a costly impact on local schools and services. Carpet manufacturers rave about the newcomers' work ethic, but some local residents have expressed concerns about costs, consequences, and unwanted change.[20]

Dalton and Gainesville are far from isolated examples of the diverse, new Hispanic migration to the South. Poultry workers in Morganton, North Carolina, include some four hundred Maya from two mountain towns in Guatemala. Arriving through chain migration, many by way of another Maya community in Florida, they have reconstituted their old communities and sustained traditional cultural values.[21] At the Smithfield Packing Company plant in Tar Heel, North Carolina, the largest hog butchering plant in the world, some three thousand Hispanic workers hack meat from hog carcasses on moving conveyor belts. Mostly Mexican and mostly illegal, according to *New York Times* investigative reporter Charlie LeDuff, the Hispanic meat cutters are replacing black workers who regularly quit in large numbers; the Smithfield plant has a 100 percent annual turnover rate.[22] In small fishing villages along the North Carolina coast, hundreds of Mexican women with special H-2B visas have replaced African American women in the seasonal crab processing industry.[23] Throughout the Southeast, farm labor has been transformed in the past decade or so, as Hispanic workers now make up a huge percentage of the farm labor force. In Georgia, Hispanics comprise over 80 percent of the state's ninety thousand migrant and seasonal farm workers. In North Carolina, 90 percent of farm laborers are Hispanic. In rural Forest Hill, Louisiana, Mexicans fill all the laboring jobs at the state's largest plant nursery. In Morgan City, Louisiana, hundreds of Mexican skilled craftsmen work as welders, fitters, and carpenters in local shipyards. In Lexington, Kentucky, they work on horse farms and tobacco farms. In North Carolina and Virginia, tobacco growers now hire primarily Latinos for tobacco farm work. Some fifteen thousand Hispanic migrants, working on temporary visas, replant timberland for reforestation companies in Arkansas, Georgia, Alabama, and elsewhere in the South.[24] In Charleston, Memphis, Birmingham, Charlotte, Atlanta, and other cities, Hispanics fill jobs in construction, landscaping, factories, hotels, restaurants, and custodial work, and in the vast urban/suburban service sector. In suburban Fairfax County, one of the wealthiest counties in the nation, Hispanics from many different nations work as maids, janitors, landscapers, and truck drivers; they also work as computer engineers, doctors, businessmen, and government bureaucrats.[25]

Hispanics in the rural and urban South have become an important component in the region's low-wage, low-skill economy, especially in manufacturing, construction, agriculture, and food processing. They work mostly for minimal pay, often under difficult and dangerous working conditions, especially in poultry and meat processing plants. "Meatpacking," Eric Schlosser noted in his exposé *Fast Food Nation* (2001), "is now the most dangerous job in the United States." Job training and instruction in work-safety rules and regulations, especially in the Spanish language, are minimal in the slaughterhouses. "Taylorization" in poultry plants, the imposition of a time-work discipline, has speeded up the shop-floor production process and pushed workers to the limits of endurance. Repetitive work with sharp knives on the disassembly lines in these plants often results in serious lacerations, back and shoulder problems, and disabling carpal-tunnel injuries. At one poultry plant in North Carolina, company personnel reported as early as 1989 that it was "normal procedure" for 60 percent of the workers "to visit the company nurse every morning to get painkillers and have their hands wrapped." Farmworkers are exposed to harmful chemicals and pesticides. Few such workers have access to health insurance, primarily because few employers provide such coverage. Fatality rates among Hispanic construction workers rose substantially in the late 1990s. Threats of deportation by crew chiefs and plant managers keep illegal workers in line, despite work hazards. Hispanic workers, the U.S. Occupational Safety and Health Administration (osha) reported in 2001, faced "a 20 percent greater risk of being killed on the job than black and white workers combined." [26]

Given these circumstances, labor union organizers have targeted new Hispanic immigrants in an effort to revive union activism in the traditionally anti-union South. With the number of Latino workers rising, they "represent the future" for labor unions at a time when the unionized work force nationally has experienced a deep decline, Atlanta journalist Sheila M. Poole reported in 1998. Union proponents contend that effective organizing among Hispanics will result in higher wages and safer working conditions, the outcome in a nationally profiled organizing drive among Latino janitors by the Service Employees International Union (seiu) in Los Angeles. [27]

Union organizers in the Hispanic South have not had much success. At the Smithfield plant in Tar Heel, organizers from the United Food and Commercial Workers Union (ufcw) recruited Hispanic workers during a collective bargaining election in 1997. Fearing that unionization would bring unwanted attention to their illegal immigration status, most Hispanics voted against the idea, and the union went down in defeat by a two-to-one vote. But at the Case Farms poultry plant in Morganton, North Carolina, where Maya immigrants from Guatemala comprised 90 percent of the labor force, workers staged several wildcat strikes and work stoppages in 1995 to protest low wages and abusive treatment. Organizers from the Laborers International Union of North America (liuna) seized the opportunity, and workers eventually voted for the union as its collective bargaining agent. The Morganton organizing campaign had a negative ending, however, as Case Farms engaged in obstructive antiunion tactics and in 2001 ended union negotiations altogether. However, in some areas of the South, poultry and catfish workers are represented by ufcw. In other efforts, both the Farm Labor Organizing Committee (floc) and the National Poultry Workers Organizing Committee are currently engaged in organizing North Carolina's Latino workers. In Greensboro, the Union of Needletrades, Industrial, and Textile Employees (unite) has been training Hispanic organizers and incorporating Latino culture into union programs. Reflecting this new union activism, in 2003 the Immigrant Workers Freedom Rides generated considerable support for immigrant rights in southern states such as Georgia and North Carolina. [28]

As these organizational efforts suggest, building a Latino union base in the South has been a difficult process, with few success stories. Some labor leaders, such as Kevin Blair of the floc, believe that "employers pit African American and Latino farmworkers and meatpackers against each other to increase productivity and to keep them from organizing labor unions." Yet the new immigrant workforce in the region remains ripe for organization, which may be speeded by a major policy shift by the national AFL-CIO. Long opposed to immigration and critical of immigrant job competition, in February 2000 national labor leaders reversed course, supported a more lenient immigration policy, and vowed to "make immigrants more enthusiastic about joining unions." Labor economist Vernon M. Briggs Jr. has challenged that policy shift, contending that "as long as mass immigration is allowed to flood low wage labor markets," little pressure can be asserted to improve wages and working conditions for American workers.[29]

The surge of Hispanic workers in the South has placed wage issues in the spotlight. Black spokespersons and some scholars have argued that Hispanics have displaced black workers and kept wages low for all workers. As early as 1979, *Ebony* magazine complained that undocumented Mexican immigrants in southern agricultural states such as Florida and North Carolina posed "a big threat to black workers." In many southern places, Hispanics now fill the jobs that used to be held by blacks. Employers' seeming preference for Hispanic workers, often praised as being more compliant and having a strong work ethic, has rankled black communities across the South. Similarly, in many part of the urban South, Hispanics have been settling in traditionally black neighborhoods where rents seem more reasonable. Not surprisingly, black resentment about job competition and unwelcome neighbors has surfaced in the urban and rural South.[30]

These issues have emerged in striking ways in Tar Heel, North Carolina. Charlie LeDuff's report on the Smithfield packing plant there portrayed a tension-filled shop-floor situation. Blacks resented Hispanic job competition and blamed the newcomers for declining wage rates. Smithfield's Hispanic workers—who now make up 60 percent of the plant's workforce—had resentments and suspicions of their own. Verbal and physical confrontations between the two groups became commonplace by the end of the 1990s. As LeDuff wrote in 2000, "While Smithfield's profits nearly doubled in the past year, wages have remained flat. So a lot of Americans here have quit and a lot of Mexicans have been hired to take their places. But more than management, the workers see one another as the problem, and they see the competition in skin-tones. . . . The enmity spills out into the towns." LeDuff captured Tar Heel's uneasy racial standoff in a comment from one of his black informants from the plant: "There's a day coming soon where the Mexicans are going to catch hell from the blacks, the way the blacks caught it from the whites." The sudden surge of Hispanic workers and their dominance in many workplaces has nurtured black concerns about job competition and low wages.[31]

Many immigration scholars, however, reject the wage-competition argument. They contend that the new Latino immigrants are filling jobs that no one else wants. Job turnover in the fields and in food processing plants has been extremely high, they contend, as much as 100 percent a year in some industries. Hispanics, they say, are filling "replacement" jobs abandoned by black workers who have rejected low pay and excessively demanding work. Some labor researchers have described a pattern of ethnic succession in southern labor markets in which Hispanics "are replacing African American or white workers who leave the worst jobs in those industries [textiles, furniture manufacturing, custodial, and meat processing], rather than displacing them from the more desirable jobs in the industry." A North Carolina sociologist echoed that view in 2000: "It looks like the whites are moving out, the blacks are moving up, and the Latinos are filling in at the bottom." [32]

In many metro areas, Hispanics have filled new jobs created by expanding urban and regional economies during the 1990s. For example, a Russell Sage Foundation study in 1996 concluded that new immigrants "are fitting into occupational slots created by economic and demographic growth." Similarly, a University of Memphis study, conducted in 2000, reported that given the growing labor market in the South, "Latino workers have tended not to displace local workers, but rather to fuel economic growth in most regional economies." [33] But not all experts agree on this subject. Indeed, the economic consequences of immigration have been a hotly debated subject among economists and policy experts for more than a decade, with some emphasizing the positive benefits of immigration and others the economic costs as measured in job losses and wage cuts among American citizens. [34]

Whatever the reality, blacks and Hispanics have been at odds over jobs, neighborhoods, and cultural differences for almost a decade. In some places, emerging hostility has led to open conflict and black-on-Hispanic violence. In other places, civic leaders, union organizers, and advocacy groups have sought to mediate emerging ethnic and racial conflicts. In North Carolina, groups such as Black Workers for Justice and the Latino Workers Association created an African-American/Latino Alliance to find common ground among blacks and Hispanics. In Durham, the Piedmont Peace Project, the North Carolina Black-Latino Reconciliation Project, and the Operation TRUCE Campaign engaged in similar work. In April 2002 in Raleigh, the Martin Luther King Jr. Resource Center sponsored a "town hall meeting" discussing issues dividing blacks, whites, and Hispanics. In Birmingham, the Civil Rights Institute, the Community Foundation of Greater Birmingham, and Operation New Birmingham have each reached out to Hispanic newcomers and sought to ease tensions over jobs and housing. Nevertheless, as a consequence of recent Hispanic migration, new patterns of racial and ethnic conflict linger unresolved throughout the South. [35]

Interracial conflict in southern factories and farms has intensified concern about the impact of illegal immigration to the region. Many of the newcomers are legal or amnestied immigrants; others are "guest workers" who work in the

United States on H-2A or H-2B visas, special federal programs that permit entry of seasonal agricultural or seafood workers when U.S. Department of Labor officials certify that no Americans can be found to do those jobs. However, a large but unknown number of Hispanic workers in the South are illegal immigrants. Teodoro Maus, Mexico's consul general in Atlanta, admitted to a reporter in 2000 that probably more than half of Georgia's almost half-million Latinos were illegal. In small north Alabama towns, illegals make up half or more of all Hispanic newcomers. IRCA, passed in 1986, required employers to ask new employees for documentation proving their eligibility to work in the United States. Virtually all large employers comply with this requirement, but they have no obligation to verify the documentation provided by new employees. The business of providing false documentation—social security cards or green cards, for instance—thrives in new immigrant communities. In Memphis, for example, undocumented workers can buy fake social security cards for as little as $100 that will pass muster at company hiring offices. In Chapel Hill, North Carolina, the cost of fake social security and resident alien cards ranges from $50 to $150. Once they successfully navigate the border crossing from Mexico, illegals easily travel to southern states on a Hispanic network of bus and van routes traversing the interstate highways. From a tiny bus station on Buford Highway, for instance, regular bus and van service connects Atlanta with more than four dozen Mexican destinations. In Memphis, four bus companies provide regular transportation service to numerous Mexican cities. Their destinations already determined through home-village networks, the newly arrived quickly find work in the ethnic niches already carved out in local economies.[36]

Enforcement efforts to combat illegal Latin immigration have been weak to nonexistent. In Georgia, INS district officials agreed that carpet and poultry processing firms heavily employed undocumented workers, but they also admitted, as the *Atlanta Journal-Constitution* reported in 2000, that those industries "haven't faced major raids in years." Reporter Matt Kempner interviewed one Mexican worker who said he had "been moving back and forth between countries for more than eight years, traveling to South Carolina, Florida, North Carolina, and Georgia. He's never run into overly curious immigration agents or bosses too picky to accept his false documents." After one highly publicized raid in 1992 on two large farms in North Carolina, the INS did little through the rest of the 1990s to enforce immigration law in the state. In Alabama, INS raids on workplaces have been few and far between, but occasional raids on poultry plants typically round up hundreds of illegal workers for deportation. In June and September 1995, for instance, the INS raided Hudson Foods and Gold Kist poultry plants in northeast Alabama, arresting and deporting more than 250 illegal workers. In July 1997, an INS raid at the Tyson Foods plant in Ashland, Alabama, netted 106 illegal Hispanic workers—72 Mexicans, 33 Guatemalans, and

1 Honduran. Another 50 or so workers ran off and eluded capture. Those arrested numbered about 15 percent of the Tyson plant's workforce, suggesting the sizeable dimensions of illegal immigration in the poultry industry. Tyson Foods claimed that it followed the letter of the law by demanding documentation and denied any efforts to recruit illegal workers. Nevertheless, in December 2001 the U.S. Justice Department charged Tyson Foods and six of its managers with running a smuggling ring that recruited illegal Hispanic workers for fifteen Tyson plants in ten, mostly southern, states. In March 2003, a federal judge dismissed some charges, and a jury eventually acquitted Tyson Foods and its managers of the remaining charges. Immigrant smuggling became an issue in Alabama, too. In 1999 when INS agents raided an apparel plant in Henegar, Alabama, they uncovered not only illegal workers but also a company-run smuggling ring that for over a decade had recruited hundreds of Mexicans from the central Mexican town of Queretaro for work in company plants in Georgia and Alabama.[37]

Although government prosecutors lost the Tyson case, the indictment of the big chicken processor in 2001 and a subsequent INS investigation in 2003 of hiring practices at Wal-Mart, the nation's largest employer, seemed to represent a new determination on the part of the INS to enforce immigration law after years of benign neglect. Indeed, throughout the urban and rural South, an underground labor market built on illegal immigrant workers has thrived without much regulation or control. As one Border Patrol agent in Mobile noted in 2000, "I couldn't tell you a corner of the state of Alabama that doesn't have some illegal immigration population." Yet until recently Alabama had only one permanent INS agent, stationed in Birmingham, and six Border Patrol agents, all assigned to Mobile. North Carolina, one of the top destinations for Hispanic migrants in the 1990s, had only eighteen immigration agents in 2000. National efforts to beef up the Border Patrol and crack down on illegal immigration have failed miserably, but perhaps this was a purposeful national strategy during the 1990s when labor markets were tight. The fact is, as a writer for *Foreign Affairs* put it, "Immigration policy today is driven by businesses that need more workers—skilled and unskilled, legal and illegal. Somehow, the process has gotten out of control." The sense that illegal Hispanic migration in the South is "out of control" has brought demands for INS action and intensified anti-immigrant feelings in some places. These perceptions have hardened in the wake of the September 2001 terrorist attacks on the United States.[38]

Not surprisingly, given their often tenuous immigration status, low incomes, language difficulties, and cultural differences, Hispanics in the South have experienced adjustment problems. However, churches, schools, libraries, and public agencies have responded in positive ways to the new immigrants. The Catholic Church and numerous Protestant denominations have embraced the newcomers, offering Spanish-language religious services, English classes, employment assistance, and varied social services. Migrant Head Start programs in many southern communities provide educational and nutritional benefits to the children of migrant farmworkers. Public schools in small towns and large cities are struggling to provide ESL classes to a growing number of Latino children. Public health agencies are confronting serious problems in serving a new population without proper immunizations and mostly without health insurance. Medical providers, police, and emergency management personnel are getting training in Spanish.[39] The League of United Latin American Citizens (LULAC) now has state directors in several southern states. Various public and private nonprofit groups have also organized to serve and advocate for new Latino southerners: the Hispanic Interest Coalition of Alabama in Birmingham, El Centro Legal Latino in Birmingham, the North Alabama Hispanic Association in Huntsville, the Alabama Democratic Hispanic Caucus, the National Interfaith Committee for Worker Justice, the Georgia Poultry Alliance, the Hispanic Center for Social Assistance in Memphis, the Latino Memphis Conexion, the Latin American Resource Center in Raleigh, El Pueblo Inc. in North Carolina, the Mexican American Legal Defense and Educational Fund and the Latin American Association in Atlanta, the Mississippi Immigrants Rights Alliance, and dozens of similar groups throughout the South. When the National Council of La Raza held its national meeting in Miami in July 2002, Latino leaders from southern states met to plan a Southeast regional network linking diverse local Hispanic organizations.[40]

While many agencies and groups have responded positively to the South's Hispanic newcomers, a more hostile response has also become evident in some places. For instance, Spanish language use has become controversial. Every southern state except Texas and Louisiana enacted official English legislation in the 1980s and 1990s. In Alabama, after a north Alabama legislator complained that "the Spanish are creeping in," the state legislature in 1989 initiated a statewide referendum on an official English amendment to the state's constitution. Supported by the Alabama English Committee, an affiliate of the national organization U.S. English, the amendment was approved by 88.5 percent of Alabama voters in 1990. Throughout the 1990s, language debates flared in Alabama over such issues as Spanish-language driver's tests and homestead tax exemptions for non-English speakers. When a Birmingham area auto dealership ran Spanish-language ads on television in 2000, local talk radio personalities discovered Birmingham's "immigration problem." They attacked the car dealership for pandering to foreigners and incited a controversy over the rising number of immigrants in the city. Hispanic activist Hernan Prado shot back a response in the Spanish-language newspaper, *El Reportero,* blasting the race-hate mentality that would "drag this state back to the shameful days when Alabama was best known for its Ku Klux Klan rallies and church bombings in Birmingham." A *Washington Post* reporter noted at the time that "many in the Birmingham area are uncomfortable with the notion that their city could take on the characteristics of a Miami."[41]

More overt expressions of anti-immigrant sentiment surfaced, as well. In May 1997 in Oneonta, Alabama, a small town north of Birmingham, a local white supremacist group affiliated with the America First Committee announced plans for a demonstration march to protest the "Mexican invasion" of the area. At the time, Oneonta had several hundred Hispanic families, but the number rose during summers as migrant workers arrived to pick strawberries, tomatoes, and other crops. William Riccio, state organizer and spokesman for the white supremacist group, lived in Birmingham, not Oneonta, and he had an unsavory background. A former Grand Dragon of the Alabama Ku Klux Klan, he had been associated with various KKK, "militant patriot," and skinhead hate groups since the 1970s. The demonstration was needed, Riccio asserted, because the Hispanics were "causing the crime rate to go up and creating a drain on the economy." Many were illegal immigrants, he said; they were "holding jobs that should go to white residents," and their presence affected "the stability of Blount County." Riccio's request for a parade permit anticipated that three hundred to five hundred people, including Klansmen and skinheads, would march in Oneonta's anti-immigrant demonstration. As townspeople began to perceive the planned demonstration as a Klan event, many of them defended local Hispanics as hardworking and law-abiding neighbors. The America First parade was postponed and then cancelled altogether, and subsequent plans for an anti-immigrant rally at the courthouse in downtown Oneonta were also cancelled. But the controversy revealed underlying resentment in some quarters about the way Alabama was changing.[42]

Anti-immigrant hostility also flared up in nearby Cullman, Alabama. Almost 99 percent white, Cullman County had fewer than one thousand Hispanics in 1999, according to U.S. Census estimates. That was too many for some people. In January 1998, after an immigration protest meeting, three men were arrested for burning the Mexican flag, as well as flags of the United Nations and the Communist party. Many of those attending the rally were KKK leaders and right-wing militia members, some from Georgia and a few from as far away as California and Canada. James Floyd, the local leader of the "Stand Up for Cullman" protest, vociferously argued for a permanent halt to Hispanic immigration, which, he believed, would ultimately challenge Cullman's white majority population. "I like my own people more than others," Floyd later asserted, "and I'm not ready for a world without borders." Apparently, he was not alone; at least one hundred people who sympathized with that view attended the Cullman protest. So much for globalization in that part of Alabama.[43]

In Siler City, North Carolina, a small town of about five thousand west of Raleigh, similar anti-immigrant sentiment flared in 2000. Hispanic migration in the late 1990s took the local community by surprise, so much so, one writer noted, that "longtime residents can scarcely grasp what has happened." Mexicans, Guatemalans, and Nicaraguans made up 80 percent of the workforce in Siler City's two poultry plants; Hispanic children comprised over 40 percent of the town's elementary school students. The town's almost abandoned downtown retail district began to sprout Hispanic shops and restaurants. Siler City's lone radio station aired complaints about the newcomers on morning talk shows but turned the airwaves over to Spanish-language music and programming in the evening. One woman seemed to sum up the general attitude in a complaint to a reporter: "They just came in and took over." Chatham County commissioners demanded that the INS crack down on Hispanic illegals, without result. In February 2000, a local white supremacist invited David Duke to Siler City to address an anti-immigration rally. The notorious ex-Klansman from Louisiana, who had just organized his own anti-immigrant group, the National Organization for European American Rights, jumped at the opportunity to promote white supremacy. A few hundred people showed up to hear Duke denounce the Hispanic newcomers: "To get a few chickens plucked, is it worth losing your heritage?" Duke asked. Two years later, in July 2002, a white-supremacist group called National Alliance, based in West Virginia, conducted an anti-immigrant rally in Gainesville, Georgia. "Hispanics in Gainesville have completely taken over," rally organizer Chester Doles complained, and he went on to say "we will take our borders back." Another white, anti-immigrant group, Georgians for Immigration Reduction, has lobbied state lawmakers to curb illegal immigration. One member of the organization expressed his concerns to an Atlanta reporter during a demonstration: "We're not out here waving the rebel flag. Our only concern about the [Georgia] flag is that it might be a Mexican flag one day." Although not widespread, anti-immigrant activities such as those in North Carolina, Georgia, and Alabama have exposed deep-seated concern in some places about the way Hispanic newcomers have been changing traditional patterns of small-town southern life.[44]

The new American nativism has not deterred Hispanics from seeking a new and better life in the American South. Like other immigrants to the United States in earlier times, they have found strength in their communal activities and cultural heritage. They have quickly created a vibrant cultural life based on homeland foodways, kinship activities, and musical traditions—a cultural life centered not just in the home but in hundreds of restaurants, grocery stores, music and dance clubs, and in traditional holiday festivals. Mexican national holidays and important religious events become occasions to celebrate ethnic culture. Customary religious practice, such as universal veneration of the Mexican national patron saint, the Virgin of Guadalupe, has sustained cultural persistence. Latin groceries and many restaurants supply not only familiar food but Spanish-language newspapers, Latin movie videos, music tapes and CDs, religious icons, home-style clothing (from white baptism dresses to cowboy boots and hats), and check-cashing and money-wiring services. They also serve as community gathering places, and they provide employment to some as cooks, waiters, and food service workers. Latin soccer teams and leagues all over the South provide leisure time activities for young men and Sunday outings for entire families, smoothing the transition to life in America. Some thirty-two soccer teams, for instance, make up the Latin American Soccer League of Birmingham, each team complete with sponsors and colorful uniforms. In 2002 in North Carolina, organizers from twenty-six Hispanic soccer leagues sponsored a statewide Hispanic soccer championship play-off, the North Carolina Copa Tecate Fiesta del Futbol. Hispanic bands and dance clubs offer familiar forms of weekend entertainment. Spanish-language newspapers and radio stations have sprouted all over the South, keeping the newcomers informed and sustaining language, culture, and tradition.[45]

The South's growing Hispanic population has important political implications. For European immigrants of the industrial era, participation in the American political process served as an integrating and Americanizing force — a pattern that may eventually emerge among Hispanics in the South. With about 50,000 registered Hispanic voters in 2002, Georgia stands on the cutting edge of Latin politicization in the region. Political analysts project 250,000 Hispanic voters in the state in the next decade, so Republican and Democratic party leaders are gearing up for the future. And, as Walter Woods of the *Atlanta Business Chronicle* suggested in 2002, "the future is in the numbers." Indeed, Woods wrote, "Georgia politics in 2015 may look a lot like present day Texas, New York and California, where the Hispanic vote decides elections." The 2002 election provided a preview of that future, as three Hispanic candidates — two Democrats and one Republican — were elected to the Georgia legislature from metro Atlanta districts. Equally important, both parties scrambled for votes among Georgia's Hispanics, who are considered liberal on social issues but conservative on economic matters. Some African Americans resented efforts to lure Hispanic voters into the Democratic corner, fearing loss of position and power to new ethnic rivals, but other Atlanta black leaders have been more welcoming, suggesting the potential for coalition politics. The new ethnic politics is unlikely to disappear from the southern political scene anytime soon. Indeed, the recent success of Hispanic candidates in Georgia signals the arrival of a new political force in the South — one that will only strengthen over time as the citizenship process inevitably produces more Hispanic voters. More immediately, Georgia's new Hispanic legislators have the opportunity to bring issues of importance to their constituents to the political arena—controversial issues such as redistricting, affirmative action, minority contracting, jury service, driver's licenses for illegal immigrants, and tuition and scholarships for undocumented students. Georgia has taken the lead among southern states in bringing new Latino residents into the political arena, but in Alabama and other states political parties are also recruiting potential Hispanic voters.[46]

Globalization has brought a transnational, low-wage Hispanic labor force to the land of Dixie—a pattern of human migration that has produced substantial cultural and demographic change in a region where change has always been slow and received with skepticism, if not hostility. As the twenty-first century begins, this process of southern ethnic and cultural change has been intensifying. Farms and factories and employers of all kinds now seek out Latino workers for their work ethic and their willingness to work for low pay. After a decade or more of intense Hispanic immigration to the South, people now generally seem more aware of the ways the region is changing, but the speed and strength of these changes in some places, especially in small towns, has caught many white and black southerners by surprise. Local print media and television have begun to pay closer attention to the impact of Hispanic migration, as have businessmen and politicians. Several southern states have created offices of Hispanic or Latino affairs. Southern university scholars have begun analyzing the policy implications of the new Hispanic immigration.[47] As the Latino newcomers become more numerous, more settled, and more established, they will undoubtedly become more organized, more politically mobilized, and perhaps more amenable to union organization. Many black southerners believe that Hispanics have taken jobs and depressed wages, but there are also signs of interracial activism and alliance among the two groups. Ethnic and linguistic change has also spawned new forms of nativism and stoked concerns about the social and economic costs of immigration. This is the nuevo New South. Ready or not, Dixie appears to be on the cusp of a long-term process of Latinization, mirroring what has already happened in other parts of the United States.

Notes

A slightly different version of this article appeared under the same title in the *Journal of American Ethnic History* 22 (Summer 2003): 31–66. A few paragraphs in this essay have been adapted from my earlier article "Latinization in the Heart of Dixie: Hispanics in Late-Twentieth-Century Alabama," *Alabama Review* 55 (October 2002): 243–74.

1. Rose Livingston, "Russellville Blends Hispanic Flavor," *Birmingham News,* October 5, 1997; Livingston, "Hispanic Families Seek Better Life Here," *Birmingham News,* October 5, 1997.

2. Livingston, "A New Home," *Birmingham News,* October 5, 1997; Livingston, "Meeting Needs of New Residents," *Birmingham News,* September 21, 1997; Patty

Fernandez-Rocha, "Hispanic Resident Sets High Goals," *Florence (Ala.) Shoals Times-Daily,* August 28, 2000.

3. Livingston, "Settlers Build a Lifestyle," *Birmingham News,* September 18, 2000; Manuel Torres, "The Latinization of the South," *Mobile Register,* June 28, 1999.

4. James C. Cobb, "The Sunbelt South: Industrialization in Regional, National, and International Perspectives," in *Searching for the Sunbelt: Historical Perspectives on a Region,* ed. Raymond A. Mohl (Knoxville: University of Tennessee Press, 1990), 25–46; David R. Goldfield and Thomas E. Terrill, "Uncle Sam's Other Province: The Transformation of the Southern Economy," in *The South for New Southerners,* ed. Paul D. Escott and David R. Goldfield (Chapel Hill: University of North Carolina Press, 1991), 135–56; Karsten Hulsemann, "Greenfields in the Heart of Dixie: How the American Auto Industry Discovered the South," in *The Second Wave: Southern Industrialization from the 1940s to the 1970s,* ed. Philip Scranton (Athens: University of Georgia Press, 2001), 219–54; Douglas S. Massey, "March of Folly: U.S. Immigration Policy after NAFTA," *American Prospect,* no. 37 (March–April 1998): 22–33; Robert D. Manning and Anna Cristina Butera, "Global Restructuring and U.S.-Mexican Economic Integration: Rhetoric and Reality of Mexican Immigration Five Years After NAFTA," *American Studies* 41 (Summer/Fall 2000): 183–209; Altha J. Cravey, "The Changing South: Latino Labor and Poultry Production in Rural North Carolina," *Southeastern Geographer* 37 (November 1997): 295–300; "The Globalization Game," *Southern Exposure* 26 (Summer/Fall 1998): 21–58; James Green, "Gone South," *American Prospect* 11 (November 20, 2000): 51–53.

5. Kitty Calavita, "Mexican Immigration to the USA: The Contradictions of Border Control," in *The Cambridge Survey of World Immigration,* ed. Robin Cohen (Cambridge: Cambridge University Press, 1995), 236–44, 236; Thomas Weaver, "Time, Space, and Articulation in the Economic Development of the U.S.-Mexico Border Region from 1940 to 2000," *Human Organization* 60 (Summer 2001): 105–20, 111; Paul Ehrlich, Loy Bilderback, and Anne E. Ehrlich, *The Golden Door: International Migration, Mexico, and the United States* (New York: Ballantine Books, 1979); Philip Martin, "There Is Nothing More Permanent than Temporary Foreign Workers," Center for Immigration Studies, *Backgrounder* (April 2001): 1–3.

6. Douglas S. Massey, Inge Durand, and Nolan J. Malone, *Beyond Smoke and Mirrors: Mexican Immigration in an Era of Economic Integration* (New York: Russell Sage Foundation, 2002), 24–51, 105–41, 127; Alejandro Portes, "Labor Functions of Illegal Aliens," *Society* 14 (September/October 1977): 31–37; Terrence Haverluk, "The Changing Geography of U.S. Hispanics, 1850–1990," *Journal of Geography* 96 (May/June 1997): 134–45; Jorge Durand, Douglas S. Massey, and Emilio A. Parrado, "The New Era of Mexican Migration to the United States," *Journal of American History* 86 (September 1999): 518–36; Jean-Claude Buhrer, "The U.S. Honey-Pot Lures Mexico's Dispossessed," *Manchester Guardian Weekly,* December 27, 1987; Wade Graham, "Masters of the Game: How the U.S. Protects the Traffic in Cheap Mexican Labor," *Harper's,* July 1996, 35–50; David M. Heer, *Undocumented Mexicans in the United States* (Cambridge: Cambridge University Press, 1990); Thomas J. Espenshade, "Unauthorized Immigration to the United States," *Annual Review of Sociology* 21 (1995): 195–216; Jorge Durand, Douglas S. Massey, and Fernando Charvet, "The Changing Geography of Mexican Immigration to the United

States, 1910–96," *Social Science Quarterly* 81 (March 2000): 1–15; Gilbert G. Gonzalez and Raul Fernandez, "Empire and the Origins of Twentieth-Century Migration from Mexico to the United States," *Pacific Historical Review* 71 (February 2002): 19–57; Rob Chambers, "Wages Are Driving Force Behind Latest Emigration," *Atlanta Journal-Constitution,* April 19, 1998; Robert Robb, "Tightened U.S. Border Policy Keeps Mexicans Trapped Here," *Arizona Republic,* December 3, 2002.

7. Massey, Durand, and Malone, *Beyond Smoke and Mirrors,* 49–50, 136–38; Calavita, "Mexican Immigration to the USA," 238–41; Jeffrey S. Passel and Wendy Zimmerman, *Are Immigrants Leaving California? Settlement Patterns of Immigrants in the Late 1990s* (Washington, D.C.: Urban Institute, 2001), 13; "Hispanics Drawn to Triangle More Than Other Large Communities," Associated Press, July 31, 2002.

8. David Griffith and David Runsten, "The Impact of the 1986 Immigration Reform and Control Act on the U.S. Poultry Industry: A Comparative Analysis," *Policy Studies Review* 11 (Summer 1992): 118–30, 124; Neil Taylor (immigration attorney in Russellville), telephone interview with the author, January 13, 2003; Kirk Ross, "Economic System Rests on Fragile House of Cards," *Chapel Hill News,* March 31, 2002; Hector Figueroa, "The Growing Force of Latino Labor," *NACLA Report on the Americas* 30 (November/December 1996): 18–22, 22; David Griffith, "Consequences of Immigration Reform for Low-Wage Workers in the Southeastern U.S.: The Case of the Poultry Industry," *Urban Anthropology* 19 (Spring–Summer 1990): 155–84; Carlos A. Heredia, "Downward Mobility: Mexican Workers after NAFTA," *NACLA Report on the Americas* 30 (November/December 1996): 34–38; Massey, "March of Folly"; Manning and Butera, "Global Restructuring and U.S.-Mexican Economic Integration"; Jeff Faux, "How NAFTA Failed Mexico," *American Prospect* 14 (July/August 2003): 35–37; James H. Johnson Jr., Karen D. Johnson-Webb, and Walter C. Farrell Jr., "Newly Emergent Hispanic Communities in the United States: A Spatial Analysis of Settlement Patterns, In-migration Fields, and Social Receptivity," in *Immigration and Opportunity: Race, Ethnicity, and Employment in the United States,* ed. Frank D. Bean and Stephanie Bell-Rose (New York: Russell Sage Foundation, 1999), 263–310.

9. "Folks Very Much Like Us," *Huntsville Times,* February 25, 2000; Suzi Parker, "Hispanics Reshape Culture of the South," *Christian Science Monitor,* June 1, 1999; Richard Rodriguez, *Brown: The Last Discovery of America* (New York: Viking, 2002), 35; Sue Anne Pressley, "Hispanic Immigration Boom Rattles South," *Washington Post,* March 6, 2000; Anne Hull, "Old South Goes with the Wind," *Washington Post,* December 8, 2002; Hull, "Highway: A Haven for Immigrants," *Washington Post,* December 9, 2002; Elizabeth Kurylo, "Immigrants Shaping Face of Atlanta," *Atlanta Journal-Constitution,* February 23, 1997. See also Barbara Ellen Smith, "The Postmodern South: Racial Transformations and the Global Economy," in *Cultural Diversity in the U.S. South: Anthropological Contributions to a Region in Transition,* ed. Carole E. Hill and Patricia D. Beaver (Athens: University of Georgia Press, 1998), 164–78; Eric Bates, "Beyond Black and White," *Southern Exposure* 22 (Fall 1994): 10–15; Steven A. Holmes, "Figuring Out Hispanic Influence," *New York Times,* August 16, 1998.

10. Frank D. Bean and Marta Tienda, *The Hispanic Population of the United States* (New York: Russell Sage Foundation, 1987), 152–63; Mike Davis, *Magical Urbanism: Latinos Reinvent the U.S. Big City* (London: Verso, 2000), 1–9. On Hispanics in Texas, see

Emilio Zamora, *The World of the Mexican Worker in Texas* (College Station: Texas A&M University Press, 1993) and David Montejano, *Anglos and Mexicans in the Making of Texas, 1836–1986* (Austin: University of Texas Press, 1987). On Hispanics in Florida, see Raymond A. Mohl, "The Latinization of Florida," in *Florida's Heritage of Diversity: Essays in Honor of Samuel Proctor,* ed. Mark I. Greenberg, William Warren Rogers, and Canter Brown Jr. (Tallahassee: Sentry Press, 1997), 151–68, 230–34; Larry Rohter, "A Puerto Rican Boom for Florida," *New York Times,* January 31, 1994.

11. U.S. Census, 1990, 2000. Census data on Hispanics for 1990 and 2000 is available on the Internet at http://factfinder.census.gov. See also Lynette Clemetson, "Hispanics Now Largest Minority, Census Shows," *New York Times,* January 22, 2003; Andres Viglucci and Tim Henderson, "Hispanics Become Largest Minority in U.S.," *Birmingham News,* June 19, 2003; Mark Bixler, "Georgia Tops Nation in Hispanic Growth," *Atlanta Journal-Constitution,* September 18, 2003; Erin Sullivan, "Hispanic Population Boom," *Birmingham Post-Herald,* June 19, 2003; Jay Reeves, "Black, Hispanic Numbers Growing," *Birmingham News,* September 19, 2003.

12. U.S. Census, 2000; Deirdre A. Gaquin and Katherine A. DeBrandt, eds., *County and City Extra: Special Decennial Census Edition* (Lanham, Md.: Bernan, 2002); MDC, Inc., *The State of the South, 1998* (Chapel Hill: MDC, Inc., 1998), 10–12; Audrey Singer et al., *The World in a Zip Code: Greater Washington, D.C. as a New Region of Immigration* (Washington, D.C.: Brookings Institution, 2001); Micki Neal and Stephanie A. Bohon, "The Dixie Diaspora: Attitudes Toward Immigrants in Georgia," *Sociological Spectrum* 23, no. 2 (2003): 181–212; Rafael A. Olmeda, "Latinization of the United States Spreads into Some Unexpected Regions," *Fort Lauderdale Sun-Sentinel,* July 31, 2002; Haya El Nasser, "Immigrants Emigrating from Calif. and N.Y.," *USA Today,* August 22, 2003.

13. U.S. Census, 2000; Evelyn Nieves, "Hispanics Polled See Themselves as Diverse," *Washington Post,* December 18, 2002.

14. Deborah Bulkeley, "Spanish-Speaking Households on the Rise in Mississippi," Associated Press, September 30, 2002; Michael Paulk, "The Latino Connection," *Memphis Business Journal,* September 23, 2002; Jim Parker, "Hispanic Workers," *Charleston Post and Courier,* October 21, 2002; James Shannon, "The Changing Face of Upstate: The Hispanics," *Greenville News,* September 24, 2002; Brian Basinger, "Latino Candidates Eye Offices, History," *Athens Banner-Herald,* July 7, 2002; Bates, "Beyond Black and White," 12–13; Leah Van Wey, "Newcomers in Numbers," *Southern Exposure* 27 (Summer 1999): 21; Carlos Conde, "Down for the Count?" *Hispanic* 12 (October 1999): 60–66; Bailey Thompson, "Can the South Cope with Yet Another Cultural Challenge?" *Huntsville Times,* February 6, 2000; Mike Salinero, "Distrust of Officials Makes Counting Hispanics Hard," *Huntsville Times,* March 21, 2000; Jay Reeves, "Census: Undercount in AL," *Huntsville El Reportero,* April 1, 2001; Haya El Nasser, "Political Fight Brews Over Census Correction," *USA Today,* February 15, 2001; "Undercount Examined," *USA Today,* March 28, 2001; Cindy Rodriguez, "Revised Census Estimate Points to Total of 285M," *Boston Globe,* February 15, 2001; and, more generally, Barry Edmondston, "The Case for Modernizing the U.S. Census," *Society* 39 (November/December 2001): 42–53.

15. Marie Jones, "Habla Espanol? Hispanic Culture Integrating Itself into Birmingham," *Birmingham Weekly,* March 5, 1998, 10–11; Jamie Kizzire, "Hispanics' Clout Rising in Alabama," *Birmingham Post-Herald,* June 27, 2000; Manuel Torres, "Hispanic

Presence Grows in Mobile," *Mobile Register,* June 28, 1999; Rebecca Charry, "Cultures Clash and Adjust," *Birmingham Post-Herald,* March 18, 1997; "Official: State Lacks Agents for Immigration," *Decatur Daily News,* March 16, 2000; Rose Livingston, "Seeking a Better Life," *Birmingham News,* April 30, 1996; Jeb Phillips, "Habla Espanol?" *Birmingham Post-Herald,* March 15, 2001; Benjamin Niolet and Rose Livingston, "Hispanic Figure Still Low," *Birmingham News,* March 15, 2001; Livingston, "Franklin Official: Hispanic Count Off by Thousands," *Birmingham News,* March 16, 2001; "Changing Alabama," *Birmingham Post-Herald,* March 17, 2001.

16. George J. Borjas, *Heaven's Door: Immigration Policy and the American Economy* (Princeton: Princeton University Press, 1999), 86; Alejandro Castro (teacher and community organizer), interview with the author and Eric Knudsen, Birmingham, March 19, 1997.

17. Manuel Torres, "The Latinization of the South," *Mobile Register,* June 28, 1999; Carol Robinson, "Hispanic Community Grows," *Birmingham News,* March 21, 1999; Rose Livingston, "The Migrant Stream," *Birmingham News,* July 12, 1999; Connie Baggett, "Changing Work Force," *Mobile Register,* August 8, 2000; Steve Mayo, "Migrant Work Force Declining," *Montgomery Advertiser,* November 19, 2000; Bill Caton, Niki Sepsas, and Chianti Cleggett, "Searching for Magic: Hispanics in the City," *Birmingham Magazine,* May 2001, 100–107; Dale Short, "Mexico in the Heart of Dixie," *UAB Magazine,* Summer 2001, 2–9; Roy L. Williams, "Employers Say Immigrants Ease Critical Worker Shortage in Area," *Birmingham News,* September 9, 2001; Glenny Brock, "Service Stronghold," *Birmingham Weekly,* July 10, 2003, 6–7. On the "settling out" pattern where Hispanic farm workers move into permanent jobs and create stable communities, see Daniel Rothenberg, *With These Hands: The Hidden World of Migrant Farmworkers Today* (New York: Harcourt Brace, 1998), 181–204.

18. Marcos McPeek Villatoro, "Mexican in Alabama," *Southern Exposure* 22 (Fall 1994): 26–27; Villatoro, "Birth of a Mestizo Nation," *Southern Exposure* 27 (Summer 1999): 18–20. For a fascinating study of chain migration patterns in the Atlanta area, see Mark Bixler, "The Latino Network," *Atlanta Journal-Constitution,* April 15, 2001.

19. Greig Guthey, "Mexican Places in Southern Spaces: Globalization, Work, and Daily Life in and around the North Georgia Poultry Industry," in *Latino Workers in the Contemporary South,* ed. Arthur D. Murphy, Colleen Blanchard, and Jennifer A. Hill (Athens: University of Georgia Press, 2001), 57–67; Hayes Ferguson, "The Nuevo South: Changing Faces," *New Orleans Times-Picayune,* December 29, 1997; *Gainesville Times,* November 3, 2002.

20. Ruben Hernandez-Leon and Victor Zuniga, "'Making Carpet by the Mile': The Emergence of a Mexican Immigrant Community in an Industrial Region of the U.S. Historic South," *Social Science Quarterly* 81 (March 2000): 49–66; James D. Engstsrom, "Industry and Immigration in Dalton, Georgia," in *Latino Workers in the Contemporary South,* 44–56; Victor Zuniga and Ruben Hernandez-Leon, "A New Destination for an Old Migration: Origins, Trajectories, and Labor Market Incorporation of Latinos in Dalton, Georgia," in *Latino Workers,* 126–35; Jim Dyer, "The Dreams of Rigo Nunez," *Atlanta Journal-Constitution,* January 24, 1999.

21. Leon Fink and Alvis Dunn, "The Maya of Morganton: Exploring Worker Identity within the Global Marketplace," in *The Maya Diaspora: Guatemalan Roots, New*

American Lives, ed. James Loucky and Marilyn M. Moors (Philadelphia: Temple University Press, 2000), 175–95; Leon Fink, *The Maya of Morganton: Work and Community in the Nuevo New South* (Chapel Hill: University of North Carolina Press, 2003); Allan F. Burns, *Maya in Exile: Guatemalans in Florida* (Philadelphia: Temple University Press, 1993).

22. Charlie LeDuff, "At a Slaughterhouse, Some Things Never Die," *New York Times,* June 16, 2000.

23. Lane Windham and Eric Bates, "H-2B," *Southern Exposure* 20 (Spring 1992): 57–61; David Griffith, *The Estuary's Gift: An Atlantic Coast Cultural Biography* (University Park: Pennsylvania State University Press, 1999), 71–98; David Griffith, *Jones's Minimal: Low-Wage Labor in the United States* (Albany: State University of New York Press, 1993), 51–81, 115–47; Griffith, "New Immigrants in an Old Industry: Blue Crab Processing in Pamlico County, North Carolina," in *Any Way You Cut It: Meat Processing and Small-Town America,* ed. Donald D. Stull, Michael J. Broadway, and David Griffith (Lawrence: University Press of Kansas, 1995), 153–86; Anne Hull, "Una Vida Mejor," *St. Petersburg Times,* May 9, 10, 11, 1999; Emily F. Selby, Deborah P. Dixon, and Holly M. Hapke, "A Woman's Place in the Crab Processing Industry of Eastern Carolina," *Gender, Place and Culture* 8 (2001): 229–58; Andrew Olsen, "Clawing Their Way Out," *Washington Times,* September 9, 2002.

24. Debra Sabia, "Challenges of Solidarity and Lessons for Community Empowerment: The Struggle of Migrant Farm Workers in Rural South Georgia," *SECOLAS Annals: Journal of the Southeastern Council on Latin American Studies* 30 (March 1999): 95–109; John D. Studstill and Laura Nieto-Studstill, "Hospitality and Hostility: Latin Immigrants in Southern Georgia," in *Latino Workers,* 68–81; Thomas A. Arcury et al., "Pesticide Use and Safety Training in Mexico: The Experience of Farmworkers Employed in North Carolina," *Human Organization* 60, no. 1 (2001): 56–65; Ned Glascock, "Foreign Labor on Home Soil," *Raleigh News and Observer,* August 29, 1999; Hayes Ferguson, "The Nuevo South: Chasing American Dream to a Small La. Town," *New Orleans Times-Picayune,* December 28, 1997; Katherine M. Donato, Carl L. Bankston, and Dawn T. Robinson, "Immigration and the Organization of the Offshore Oil Industry: Southern Louisiana in the Late 1990s," in *Latino Workers,* 105–13; Valarie Honeycutt and Andy Mead, "From the Border to the Bluegrass: Why Hispanics Come and What They Leave Behind," *Lexington Herald-Leader,* December 20, 22, 1998; Chris Poynter, "More Hispanics Find a Job—and a Home," *Louisville Courier-Journal,* July 20, 1999; Steven Greenhouse, "Migrants Plant Pine Trees but Often Pocket Peanuts," *New York Times,* February 14, 2001; Rick Mines, "Ethnic Shift in Eastern Crop Agriculture: Replacement or Displacement?" (unpublished paper, Changing Face Conference, Newark, Delaware, September 1997), http://migration.ucdavis.edu/rmn/.

25. Keith F. West, "Hispanic Population Boom Portends Change," *Charleston Regional Business Journal,* April 9, 2001; Michael Kelley, "Latino Memphis," *Memphis Commercial Appeal,* September 21, 1997; Rebecca J. Dameron and Arthur D. Murphy, "An International City Too Busy to Hate? Social and Cultural Change in Atlanta, 1970–95," *Urban Anthropology* 26 (Spring 1997): 43–69; Jane Kitchen, "The Hispanic Boom," *Hispanic* (January–February 2002): www.hispaniconline.com/magazine; Peter Whoriskey and Sarah Cohen, "Immigrants Arrive from Far and Wide," *Washington Post,*

November 23, 2001; "Boom in Immigrants Transforming County," *Washington Post,* June 6, 2002.

26. Joe Fahy, "No Pain, No Gain," *Southern Exposure* 17 (Summer 1989): 35–38; Eric Schlosser, *Fast Food Nation: The Dark Side of the All-American Meal* (Boston: Houghton Mifflin, 2001), 169–90, 172; Steve Stiffler, "Inside a Poultry Plant: An Ethnographic Portrait," *Labor History* 43 (August 2002): 305–13; Barbara Goldoftas, "Inside the Slaughterhouse," *Southern Exposure* 17 (Summer 1989): 25–29, 27; Javier Lopez, "Diary of a Poultry Worker," *Southern Exposure* 31 (Spring 2003): 48–53; E. Richard Brown and Hongjian Yu, "Latinos' Access to Employment-based Health Insurance," in *Latinos: Remaking America,* ed. Marcelo M. Suarez and Mariela M. Paez (Berkeley: University of California Press, 2002), 236–53; Dave Williams, "Uninsured Hispanics Are a Growing Concern Among Health Leaders," *Savannah Morning News,* October 2, 2002; Thomas A. Arcury and Sara A. Quandt, "Chronic Agricultural Chemical Exposure Among Migrant and Seasonal Farmworkers," *Society and Natural Resources* 11 (1998): 829–43; Sara A. Quand et al., "Migrant Farmworkers and Green Tobacco Sickness: New Issues for an Understudied Disease," *American Journal of Industrial Medicine* 37 (March 2000): 307–15; Thomas A. Arcury et al., "Farmworker Reports of Pesticide Safety and Sanitation in the Work Environment," *American Journal of Industrial Medicine* 39 (May 2001): 487–98; Rebecca C. Elmore and Thomas A. Arcury, "Pesticide Exposure Beliefs Among Latino Farmworkers in North Carolina's Christmas Tree Industry," *American Journal of Industrial Medicine* 40 (August 2001): 153–60; Joyce Hedges, "Hispanic Workers Face Disparate Risk, Are Overrepresented in Hazardous Jobs," *Occupational Safety and Health Reporter* 31 (January 11, 2001); Jim Hopkins, "Deaths of Hispanic Workers Soar 53%," *USA Today,* March 25, 2002.

27. Sheila M. Poole, "Unions Seek Latinos to Bolster Numbers," *Atlanta Journal-Constitution,* April 19, 1998; Harold Meyerson, "Street vs. Suite: Why L.A.'s Janitors Will Win Their Strike," *L.A. Weekly,* April 7, 2000; Meyerson, "A Clean Sweep," *American Prospect* 11 (June 19, 2000): 24–29; Roger Waldinger et al., "Helots No More: A Case Study of the Justice for Janitors Campaign in Los Angeles," in *Organizing to Win: New Research on Union Strategies,* ed. Kate Bronfenbrenner et al. (Ithaca: Cornell University Press, 1998), 102–19. See also Ruth Milkman, ed., *Organizing Immigrants: The Challenge for Unions in Contemporary California* (Ithaca: Cornell University Press, 2000).

28. LeDuff, "At a Slaughterhouse, Some Things Never Die"; Craig Whitlock, "Immigrant Poultry Workers' Struggle for Respect Draws National Attention," *Raleigh News and Observer,* November 30, 1996; Fink and Dunn, "The Maya of Morganton"; Fink, *The Maya of Morganton;* Griffith, "New Immigrants in an Old Industry," 159; Erica Hodgin, "Heat's on Farm Labor System," *Raleigh News and Observer,* August 10, 1999; "On the Line: Latinos on Labor's Cutting Edge," *NAFTA Report on the Americas* 30 (November/December 1996): 18; Yolanda Rodriguez, "Immigrants Ride for Rights," *Atlanta Journal-Constitution,* September 30, 2003; Lindsey Listrom, "Activists Rally for Immigrant Rights," *Durham Daily Tar Heel,* October 1, 2003.

29. Janita Poe, "Latino Leaders to Target Problems in South," *Atlanta Journal-Constitution,* July 24, 2002; Ian Urbina, "Southern Bellwether: Unions Won't Survive Unless They Organize Down in Dixie," *In These Times* 26 (March 4, 2002): 16–18; Vernon M. Briggs Jr., "American Unionism and U.S. Immigration Policy," Center for Im-

migration Studies, http://www.cis.org/articles/2001/back1001.htm. More generally, see Hector L. Delgado, *New Immigrants, Old Unions: Organizing Undocumented Workers in Los Angeles* (Philadelphia: Temple University Press, 1993); Vernon M. Briggs Jr., *Immigration Policy and the American Labor Force* (Baltimore: Johns Hopkins University Press, 1984); Briggs, *Mass Immigration and the National Interest,* 2nd ed. (Armonk, N.Y.: M. E. Sharpe, 1996); Briggs, *Immigration and American Unionism* (Ithaca: Cornell University Press, 2001); Ruth Milkman, "Immigrant Organizing and the New Labor Movement in Los Angeles," *Critical Sociology* 26 (2001): 59–81.

30. Jacquelyne J. Jackson, "Illegal Aliens: Big Threat to Black Workers," *Ebony,* April 1979, 33–40. See also Frank D. Bean and Stephanie Bell-Rose, "Immigration and its Relation to Race and Ethnicity in the United States," in *Immigration and Opportunity,* 1–28.

31. LeDuff, "At a Slaughterhouse, Some Things Never Die."

32. Andres Viglucci, "Hispanic Wave Forever Alters Small Town in North Carolina," *Miami Herald,* January 2, 2000; Mark Bixler, "Unwilling Neighbors," *Atlanta Journal-Constitution,* November 21, 2000; Ben Stocking, "Side By Side: Worlds Apart," *Raleigh News and Observer,* May 4, 1997; Charlie LeDuff, "Some Things Never Die," *Raleigh News and Observer,* July 2, 2000; Ned Glascock, "Latinos Now Filling Bottom-Rung Jobs," *Raleigh News and Observer,* October 29, 2000; Cynthia Tucker, "Latino Growth a Wake-up Call for Black Folks," *Atlanta Journal Constitution,* March 18, 2001; Dahleen Glanton, "Hispanic Influx in Deep South Causes Tensions—with Blacks," *Chicago Tribune,* March 19, 2001; Julianne Malveaux, "Blacks Hold Mixed Views on Immigrants," *USA Today,* August 31, 2001; Ron Nissimov, "Some Blacks Irritated by Immigrant Influx," *Houston Chronicle,* August 25, 2002.

33. Reynolds Farley, *The New American Reality: Who We Are, How We Got Here, Where We Are Going* (New York: Russell Sage Foundation, 1996), 200; Marcela Mendoza, David H. Ciscel, and Barbara Ellen Smith, "Latino Immigrants in Memphis, Tennessee: Their Local Economic Impact" (Working Paper 15, Center for Research on Women, University of Memphis, 2001), 4.

34. For key sources in the debate among the experts, see "Social Science and Public Policy: Immigration and its Consequences," *Transaction: Social Science and Modern Society* 22 (May/June 1985): 67–76; Peter H. Schuck, "The Great Immigration Debate," *American Prospect,* no. 3 (Fall 1990): 100–118; Julian L. Simon and Rita James Simon, "Do We Really Need All These Immigrants?" in *Second Thoughts: Myths and Morals of U.S. Economic History,* ed. Donald N. McCloskey (New York: Oxford University Press, 1993), 19–25; Julian L. Simon, *The Economic Consequences of Immigration* (Oxford: Blackwell, 1989); George J. Borjas, *Friends or Strangers: The Impact of Immigrants on the U.S. Economy* (New York: Basic Books, 1990); Richard A. Wright, Mark Ellis, and Michael Reibel, "The Linkage between Immigration and Internal Migration in Large Metropolitan Areas in the United States," *Economic Geography* 73 (April 1997): 234–54; Daniel S. Hamermesh and Frank D. Bean, eds., *Help or Hindrance? The Economic Implications of Immigration for African Americans* (New York: Russell Sage Foundation, 1998); Bean and Bell-Rose, eds., *Immigration and Opportunity;* George J. Borjas, *Heaven's Door: Immigration Policy and the American Economy* (Princeton: Princeton University Press, 1999); Nelson Lim, "On the Back of Blacks: Immigration and the Fortunes of African

Americans," in *Strangers at the Gates: New Immigrants in Urban America*, ed. Roger Waldinger (Berkeley: University of California Press, 2001), 186–227; Roger Waldinger and Michael L. Lichter, *How the Other Half Works: Immigration and the Social Organization of Labor* (Berkeley: University of California Press, 2003).

35. Thomas A. Tweed, "Our Lady of Guadalupe Visits the Confederate Memorial," *Southern Cultures* 8 (Summer 2002): 79–80; Stocking, "Side By Side"; Scott Jenkins, "Blacks, Hispanics Hoping to Break Cultural Barriers," *Salisbury (N.C.) Post*, May 2, 2001; Scott Jenkins, "Hispanics, Blacks Gather to Bridge Culture Gaps," *Salisbury (N.C.) Post*, May 6, 2001; Glascock, "Latinos Now Filling Bottom-Ring Jobs"; "Race Relations Topic of Town Meeting," Raleigh *News and Observer*, April 25, 2002; "Hispanic Forum Overwhelming Success," [Birmingham Civil Rights Institute] *Vision* 3 (January–March 2002): 1; Community Foundation of Greater Birmingham, *Birmingham, A City of Roots and Wings: A Special Report on Race Relations and Diversity Survey* (Birmingham: Community Foundation of Greater Birmingham, 2003).

36. Philip Martin, "Do Mexican Agricultural Policies Stimulate Emigration?" in *At the Crossroads: Mexico and U.S. Immigration Policy*, ed. Frank D. Bean et al. (Lanham, Md.: Rowman and Littlefield, 1997), 102–3; Matt Kempner, "The Big Wink: Labor Needs Bend Immigration Rules," *Atlanta Journal-Constitution*, January 23, 2000; Roberto Suro, "Boom in Fake Identity Cards for Aliens," *New York Times*, February 19, 1992; Steve Thompson, "The Paper Chase," *Chapel Hill News*, March 31, 2002; "Fake Social Security Cards Sold to Illegal Immigrants," *Athens Banner-Herald*, November 26, 2002; Mendoza, Ciscel, and Smith, "Latino Immigrants in Memphis, Tennessee," 7.

37. Kempner, "The Big Wink"; Ned Glascock and Craig Whitlock, "Law vs. Reality," *Raleigh News and Observer*, November 30, 1998; Nick Patterson, "Illegals Find It Hard to Fit into Society," *Birmingham Post-Herald*, March 17, 1997; Patterson, "Industry Says It Does Not Seek Out Illegals," *Birmingham Post-Herald*, March 3, 1997; Rose Livingston, "Illegal Aliens Arrested," *Birmingham News*, July 7, 1997; Jodi Wilgoren, "U.S. Indictment Charges Smuggling of Workers," *Fort Lauderdale Sun Sentinel*, December 23, 1997; Robert L. Jackson, "Tyson Foods Is Indicted in Immigrant Smuggling," *Los Angeles Times*, December 20, 2001; Bill Poovey, "Tyson, Managers Plead Innocent," *Birmingham News*, January 25, 2002; "Tyson Indicted," *Rural Migration News* 8, January 2002, http://migration.ucdavis.edu/rmn/; Sherri Day, "Jury Clears Tyson Foods in Use of Illegal Immigrants," *New York Times*, March 27, 2003.

38. Greg Schneider, "Grand Jury, Wal-Mart Probe Hiring of Workers," *Washington Post*, October 25, 2003; Abigail Goldman, "Wal-Mart to Review All Workers After Immigration Raids," *Los Angeles Times*, October 25, 2003; Rose Livingston, "INS Agent Shortage Called 'Dangerous' for Alabama," *Birmingham News*, March 16, 2000; Manuel Torres, "The Latinization of the South," *Mobile Register*, June 28, 1999; LeDuff, "At a Slaughterhouse, Some Things Never Die"; James Goldsborough, "Out-of-Control Immigration," *Foreign Affairs* 79 (September/October 2000): 89–101, 89.

39. On churches, see Trish Wilson, "More Latinos Leaving Catholicism for Baptist Faith," *Raleigh News and Observer*, April 23, 1995; Yonat Shimron, "Catholic Welcome of Latinos Uneven," *Raleigh News and Observer*, October 25, 1996; Jessie Burchette, "Methodists Trying to Welcome Hispanics," *Salisbury (N.C.) Post*, July 29, 1999; Greg Garrison, "Jehovah's Witnesses Draw Hispanics," *Birmingham News*, December 5, 1999;

"Church Adapts to Hispanic Immigrants," *Huntsville El Reportero*, July 16, 2000; Tom Smith, "Russellville Church Brings Multitudes of Cultures Together," *Florence (Ala.) Shoals Times-Daily*, June 28, 2000; John Gerome, "A More Ethnic City," *Birmingham News*, September 29, 2000; Leslie Scanlon, "Churches Respond to Needs, Fervor," *Louisville Courier-Journal*, January 16, 2000; Frank Roberts, "Some Build Bridges to Growing Ranks of Hispanics," *Norfolk Virginian-Pilot*, June 22, 2002; Linda Parham, "Church Offers Lifeline to Area Hispanics," *Birmingham News*, October 8, 2002; David Cho, "Energetic Worship Excites Hispanic Catholic Church," *Birmingham News*, November 29, 2002; Leigh Anne Monitor, "Faith Breaks Language Barrier," *Birmingham Post-Herald*, March 22, 2003; Patricia Campion, "One Under God? Religious Entrepreneurship and Pioneer Latino Immigrants in Southern Louisiana," *Sociological Spectrum* 23, no. 2 (2003): 279–301.

40. Raymond A. Mohl, notes from meeting of Central Alabama Alliance for Latino Health, Birmingham, April 12, 2001; "Hispanic Association Formed in Huntsville," *Huntsville El Reportero*, November 1999; Tom Smith, "Coalition Works to Eliminate Barriers," *Florence Shoals Times-Daily*, July 24, 2000; Charda Temple, "Hispanic Caucus Seeks Stronger Voice in State," *Birmingham News*, February 9, 2003; Kempner, "The Big Wink"; Kelley, "Latino Memphis"; Ned Glascock, "Estimate Alarms Hispanic Advocates," *Raleigh News and Observer*, December 21, 1997; Ruth Sheehan and Ned Glascock, "Spanish Lessons," *Raleigh News and Observer*, February 22, 1998; Rich Badie, "Latino Civil Rights Group to Open Office in Atlanta," *Atlanta Journal-Constitution*, November 29, 2001; Mark Bixler, "Face of the Future," *Atlanta Journal-Constitution*, April 24, 2002; Yolanda Rodriguez, "New Leader to Expand Latin American Association," *Atlanta Journal-Constitution*, July 24, 2002; Bulkeley, "Spanish-Speaking Households on the Rise in Mississippi"; Janita Poe, "Latino Leaders to Target Problems in the South," *Miami Herald*, July 24, 2002.

41. Raymond Tatalovich, *Nativism Reborn? The Official English Language Movement and the American States* (Lexington: University Press of Kentucky, 1995), 182–85, 194–224; Tatalovich, "Official English as Nativist Backlash," in *Immigrants Out: The New Nativism and the Anti-Immigrant Impulse in the United States*, ed. Juan F. Perea (New York: New York University Press, 1997), 78–102; Robert D. King, "Should English Be the Law?" *Atlantic Monthly*, April 1997, 55–64; Gary Strauss, "Can't Anyone Here Speak English?" *USA Today*, March 2, 1997; Carol Schmid, "Immigration and Asian and Hispanic Minorities in the New South: An Exploration of History, Attitudes, and Demographic Trends," *Sociological Spectrum* 23, no. 2 (2003): 129–57; *Birmingham News*, April 27, 1989, June 6, 1990; Mary Orndorff, "High-Court to Review English-only License Test," *Birmingham News*, September 27, 2000; Kevin Sack, "Don't Speak English? No Tax Break, Alabama Official Declares," *New York Times*, June 4, 1999; Rose Toussaint-Almanza, "American Citizen, No English? You Will Not Receive Service from Government Agencies," *Huntsville El Reportero*, November 1, 1999; Elaine Witt, "Ad Controversy Befouls Our Southern Hospitality," *Birmingham Post-Herald*, January 25, 2000; Jamie Kizzire, "Hispanics' Clout Rising in Alabama," *Birmingham Post-Herald*, June 27, 2000; Hernan Prado, "Racial Slurs from Alabama Radio Station," *Huntsville El Reportero*, May 1, 2000; Dave Bryan, "Hispanics Make Headway in Old South," *Washington Post*, October 10, 2000. See also Geoffrey Nunberg, "Lingo Jingo: English-Only and the New Nativism,"

American Prospect no. 33, July-August 1997, 40–47; William Branigin, "As Hispanic Numbers Rise, Some Say No to Spanish," *Birmingham News,* February 7, 1999.

42. Suzy Lowry, "White Supremacists Plan Oneonta March," *Oneonta Blount Countian,* May 21, 1997; Suzy Lowry, "White Supremacists Withdraw Second Application for Parade Permit," *Oneonta Blount Countian,* June 4, 1997; "Ku Klux Klan Gives Mixed Signals," *Oneonta Blount Countian,* June 18, 1997; Gita M. Smith, "Klan Targets Hispanics Welcome in Alabama," *Atlanta Journal-Constitution,* June 17, 1997.

43. Beth Lakey, "Three Arrested at Protest," *Cullman Times,* January 18, 1998; Rose Livingston, "Hispanics Fear Trouble After Cullman Rally," *Birmingham News,* January 29, 1998; Manuel Torres, "The Latinization of the South," *Mobile Register,* June 28, 1999; "Advocacy: Essential for Hispanic Ministries," United Methodist Church, General Board of Global Ministries, *Hispanic Ministries Newsletter* 6 (December 1998/January 1999); Kelly Hamilton, "Mexico Comes to Cullman, Alabama," graduate seminar paper, Department of History, University of Alabama at Birmingham, 2002.

44. Ben Stocking, "A Surging Latino Population Calls Siler City 'Home,'" Raleigh *News and Observer,* January 14, 1996; Ned Glascock and Ruth Sheehan, "Backlash Greets Newcomers," *Raleigh News and Observer,* February 23, 1998; Sue Anne Pressley, "Hispanic Immigration Boom Rattles South," *Washington Post,* March 6, 2000; Andres Viglucci, "Hispanic Wave Forever Alters Small Town in North Carolina," *Miami Herald,* January 2, 2000; Tom Steadman, "Immigration: A Small Town Struggles to Cope with Change," *Greensboro News and Record,* April 16, 2000; Sergio Bustos, "Small Towns Shaped by Influx of Hispanics," *USA Today,* May 23, 2000; Barry Yeoman, "Hispanic Diaspora," *Mother Jones,* July/August 2000, 35–41, 76; "White Supremacists to March in Hall County," *Athens Banner-Herald,* July 11, 2002; "Faces Change, But Immigration's Positive Impact Remains," *Athens Banner-Herald,* July 20, 2002; Rick Badie, "Group Says Debate Isn't About Race," *Atlanta Journal-Constitution,* February 19, 2003; Atha J. Cravey, "The Changing South: Latino Labor and Poultry Production in Rural North Carolina," *Southeastern Geographer* 37 (November 1997): 295–300.

45. Tweed, "Our Lady of Guadalupe Visits the Confederate Memorial," 72–93; Joan Flocks and Paul Monaghan, "Viva Mexico!: Mexican Independence Day Festivals in Central Florida," in *Southern Heritage on Display: Public Ritual and Ethnic Diversity within Southern Regionalism,* ed. Celeste Ray (Tuscaloosa: University of Alabama Press, 2003), 167–93; Sarah Lundy, "Festival Hispano Celebrates Cultures," *Charleston Post and Courier,* September 8, 2002; Marie Jones, "Habla Espanol? Hispanic Culture Integrating Itself into Birmingham," *Birmingham Weekly,* March 5, 1998; Carol Robinson, "Hispanic Community Grows," *Birmingham News,* March 21, 1999; Mark Bixler, "The Latino Network: Old Ties Renewed in Metro Area," *Atlanta Journal-Constitution,* April 15, 2001; Kevin Sack, "Far from Mexico, Making a Place Like Home," *New York Times,* July 30, 2001; Glenny Brock, "Taking Stock: Family Groceries Reflect Birmingham's Growing Diversity, *Birmingham Weekly,* October 18, 2001; Regina Wright, "Mexican Holiday, Decatur Style," *Decatur Daily News,* May 5, 2000; Gigi Anders, "Nuestro Mundo," *Raleigh News and Observer,* September 20, 1998; "Ethnic Diversity in Birmingham Nightlife," *Huntsville El Reportero,* October 1, 2000; Matt Tidmore, "A League of Their Own," *Birmingham News,* October 4, 2000; "Liga Latino Americana de Futbol," *Gadsden Latino,*

May 16, 2001; Jim Young, "Hispanic Soccer Title to be Decided Sunday," *Greensboro News and Record,* September 20, 2002; Dawn Wotapka, "A Latino Superstore Takes Shape," *Raleigh News and Observer,* May 26, 2000; Patricia Dedrick, "Going Gourmet with Goats," *Birmingham News,* July 18, 2003; Eric Velasco, "Bueno!" *Birmingham News,* October 17, 2003.

46. Walter Woods, "A Wave of Political Change," *Atlanta Business Chronicle,* March 22, 2002; Yolanda Rodriguez, "Atlanta's Edge: Latino Diversity," *Atlanta Journal-Constitution,* June 26, 2002; Betty Liu, "Latinos Flex Their Muscles in Georgia Poll," *Financial Times (London),* August 20, 2002; Mark Bixler, "Latino Candidates: Victories Signal Growing Clout," *Atlanta Journal-Constitution,* November 7, 2002; Yolanda Rodriguez and Sheila M. Poole, "Electoral Jolt Leaves Groups Guessing," *Atlanta Journal-Constitution,* November 20, 2002; Janita Poe, "Budding Coalition," *Atlanta Journal-Constitution,* September 24, 2003; Kim Baca, "Few Hispanics Voting in S.C., Records Show," *Columbia The State,* June 11, 2001; Tom Gordon, "Democrats Reach Out for Hispanic Vote," *Birmingham News,* October 6, 2002. For national implications of Latino voting, see Don Campbell, "The Coming Fight Over Latino Power," *USA Today,* April 23, 2001; Harold Meyerson, "The Rising Latino Tide," *American Prospect* 13 (November 18, 2002): 22–25.

47. Cruz C. Torres, *Emerging Latino Communities: A New Challenge for the Rural South* (Hattiesburg: Southern Rural Development Center, Mississippi State University, 2000); Linda Garrett, *Looking for a Better Life: Latinos in Georgia, Myths and Realities of the Immigrant Journey* (Athens: Institute on Human Development and Disability, University of Georgia, 2000); Jorge H. Antiles and Stephanie A. Bohon, *The Needs of Georgia's New Latinos: A Policy Agenda for the Decade Ahead* (Athens: Carl Vinson Institute of Government, University of Georgia, 2002).

Asian Immigrants in the South

David M. Reimers

Here in Georgia's most heavily Asian county, the future of a New South—
a multi-cultural region more California than Dixie—can be seen in communities like Duluth, a city that saw its Asian population grow in the past
decade from a few hundred families to the city's largest ethnic minority.
Jessie Mangaliman, "The South's New Cultural Landscape," *San Jose Mercury News*,
March 17, 2002.

Asian Immigration to the South before 1945

From the end of the Civil War until World War I, a global migration of
peoples occurred as millions of Europeans and Asians moved to neighboring
nations or crossed oceans to settle in South America, the Caribbean, Canada,
and the United States. Immigrants to the United States tended to avoid the
South, with the bulk of newcomers favoring the West and Northeast. The South
did attract some immigrants: Greeks, Cubans, and Italians went to Florida; Jews
settled in small towns and larger cities; Italians also located in New Orleans,
while a few settled in Mississippi's Delta. A case in point: Leroy Percy, hoping to
reduce plantation owners' dependence on black farmers, recruited Italians to
work his plantation in Arkansas. While at first achieving success, Percy discovered that the newcomers did not wish to labor under Percy's conditions, and the
experiment soon came to an end.[1]

This experience with Italian farmworkers partially explains why the South
recruited so few Europeans. Plantation work was identified with blacks, who for
the most part lived in poverty as sharecroppers, tenants, or farm laborers of one
kind or another. Black sharecroppers had few rights and lived in a state of acute
dependency on whites. Life in the towns and cities was little better for southern African Americans. Such dependency and poverty in the rural South were
not likely to appeal to immigrants who would have viewed blacks as competition.[2] In addition, aside from agriculture there were few jobs to attract the
foreign born. The growing textile industry employed mainly local white labor
under poor health conditions and low wages. Nor were the forest-related industries enticing. While iron and steel attracted a few immigrants, wages in the
southern United States were lower than elsewhere. Indeed, in the twentieth century, southern entrepreneurs and governmental officials were able to lure New

England cotton mills and other industries to the South because of this wage gap. While conditions for immigrants were hardly ideal in the North and West, wages were higher, and once immigrant communities were established in Pittsburgh, Chicago, Detroit, and other cities, they attracted their fellow nationals who could find familiar faces and organizations and who could help them find employment and housing.

Thus, in spite of some southern efforts to attract European immigrants, most headed to the North and West. In 1860 about 14 percent of the non-South's population was foreign born, but in the South the figure was only 5 percent. The mass immigration of the post–Civil War decades made the gap between the former Confederate states and the rest of the nation even wider. In 1910, when nearly 15 percent of the nation's peoples were foreign born (the highest percentage ever recorded), only 2 percent of the South's population hailed from abroad. Hoping to attract immigrants in the late nineteenth century, white southerners had generally opposed immigration restriction for Europeans, but they underwent "an astonishing revolution in the early twentieth century," notes John Higham, perhaps reflecting the region's inability to attract immigrants and its absorption of racist ideas about European immigrants.[3] After that time, southern senators and representatives could be counted on to vote for tight limits on European immigration.[4]

Some Asians did settle in the South, as early as the eighteenth century, before their eventual exclusion. After Spain conquered the Philippines, the Spanish taught Filipinos the Spanish language and then recruited many men as sailors on Spanish vessels plying the route between China and Manila. Some ships in this galleon trade made it to the New World where Filipino sailors jumped ship and settled in Mexico. A few eventually found their way to the United States. According to Marina E. Espina, Filipinos "lived along the southeastern coast of Louisiana" as early as 1765, which made them the first modern Asians to set foot on American soil.[5] The most famous settlement, according to Espina, was "Manila Village" in Jefferson Parish, where the immigrants survived as fishermen. Some three hundred Filipinos lived there at one time or other, along with some Chinese and Spaniards. In 1883 *Harper's Weekly* claimed that four hundred Filipinos had created another Louisiana outpost "known as St. Maolo."[6] They were usually Roman Catholics who spoke Tagalog, Cebuano, and Spanish and lived off the shrimp and fishing trade.[7]

These immigrants formed the first Filipino American benevolent society, *La Union Filipina,* headquartered in New Orleans. One authority estimated the Filipino population in Louisiana to be two thousand in 1906, though the census figure is much lower than that amount.[8] Living mainly by fishing, they kept to themselves. In 1915, the village at St. Maolo was destroyed by a hurricane, a disaster that fostered a movement of Filipinos to New Orleans.

Asians made inroads elsewhere in the South. According to Raymond A. Mohl's account, Kamosu Jo Sakai arrived in Florida in 1903 to organize a Japanese agricultural colony.[9] He had been educated western style and converted to Christianity. In Florida, Sakai found support from the Jacksonville business community, who offered him free land. Instead he purchased land and then returned to Japan to procure laborers, but he persuaded only a few to venture to Florida. For a few years this colony, called "Yamota," struggled successfully, yielding pineapples. Sixty Japanese lived in the colony in the 1920s, but it ended only a few years later.[10]

Other Japanese migrated to Texas in the late nineteenth century. These were sons who did not stand to inherit in Japan and who had heard of possibilities in Texas. Seito Saibara founded a colony in Harris County and enticed others to follow. A few grew rice successfully, but the Great Depression made their enterprises difficult. Some of these Japanese were arrested and sent to the relocation camps during World War II.[11]

The small number of Japanese in Florida and Texas reflected the Japanese presence in the entire South. The census from 1890 to 1910 located few southern Japanese—in Georgia, for example, no Japanese were counted in 1890, and only one was counted in 1910.[12] The Dillingham Commission on Immigration, reporting in 1911, found only one Japanese woman working in the whole South; she was employed in the cigar and tobacco manufacturing industry.[13]

The first Asian Indian to come to America probably did so in 1790, and he was followed by only a few others.[14] Both the Bureau of the Census and the Dillingham Commission found only handfuls of Asian Indians and virtually no Koreans when they submitted their reports. The 1910 census listed only 4,006 Indians arriving from 1900 to 1910, with very few, if any, settling in southern states.[15] The Dillingham Commission reported that the first Indians coming to the United States were professionals, travelers, and merchants who resided mostly in New York and other northeastern states.[16] If any of these people settled in the South, nothing is known about them, and their numbers were very small. Before 1915, only 1,000 Koreans had immigrated to the continental United States, most of whom lived in California.

Chinese, by far, made up the largest number of Asian immigrants who settled in the South before World War II. Southerners had had direct contact with the Chinese before the Civil War because several Chinese had attended schools in the South, and a few had traveled through the southern states as entertainers.[17] Some white southerners looked to China as a favorable field for Christian missionaries and even hoped to train Chinese immigrants to return to their homeland to preach the Gospel. These southern religious leaders brought converted Chinese with them when they toured the South.[18]

In part, however, the growth of this population resulted from economics, not religious trends: active recruitment by post–Civil War planters who wanted to replace newly freed slaves played an important role in bringing Chinese immigrants to the southern states. Some white southerners believed that blacks would no longer provide muscle for their needs or would demand high wages. In the 1860s several southern conventions addressed future race and labor issues and called for the importation of Chinese plantation workers. Newspapers also took up the call. The *Vicksburg (Miss.) Times* declared, "Emancipation has spoiled the negro, and carried him away from fields of agriculture. Our prosperity depends entirely upon the recovery of lost ground, and we therefore say let the [Chinese] Coolies come, and we will take the chance of Christianizing them."[19]

Some of the first Chinese brought to Mississippi were recruited directly from China (and Cuba, where they were working as contract laborers), but such a trip across the Pacific was long and costly. The few who did settle in the South provided networks for relatives and other Chinese immigrants who needed employment after the California mines and railroads no longer had many openings. And some, according to James Loewen, arrived with enough money to open small businesses.[20]

In spite of planter enthusiasm, white Mississippians were unable to attract many Chinese agricultural workers, and white planters soon abandoned their attempts to find labor among Asian immigrants; instead they continued to rely upon African Americans to become sharecroppers or plantation workers. As for the Chinese themselves, they quickly left the farms, which paid low wages and offered only a very limited future, and opened small grocery stores in the Mississippi Delta.[21] Loewen reports that the first Chinese grocery began operating in the early 1870s. A modest enterprise, opened with as little as a hundred dollars, the Chinese grocery generally served blacks and working-class whites. It was hard to make a profit, but by living frugally, residing in the back of the store or upstairs, the Chinese managed to earn enough money to last beyond the first generation. Loewen reports that new immigrants from China, mostly male relatives, migrated to the Mississippi Delta to work in existing shops or to open their own businesses. Some went to Mississippi because the restrictive laws limiting Chinese immigration still permitted merchants to settle in the United States. While the groceries were the core of the Mississippi Chinese community, some Chinese became Christians and organized Protestant churches.

When the gates opened again for substantial Chinese immigration after World War II, few chose to settle in Mississippi. Yet the Delta Chinese community, while shrinking in size, still existed by the end of the twentieth century. The number of stores peaked in 1960 when twelve hundred Chinese operated businesses in twelve Delta counties. The Chinese Baptist Church of Cleveland, Mississippi, was not a symbol of the new immigration, but a sign that the original community remained. The post-1960 generation, however, was not likely to follow their ancestors by operating grocery stores in the Delta.[22]

The experience of the Mississippi Chinese was not encouraging to other potential immigrants. In addition to having to struggle to make a living, Chinese immigrants were "between black and white" and not considered equal to whites. Some Chinese merchants were able to bring over their families, but the Mississippi Chinese community did not have enough Chinese women for Chinese men. Faced with a shortage of Chinese women, the men married African Americans, or in a few cases, white southerners. Delta whites saw the children of African Americans and Chinese as blacks and relegated the youth to separate schools or black schools. In other ways, too, Chinese merchants deferred to whites, and not until the 1930s and 1940s did the Chinese and their children become "white," or white enough to enroll in white schools and patronize white churches and public facilities. The number of Chinese, of course, was small, and indeed in some communities before 1930, where only one or two Chinese children lived, whites did permit them to attend white schools. What would have happened if their numbers had been large is left to speculation.[23]

Planters elsewhere in the South after 1865 believed that Chinese immigrants might solve their perceived labor difficulties, but they found few who were willing to leave China or California, especially for the low wages landowners had in mind. Federal government restrictions on the "coolie trade" also hindered efforts at recruitment. A few Louisiana planters brought Chinese from Cuba, and the early success of Louisianans prompted others to seek Chinese immigrants, but the number recruited for farm work was small. Although planters failed to find eager tenants or farmworkers among Chinese immigrants, the newcomers nonetheless found employment on railroads or in cotton mills.[24]

Florida, with its more diverse economy, was another point of Chinese entrance. There, too, eager recruiters claimed that Chinese immigrants would solve the state's shortage of workers. However, only a few came to work in the fields, drain water, and labor in the turpentine industry. After working on plantations or under their initial contracts, Chinese immigrants moved to cities or small towns. There, as elsewhere, they operated grocery stores or laundries. As they had for the Mississippi Delta migrants, the grocery stores became the center of their lives: "After the Chinese moved from the places of first employment to scattered sharecropping sites or locations in towns and cities, few symbols of their culture remained except Chinese stores."[25]

In Texas planters also attempted to recruit Chinese laborers to take the place of African Americans. In addition, railroad workers from China arrived in 1870, and a second and larger contingent came in 1881. Some did labor as farmers and on the railroads, but eventually most ended up in towns where they followed the path of the Mississippi Chinese and became owners of small shops.

As elsewhere they were mostly young men. They numbered only 1,031 in the 1940 census.[26]

If Asians found social and economic conditions unappealing in the southern states, the issue became moot when Congress moved to bar them from entering the United States as immigrants in the late nineteenth century. The Chinese Exclusion Act of 1882 marked the first time Congress barred a specific nationality group. The movement to ban Chinese immigrants had begun in California, but it quickly gained wide support. While some southern conventions had tried to encourage Asian settlers in the 1860s, by the 1880s southern congressmen supported the restrictions. Daniel J. Tichenor noted, "For their part, Southern congressional Democrats promoted a 'political alliance of the South and the West' dedicated to white supremacy and defeat of Northeastern 'radicalism.'"[27] In the House of Representatives southerners voted sixty to two (twenty not voting) for the bill. In the Senate only one southern Democrat voted against it. Sen. Green Harris (D-Tenn.) typified the shift in the South: in 1869 he chaired the Memphis Chinese Labor Convention, but thirteen years later he voted for Chinese exclusion. The racist overthrow of Radical Reconstruction was capped off with the exclusion of the Chinese.[28] Indeed, a few Congressional southern representatives tried, unsuccessfully, to ban blacks, most of whom came from the Caribbean, from immigration to the United States.[29]

Later acts prohibited most other Asians from entering. The Gentleman's Agreement between the United States and Japan (1907–8) barred Japanese laborers, which included Koreans because Japan controlled Korea at that time. Korean and Japanese "picture brides" still arrived until Congress halted this flow in the 1920s. Indians were blocked from entering by a major immigration act enacted in 1917. Legislators attempted to eliminate nearly all Asian migration in 1924 when they barred all "aliens ineligible for citizenship." The Naturalization Act of 1870 had limited naturalization to persons of African descent and free "white persons," and federal courts held that Asians were not white. Thus Congress simply used those judicial decisions to halt Asian immigration when it excluded all aliens ineligible for citizenship from coming to the United States. These measures won universal support from Congress, including southern representatives and senators. Most of the critics of the Johnson-Reed Act of 1924, which virtually barred Asians and established a national origins system favoring northern and western Europe, came from areas with ties to immigrants from southern and eastern Europe.[30]

Filipinos were nationals, not aliens, and hence were not covered by the 1924 law. However, the Tydings-McDuffie Act of 1934 limited the number coming from the Philippines to fifty annually until independence was achieved, scheduled ten years down the road. Then Filipinos would become aliens, not permitted to immigrate to the United States at all.

Overall, the cited legislation and the Gentlemen's Agreement severely cur-
tailed immigration from Asia. A second generation of Asians came of age in the
United States in the early twentieth century, but the total population remained
small, and the Chinese population decreased for several decades after the 1882
ban was passed.

The New Asian Immigration to the South

In his history of the New South, published in 1995 and covering the period 1945 to 1980, Numan Bartley does not even mention immigration.[31] While
numbers of Asian immigrants grew slowly after a more relaxed immigration
policy went into effect in 1968, it was not until the 1980s that Asians were settling in the South in substantial numbers. The 2000 census reported 10,242,998
million Asians (both immigrants and resulting subsequent generations) in the
nation. Census forms that year permitted persons to check off more than one
race, and another 1.7 million respondents claimed that they were partly Asian,
thus driving the total number of Asians to 11.2 million or 4.2 percent of the
American people.[32] In 2000 Mexico was the leading source for immigration to
the United States, but the next four nations were Asian: the Peoples' Republic of
China, the Philippines, India, and Vietnam. These countries also had backlogs
of those awaiting visas.[33]

The census also noted a concentration of immigrants in six states and key
metropolitan areas. Immigrants clustered in California, New York, New Jersey,
Illinois, and two southern states, Texas and Florida. These six areas comprised
the destination of 66 percent of immigrants in 2000, a pattern similar to other
years.[34] Among the top ten metropolitan areas receiving immigrants in the
1990s were New York, Los Angeles–Long Beach, Orange County (California),
Chicago, Washington, D.C. (which can be included as part southern), and Miami, Houston, and Dallas in the South.[35]

About one half million Asians lived in the South in 1980, a number that grew
to slightly over one million in 1990. The figure more than doubled by 2000 to
over two million, which represented two percent of the South's population. In
that year the southern states with the most Asians were Florida, Texas, Virginia,
and Georgia.[36]

Since 1980 immigrants, Asians among them, have been spreading to new and
different regions, states, and cities, and new immigrants are appearing in places
where their presence was scarcely observed forty years previously. Table 1 indicates the Asian growth in selected southern states. The figures are certainly an
undercount, though the degree to which Asians are undercounted is not clear.

These figures are for all Asians, not simply the foreign born, and they include
those who said they were Asian or Asian and some other race. In 2000 roughly

TABLE 1
Asians in the South, Selected States, 1990–2000

State	Number in 1990	Number in 2000	% Increase
Texas	311,918	644,193	207%
Florida	149,856	333,013	222%
Virginia	156,036	304,559	195%
Georgia	73,764	199,812	271%
Mississippi	12,679	23,281	184%
Alabama	21,088	39,458	187%

Source: U.S. Census, 2000.

60 percent of Asians in the United States were foreign born, and the percentage of foreign-born Asians in the South is likely similar. Only Japanese Americans had a majority born in the United States. The foreign-born population included the so-called "1.5 generation," those who arrived at an early age and were educated in American schools, beginning as young children. The 1.5 generation, in many ways, resembled the native-born population.

The Immigration and Naturalization Service (INS) stopped collecting residence information for immigrants more than twenty years ago, but it does annually report the "intended residence" of incoming immigrants. The leading metropolitan areas for Asian immigrants (and Latinos) were located in California. In 2000 the Los Angeles–Long Beach area was the intended destination of 2,409 Indians; another 1,266 listed Houston and 1,215 were headed for Dallas.[37] Overall, as the twenty-first century dawned, one fifth of Asian immigrants told the INS that the South was their intended destination, a figure similar to that reported in 1990. Table 2 indicates the intended place of residence for several nationalities in two southern states for 2000. For the most part, the intended residence did not vary much from 1980 to 2000.

How does one explain these extraordinary changes in the South? Three factors—one national and two regional—were key to opening the South to the new global immigrants. First, at the national level, tightly enforced immigration restrictions were loosened. The repeal of the Chinese exclusion acts in 1943 permitted Chinese naturalization and immigration, though the number of newcomers allowed was small (only 105 annually). Then India and the Philippines were granted similar quotas in 1946. Six years later the McCarran-Walter Immigration Act abolished the racial prohibitions and gave all other Asian nations small quotas. Some Asians were also included in the special refugee laws enacted in the 1950s, but the major change in policy came in 1965 when Congress did away with the entire national origins quota system and granted all nations in the Eastern Hemisphere the same annual number of visas.[38] Refugees were included in the 1965 act, but Congress also established a new and more gener-

TABLE 2
Intended Residence of Immigrants in Alabama and
Virginia, 2000

State	Nationality	Number
Alabama	Bangladeshi	17
	Chinese	96
	Filipinos	45
	Indians	129
Virginia	Bangladeshi	266
	Chinese	426
	Filipinos	812
	Indians	956

Source: Immigration and Naturalization Service (INS), Statistical
Yearbook, 2000.

ous refugee policy in 1980.[39] All of these measures were pushed by ethnic organizations and helped along by growing awareness in the United States of the
nation's role in international affairs. Congress and presidents wanted to aid
postwar allies in Europe by admitting refugees and by answering communist
claims that American immigration laws discriminated against Asians. In attempting to manage the growth of undocumented or illegal immigration, Congress granted an amnesty to nearly three million persons in 1986 yet simultaneously outlawed the hiring of undocumented immigrants. In 1990 legislators
went further and increased immigration quotas by 35 percent and increased individual country limits to 26,250. All of these changes made huge increases in
immigration possible, and Asians were quick to take advantage. The Asian population of the United States in 1940 was small indeed, comprised of only a few
thousand Koreans and Indians, somewhat more Filipinos, and about one hundred thousand Chinese, and several hundred thousand Japanese in Hawaii and
along the West Coast. By that date a second generation (and hence, American
citizens) was emerging in the Asian communities. On the eve of enactment of
the 1965 act, about twenty thousand Asians entered the United States as refugees
and regular immigrants. Between 1968, when the new law was fully in place, and
2001, seven million Asian immigrants entered the United States.[40]

Yet without two significant changes in the South, few Asian immigrants would
have gone there. The newcomers had little desire to settle in a land with rigid,
often violent racism. During the 1940s southern blacks began to challenge the
oppressive Jim Crow system of race relations in the eleven former confederate
states.[41] Finally, African Americans directly challenged the "separate but equal"
educational doctrine of Plessy v. Ferguson (1896). In Brown v. Board of Education
(1954), the Supreme Court declared that forced separation was inherently un-

equal, but southern whites were slow to open their schools, and when civil rights workers tested universities and other public facilities, violence erupted. The Montgomery, Alabama, bus boycott made Martin Luther King Jr. the major spokesman in the southern black community and, after a struggle, desegregated the city's buses.

African Americans moved to direct action against segregation when students from the North Carolina Agricultural State College sat at white lunch counters in a Greensboro, North Carolina, Woolworth store. Freedom rides of interstate buses to test desegregation followed, as did attempts to open more southern universities to blacks. Racist whites formed white citizens councils in retaliation, and mobs greeted those trying to open the University of Alabama and ride the buses.[42] The administration of John F. Kennedy was forced to respond, and following Kennedy's assassination in 1963, President Lyndon Johnson pushed Congress to pass the Civil Rights Act of 1964 and the Voting Rights Act the next year. Actual desegregation proceeded slowly, but gradually African Americans gained access to the public facilities and employment opportunities that had been closed to them. They also gained better access to the vote once the federal government began enforcing the Fifteenth Amendment. By the 1980s, these improvements—if not actual racial equality—made it clear that a new South was emerging.[43]

That the major pieces of civil rights legislation occurred at the same time as liberalization of immigration policy was no accident. "We have removed all elements of second-class citizenship from our laws by the Civil Rights Act," Vice President Hubert Humphrey said. "We want to bring our immigration law into line with the spirit of the Civil Rights Act of 1964."[44]

Responding to the changing social climate, the Civil Rights Commission and Congressional committees probed discrimination against Asian immigrants and Asian Americans. Administrations after 1965 extended equal protection of the law to Asians and Latinos and even granted them a place in affirmative action programs.[45] The Equal Employment Opportunity Commission and other federal agencies developed new criteria for affirmative action, moving from a nondiscrimination model to an underutilization one. Federal agencies found that Asians were underrepresented in many white-collar occupations and in top business positions and urged changes in these positions to include more Asians. Asian groups also succeeded in gaining access to Small Business Administration programs for minorities. Since most of the issues involving employment, small businesses, contractors and college and universities admissions were found in nearly all parts of the United States, Asians could now find opportunities in the South fostered by the federal government.[46]

As southern race relations evolved, so did the economy, in ways that made the South attractive to Asian immigrants. In the late nineteenth century, as noted, southern states, relying on plantations growing cotton and other crops, extractive industries, and mill towns, had not attracted many Asian immigrants. However, after the 1960s and the emergence of mass immigration across the globe, a new South beckoned to foreigners. The southern economy had received a boost during World War II, and the major changes begun then continued at a rapid pace after 1945. By 2000 cotton was no longer king. Southern wages, which had always been lower than those in the North, began to catch up. In 1950 southern per capita income had been only 69 percent of the national average, but by 2000 it had reached 86 percent of the rest of the nation.[47]

Mechanization of agriculture sent hundreds of thousands either to the North or to southern cities in search of a better life. Retailing expanded, and the world's largest retailer, Wal-Mart, opened in the South and then expanded to the rest of the nation and even overseas. The petroleum industry also provided a stimulus, as did the growth of the textile industry. Indeed, by the 1990s, after luring northern textiles, southern mills found themselves in sharp competition with cheap Asian, Mexican, and South American factories overseas. High-tech, banking, and commercial centers in such places as Houston, Dallas, and Atlanta all had need of skilled labor. Asian immigrants, whose general educational levels were equal to or slightly above most native-born Americans, could answer the needs of the new global economy in southern cities and towns.

As the southern states developed within the Sun Belt, southern governments and communities attempted to attract outside capital, whether from elsewhere in the nation or abroad.[48] When looking to invest in the United States, German and Japanese firms were attracted by the wage gap and the lack of a strong union movement in the South. Japan's Nissan looked at several Georgia and Tennessee sites before building a new plant in Smyrna, Tennessee, where the company was able to avoid the United Auto Workers organizational drive.[49] In addition, Toyota and Hyundai announced plans to open auto plants in several southern states in the near future.[50]

Air-conditioning, better transportation and communication systems, and improved education all stimulated these major changes in the former Confederate states. Dallas, Houston, Miami, Atlanta, and New Orleans emerged as major metropolitan centers.[51] A traveler to the South's major metropolitan areas cannot help but notice the presence of national chain stores, fast food eating places, familiar hotel chains such as Holiday Inn, and clothing styles worn throughout the rest of the nation.

Aside from political, social, and economic incentives, personal issues also motivated immigrants to settle in the South. Some of the newcomers entered the United States as wives of American service personnel. Most of the four to five thousand Japanese immigrants entering annually after World War II were married to American servicemen, and many others came from Korea and the

Philippines, where the United States also had military bases. An even smaller number came from Vietnam. Scholars do not agree on the exact number, let alone where they settled. Some of these "war brides" ended up on southern military installations but perhaps only while their husbands were on temporary duty. However, some also settled permanently in the southern states. While the precise fate of these women is not known, Asian war brides experienced difficulties in living in the United States, and they earned little compared to other Asian wives.[52] Their numbers were not especially large; but if they naturalized, they were eligible to sponsor their parents, brothers, and sisters as new immigrants. These networks helped to establish new ethnic communities.

Other Asian women "met" their future spouses through "mail-order bride" services. They used "pen pal" clubs or organizations that specialized in finding foreign spouses, and individual women also simply advertised in newspapers to meet and find future husbands. Most of the women available through these services were Asians, mainly from the Philippines, Korea, and Japan. Some of the tens of thousands of them who placed advertisements and used specialized "mail-order bride" agencies did find an American citizen to marry and thus became immigrants.[53] The INS and Congress believed that many of these unions were nothing more than fraudulent ways of migrating to the United States. However, such international marriages arranged through agencies accounted for only a fraction—four to six thousand—of those American citizens marrying foreign-born spouses in any one year of the 1990s.[54] It is not known how many of these Asian women married southern men.

Orphans adopted from abroad also account for another few thousand immigrants annually. The adoption of foreign children grew slowly but steadily in the 1980s and 1990s and accounted for eighteen thousand new citizens annually by 2000. Between 1970 and 2000 most came from Asia, with Korea and later China the leading nations for foreign adoptions. The INS reports do not indicate where these children settled.[55]

Refugee admissions and their subsequent family migration are also an important aspect of the South's new Asian immigration.[56] Among the first Asian refugees to settle in the South were Indians who had been expelled from Uganda in 1972 by the racist regime of Idi Amin. The Ugandan Indians, who had been living in Africa for several generations, were given little time to leave, and most who did were only able to take a small amount of money and just a few possessions with them. The vast majority of the seventy thousand or so who escaped settled in Great Britain and Canada, but the United States also agreed to accept some of these refugees. They were admitted under the authority of the attorney general and did not have to go through regular refugee procedures.[57] Some of those who had gone to Great Britain later emigrated to the United States.[58]

Many of these Ugandan Indians followed the same career path upon reaching the United States, that of small motel operator. In fact, when the film director Mira Nair was traveling in the Deep South, she noticed that many motels were being run by Asian Indians, some of whom had originally come from Africa after 1972. These Indians had not been operating motels in Uganda but had considerable experience in small business enterprises. So impressed was Nair that she made a movie about them, *Mississippi Masala*.[59] The film, set in Mississippi, combined both fact and fiction, but there is no doubt of the important role played by motel owners in the Indian American community. In the movie, the motel owner's daughter defied racial lines by having an affair with an African American and eventually left her family and the southern community in search of a state where such unions were more acceptable. Her parents bitterly disapproved of the affair, but in the end they could not stop it.

While the first Indian motel owner is not known, the name given is usually Kanjibhai Desai, an illegal immigrant, who bought the Goldfield Hotel in downtown San Francisco in the early 1940s. Only a handful of others opened additional properties by the end of the decade, and it was still not an especially large number by the 1960s.[60] But because the motel business was not doing well in the 1970s and 1980s when the Ugandan Indians arrived, many motels owned by independent operators could be purchased for relatively low prices. Exactly how many were bought by Indians from East Africa is not known, but most experts believe that the proportion of Indian-operated motels managed by immigrants from Africa was high, especially in the early days. One of the successful motel owners was Mit Amin who left Kenya in 1964 to settle first in London before moving to North Carolina to manage a family-owned motel. He eventually purchased, with the aid of family members, a bed-and-breakfast establishment in Atlanta.[61]

After buying up mom-and-pop motels for sale across the United States, Indians began to move into budget motel chains, such as Budget Inn, and the other major chains, such as Holiday Inn. Once the African refugees and others from India began to acquire motels, word got back to India, especially to residents of Gujarati, many with the name of Patel, who were members of a Hindu subcaste. Some were indeed related. One owner in Huntsville, Alabama, explained to a visitor that fifteen miles away his cousin ran a motel, and ninety miles down the road another cousin operated one, and an uncle was a motel owner "somewhere in Georgia."[62] These owners were not always related, but the chain migration certainly sent many immigrants named Patel to the South seeking to become small business owners and motel operators, so much so that such budget accommodations were frequently (and pejoratively) referred to as "Potels."

Mike Patel, the head of the Asian-American Hotel Owners Association, headquartered in Atlanta, said of the early years, "I hardly saw any Indians when I came here in 1984. You either saw white people or black people. If you were brown, people looked at you twice."[63] In 2001 Patel estimated that Indians own 45 percent of the nation's roadside hotels both in Georgia and the entire country. His organization represents seven thousand Indian owners.[64] In 1999 the American Hotel and Motel Association picked an Asian Indian as president, the first time that an Asian headed this organization.[65]

Another, and larger, refugee flow hailed from Southeast Asia. As late as 1969 only 3,000 Vietnamese had migrated to the United States. These were mostly war brides, diplomats, and students. When the American-backed government fell to communists in 1975, 130,000 Vietnamese managed to escape by air or boat. Several years later another exodus began, and this time it included Cambodians and Laotians. Many found shelter in refugee camps in neighboring Thailand before they were admitted to the United States. In the 1980s the governments of the United States and Vietnam agreed to an Orderly Departure Program to bring persons to America. In addition, in 1982 Congress passed legislation to admit the children of Vietnamese mothers and American GI fathers, who had been abandoned in Vietnam. After criticism about the law's flaws, legislators enacted the Vietnamese Homecoming Act in 1988, which also covered similar children in Korea, though the vast majority were Vietnamese. These children were dispersed across the nation, and several thousand ended up in southern states.[66] By 1992 over one million persons from Vietnam, Cambodia, and Laos were counted in the United States. In the 1990s the United States no longer admitted many refugees from these three nations, but thousands still entered annually under the family unification provisions of the immigration laws. In 2000 the INS recorded 26,747 newcomers from Vietnam.[67]

Faced with such a dramatic influx in the late 1970s and early 1980s United States refugee officials decided in 1975 to house the Vietnamese temporarily in four camps located in the United States. Officials wanted to avoid the kind of refugee settlement that had brought the overwhelming majority of Cubans to one region: Miami and Dade County, Florida. The government believed that if too many refugees found homes in any one locale, opposition would develop to their settlement, and they would have an adverse economic impact in these communities. As a result, after initial processing in the federal camps, Southeast Asians were dispersed throughout the United States through the work of voluntary religious and state refugee organizations (VOLAGS). Southern communities such as Fort Smith, Arkansas; Clarkston, Georgia; Charlotte, North Carolina; and Bayou La Batre, Alabama, thus witnessed new settlements of Vietnamese and Cambodians where none had existed before.[68]

In a few cases refugees were sent where Asian communities had already been established. Church groups in Georgia helped locate Vietnamese in that state, but the presence of Chinese who had worked on railroads and remained in Georgia also assisted in the decision process. Because many of the Vietnamese were ethnic Chinese, officials decided to work with these descendants of early immigrants and place the new ethnic Chinese near them. But many refugees did not wish to be sent to the selected locales. Moreover, the government could not control secondary migration, and many of the refugees moved from their original homes to California, which became the center of Vietnamese life in the United States.[69] By 1990 California was home to nearly one half million of the refugees.[70]

As a result of the dispersal policy, refugees from Southeast Asia could be found in all southern states, although their numbers were not particularly large in many cases. One of the southern centers of refugee settlement was the Washington, D.C., metropolitan area. In 1998 the nation's capital and environs was the fifth most popular center for legal immigration, lagging behind only Los Angeles, New York, Chicago, and Miami. Included in the region's newcomers were many Asians. The Vietnamese community tended to cluster in Arlington and Fairfax counties, Virginia. Unlike other Asian settlers, the Vietnamese "commonly reside in the inner suburbs," where two out of three Vietnamese lived. Virginia's Eden Center was a large shopping mall catering especially to the Vietnamese—an estimated 70 percent of the shoppers at Eden Center were Asians.[71]

Though it lagged far behind California, Texas also harbored many Vietnamese refugees, who numbered 134,961 in 2000. The North Texas Council of Governments reported that 14,000 Vietnamese lived in Tarrant County with another 17,500 in Dallas County.[72] With aid of VOLAGS Vietnamese also settled in Louisiana, with Catholic charities involved in the resettlement.[73] To the north, in Baton Rouge, 3,533 Vietnamese were counted in the 2000 census.[74] Still other Vietnamese settled in Georgia. The census reported a jump in the number of Vietnamese in Georgia from 7,801 in 1990 to 29,016 in 2000 (a 372 percent increase).[75]

Laotians (including the Hmong) were settled in a similarly cooperative effort by the federal government and the VOLAGS. In 2000 a Laotian immigrant born during the Vietnam War was settled in Morganton, North Carolina. He later became the first Asian member of the city's Department of Public Safety.[76] The Cambodians' migration process followed a similar track. Cambodian Thomas Beamesderfer was a child when the Khmer Rouge came to power and killed hundreds of thousands of Cambodians. Beamesderfer and some of his family fled, but not all escaped successfully. His father disappeared during Cambodia's civil war. As did many others, Beamesderfer crossed the border of Thailand where he lived in a refugee camp. When he was fifteen a Pennsylvania family sponsored him, and he took on his sponsoring family's name, Beamesderfer. He eventually settled in northern Virginia with the help of Refugee Resettlement and Immigration Services for the Catholic Diocese of Richmond. He lived in an apartment surrounded by other Cambodians; 1,013 were in Richmond alone. The Catholic Diocese of Richmond settled several thousand more during the 1990s.[77] Heroic stories of refugees surviving pirates at sea, the holocaust in Cambodia, or primitive conditions in Thai camps often grabbed the headlines, yet, as noted, most of the Indochinese immigrants to the South after 1990 used the regular immigration procedures for family unification and occupational skills.

Asian doctors and nurses comprised another major group of immigrants to the United States at this time. The 1965 immigration act was passed in the same year as Medicare and Medicaid. Americans had been demanding improved and more medical care, but medical schools had not kept up with the demand. States did move in the 1960s and 1970s to increase substantially the number of physicians, nurses and other medical professionals, but physicians were needed before the new and expanded medical colleges graduated more professionals. As a result, foreign doctors and nurses migrated to fill the need. The shortages were especially acute in inner cities and in isolated rural areas. After 1965, the Philippines became the largest Asian source for immigrants (except for refugees in some years) to the United States, and in the years just after the 1965 immigration law went into effect, about one quarter of Filipino immigrants entered under the occupational categories, a number of whom were medical professionals. Virginia, Texas, and Florida were the main states where Filipino medical professionals settled in the South.[78] Asian Indian physicians, both men and women, were also large users of the occupational immigrant visa categories. In 1987 the *Wall Street Journal* estimated that there were 28,000 Indian physicians in the United States, and the figure topped 30,000 as the twentieth century ended.[79]

Dr. Abdus Saleem of Pakistan was one of the Asian medical professionals who settled in the South. Saleem left Pakistan in 1971 to pursue opportunities in America. He settled first in Pennsylvania but moved to Houston in 1975, where he and his wife, also a physician, practiced medicine. Dr. Saleem became chief of hematology at Methodist Hospital and professor of pathology at the Baylor College of Medicine. After becoming an American citizen and living in the United States for 30 years, he declared, "I have spent more years in the United States than anyplace else. This is my home." He remained an active Muslim, and his family preserved ethnic practices, including eating traditional Pakistani foods.[80]

In 1976 Congress limited opportunities for immigrating medical professionals, but, responding to the urgent demands of hospitals and other health care facilities, a few years later legislators modified the rules and again permitted more medical professionals to enter the country. The changes permitted 28,000 physicians and 60,000 nurses to emigrate during the 1990s either as permanent resident aliens or as temporary workers; some of the temporary nonimmigrants were later able to get green cards.[81] By 1990 more than 50,000 foreign-born Asian physicians practiced in the United States. The 49,000 Filipino-born nurses were by far the largest number of alien nurses in American hospitals and health centers, and Asian Indians made up the largest share of foreign doctors.[82] Yet in 2002 the *Wall Street Journal* still reported shortages of physicians in rural areas, and the American Nursing Association estimated in that year that the United States faced a shortage of 126,000 nurses. Health officials looked to India to help meet the demand.[83]

Exactly how many of these professionals lived in the South is unknown, though judging from Asian immigration patterns in the 1980s and 1990s, the number is likely around twenty percent; many cities depended on these alien medical professionals. When the nursing shortage periodically turned to a glut, some foreign-born nurses entered illegally. In 1998 the INS announced that more than five hundred Korean and Filipino nurses had been smuggled into the United States over a three-year period. Although they ended up in nearly all states, one of the centers of this activity was Texas, where undocumented nurses worked for wages considerably less than American-born and legal immigrants. The INS indicted Clara Kim for furnishing undocumented nurses to the Southern Manor Nursing Home in Lubbock, Texas.[84] In other cases, the courts indicted several Indians and Pakistanis working out of Houston and Fort Worth.[85]

Medical professionals were only part of the skilled labor flow from Asia to America. In fact, Asian immigrants, except for refugees, are slightly better educated than Americans generally, and many arrived using the occupational categories for technicians, computer experts, and other highly skilled workers. Some of the educated Asians studied in the United States before locating a job and obtaining a visa; foreign student programs often have operated as an immigration network. Economist George Borgas has estimated that 13 percent of all foreign students eventually settle in the United States.[86] The first Chinese who moved to Atlanta after new immigration policies went into effect in the 1960s were highly educated; some 80 percent had "professional degrees with advanced training."[87] A large percentage of these immigrants had originally been students in the United States. As Americans have flocked to business schools and avoided graduate programs in computer science, chemistry, physics, and engineering, foreigners have moved into these fields.[88] From 1960 to the 1990s, 150,000 Taiwanese studied in America, and many remained as legal resident aliens afterwards, employed with an occupation in demand.

Chen Button was one such student. She emigrated from Taiwan in 1979 as a graduate student and then took a job as a marketing manager for Texas Instruments.[89] A growing number and proportion of immigrants in recent years had already been in the United States when they received their green cards. A study of Ph.D. degrees in science and engineering revealed that in 1993 two thirds of foreigners who received those degrees had obtained them in American universities.[90]

Students from mainland China have grown in significant numbers in the past two decades. Chinese students numbered 59,939 in 2001, the largest nationality of students from all over the globe. The next largest sources of foreign students are India, Japan, South Korea, and Taiwan.[91] The largest number of foreign students to study in the South, numbering 4,320 in the academic year 2001–2, enrolled at the University of Texas at Austin.[92]

The destruction of the World Trade Center on September 11, 2001, resulted in increased xenophobia and greater restrictions on student visas, but it did not deter foreign students from attending American colleges and universities. The Institute of International Education reported a record high of almost 600,000 foreign students studying in American institutions of higher education in 2002.[93]

Some southern colleges developed reputations that encouraged foreign students to enroll.[94] Such was the case with Virginia Tech in Blacksburg, Virginia, which was a magnet for many Asians. The advisor to the Indian Student Association said that 95 percent of the area's Asian population was "somehow affiliated with Tech." You-Xiong Wang, a senior research scientist with Tech's Fiber Optics Research Center, agreed that the school's reputation helped to attract many international students.[95]

Others entered as nonimmigrants, mostly on H-1B visas that allowed them to work only temporarily in the United States. Congress responded to business pressures in 1998 and increased the number of H-1B visas to 115,000 from the previous 65,000. The vast majority of these temporary nonimmigrants were Asian, especially Chinese, Indians, and Filipinos.[96] In 2001 Indians alone accounted for nearly one half of these temporary workers.[97] Although some found permanent employment afterward, job security did not always come easy for H-1B workers. Farhana Yesmin from Bangladesh graduated from the University of Texas at Dallas in 1999, when technology companies were scrambling for hired help. She found a job at Nortel Networks Corporation in Richardson, Texas, but when the technology industry took a downturn, she lost her position and was unable to get either another job or a green card.[98]

The most well-known destination for computer experts emigrating from China and India is, of course, California's Silicon Valley. An estimated 30 percent of the experts in Silicon Valley were immigrants from these two nations. But the new technologically focused economy was by no means limited to California. Throughout the South, urban centers such as Washington, D.C. (and northern Virginia), Atlanta, Houston, and Dallas transformed their economies after 1960. Robert Stein, the dean of social sciences at Rice University, noted that everyone knew about the rapid growth of Texas's Latinos, but many did not realize that the state also experienced a major influx of Asian immigrants, especially "computer programmers and other high-skill workers in high tech industries"; these newcomers were mainly from India and Pakistan.[99] Computer-oriented employment also attracted Sri Lankans and Bangladeshi.[100]

While Asians continued using occupational preferences to enter, these categories accounted for only 20 percent of visas under the 1965 act, and even after limits in these categories were increased under the 1990 law, those who immigrated under their auspices still represented a minority. The vast majority entered under the family unification provisions.[101] Included in the family migration flows were adult men and women who found employment, even though they were not migrating under the occupational categories.

Most Asians in the paid workforce in southern states found jobs working for other people. Yet a sizable number set up their own businesses.[102] Mention has been made of Indian motel owners, but Indians also opened stores to cater to the needs of other Indians and Southeast Asians. Asian entrepreneurs also ran mom-and-pop enterprises serving the general public, including video shops, Dairy Queens, Blimpie or Subway sandwich shops, and Dunkin' Donuts franchises.[103] The Vietnamese, for example, dominated the nail salon business in Atlanta as they did in Louisiana.[104] The popularity of Asian food enabled Indian and especially Chinese restaurants to cater to both an American and Asian immigrant clientele.[105] In northern Virginia and Washington, D.C., Vietnamese refugees have opened dozens of enterprises including restaurants as well as the previously mentioned Virginia's Eden Shopping Center.[106]

Of all immigrant groups arriving since 1970, none has a higher percentage of small business operators among its ranks than Koreans.[107] Approximately ten percent of Asians owned small enterprises, but among Koreans the figure was much higher. Chinese actually owned a greater share of small businesses in the Asian community, but the Chinese population in the United States was considerably larger than the Korean one.[108] The center of Korean business was in Los Angeles, but wherever they settled, Korean immigrants opened many new shops. Some of the first new Korean immigrants settled in the South, in El Paso, during the 1980s. Like some other Asians, many began their sojourn to America as students, studying at the University of Texas, El Paso. Others returned to El Paso after being stationed at Fort Bliss as part of the Korean military group training there. Hochan Kim opened his El Paso store in 1982 when there was only one small Korean-run store doing business. Within five years twenty-eight other Korean-operated shops had appeared, selling toys, electronics, clothes, and groceries. Many of the stores stocked goods wanted by the large Latino population in El Paso.[109] Koreans have also opened small groceries in Richmond, Atlanta, and other southern cities.[110] Just as Koreans were moving out of the green grocery business in New York and California and into more profitable dry cleaners, they have done so in southern states. As the *Atlanta Journal-Constitution* put it, "Drop off a load of dirty clothes at practically any local dry cleaners and the business owner is likely to be Asian—Korean actually."[111] Dry cleaners were only one of the businesses run by Korean immigrants. For example, the Korean Directory of Atlanta for 1997 was 500 pages in length and included everything "from wedding photographers to real estate agents and includes a full-page ad for local golf clubs that welcome foreigners."[112]

The Korean community in Annandale, in Fairfax County, Virginia, illustrates many of the aspects of Korean immigrant entrepreneurship. Once the first Korean stores and churches appeared, others followed. According to the *Washington Post,* these included "19 Korean churches, 16 beauty salons, 10 weekly newspapers, nine acupuncturists, eight women's clothing shops and two bridal shops." The city also attracted many Korean professionals who opened their offices in Annandale. As Koreans became the largest foreign-born group in Annandale, the older Chinatown began to lose business to the Koreans.[113] In 2002 a New Jersey bank announced its intentions to open a branch in Annandale to serve the needs of the city's Koreans. Bank officials said they would employ bilingual workers because so many of the immigrant Koreans spoke English that "is not that fluent."[114]

Scholars often call these small businesses "economic niches," where minorities, if they are willing to work long hours, can make a living. These niches depend upon the labor of family members or low-wage Latinos in some cases. They also rely upon financial assistance from relatives or their ethnic communities. Not infrequently, Asians, especially Koreans, worked for a few years in Korean stores, saved, and then struck out on their own. Yet there was another source of funding—the Small Business Administration (SBA) of the federal government. Asian entrepreneurs successfully petitioned to be included in minority programs backed by the SBA and thus gained better access to banks and federal government contracts.[115]

Winning federal contracts and the support of the SBA has not come without controversy. The SBA considers Asians to be socially disadvantaged, but Asian entrepreneurs are generally better educated than blacks or Hispanics, and many are recent immigrants who have not faced the severe discrimination suffered by their predecessors. In addition, their firms are larger with more capital than those of Latinos and African Americans. In Alabama, for instance, where high-tech expertise paid off, Asian firms overtook black ones. In 1984 Asian firms received only 2.6 percent of SBA funding for that year compared to African Americans' share of 88 percent, but a decade later Asians received nearly half of the awards and blacks only one third. "Almost all of my firms are in high tech," explained one SBA official. Alabama Asians captured most of the new firms related to installations of the Strategic Defense Command, the Army's Missile Command, and the Marshall Space Flight Center.[116] In 2001 in Georgia, Asians, who made up about 2 percent of the state's population, received twice as many SBA loans as African Americans, who made up 30 percent.

Rajubhai Patel's is a typical case. Patel left the Indian state of Gujarat to emigrate to America, where his brother employed him at a motel he owned in Tennessee. With this experience and a small amount of savings, Patel purchased a Blimpie franchise and later a convenience store and dry cleaner. Then with the aid of the SBA he bought another Blimpie food shop.[117]

Overall, the growth of Asian-owned firms in the last twenty years has been impressive. While the Asian population was considerably smaller than the African-American or Latino population, Asian firms accounted for one third of minority business firms. Moreover, on average, the Asian firms had larger capitalization, more employees, and higher sales figures.[118] The surge of Asians into small businesses in the South was part of a national trend. Nationally, Asian businesses had an average revenue of $336,299 versus $155,200 for Hispanic enterprises and only $86,500 for black-owned companies.[119]

Because of the high educational levels of most Asians and their entrepreneurial activities, their family incomes were higher than African Americans, Latinos, and many white Americans. In addition, Asian families were more likely to have more than one wage earner, especially in the mom-and-pop businesses that require long working hours. Knowledge of English is clearly another factor influencing income. Asian Indian family incomes were among the highest in the nation, but these immigrants were highly educated and already spoke English when they arrived. Many Koreans arrived with college degrees but with practically no knowledge of English, which limited their earning capacities.

Some poor Asians also arrived. Because they could not qualify under the immigration laws, many of these less-educated persons were willing to become undocumented aliens in order to find jobs in the American economy. Estimates vary, but in 2000 the U.S. Census Bureau put the illegal population at nearly nine million, considerably higher than the INS estimates of the middle to late 1990s. Illegal aliens hail from the nations that furnish most immigrants, and they tend to settle in the same states and metropolitan regions as legal immigrants.[120]

Among the most desperate immigrants were Chinese from Fuzhou, the capital of China's Fujian province. Paying thousands of dollars to smugglers who promised to get them into the United States by air or sea, these undocumented aliens then were obligated to pay off substantial debts. Estimates of the number of arrivals in the 1990s ran as high as 100,000 young Chinese, most of whom settled in New York City.[121] They drew national attention when the ship *Golden Venture* ran aground off Queens, New York, in 1993 with 298 Chinese illegal aliens aboard.

The next year federal authorities intercepted a trawler loaded with illegals headed for Virginia. Then, in 1999, the Coast Guard, acting on a tip, found 132 men and boys hidden in a secret compartment on a ship docked at Savannah, Georgia. The aliens had each paid between forty and fifty thousand dollars to take them from China to the United States. A grand jury in Atlanta indicted seven of the crew for trying to smuggle the Chinese into the country. Hoping to avoid deportation, some of the captured aliens claimed asylum, a tactic that had been successful for several of the *Golden Venture*'s passengers.[122]

Other Asians were taken from China to Mexico, where they attempted to cross the border and find employment in Texas. Still others first landed in Cuba and then, like so many Haitians and Cubans, made the journey to Florida by boat. In 1998, the federal government announced that it had broken a smuggling ring that had brought thousands of Asians—as many as three hundred a month—into the United States over a three-year period. The aliens were mostly Indian but included Pakistanis as well. They had been taken to Moscow, then to Cuba, and finally to Mexico, where they attempted to cross the Mexican-U.S. border. Some had managed to end up in Dallas.[123]

By following immigrant networks developed in the post-1970 New South, Asians have become a presence throughout the South, though their patterns of settlement are concentrated in a few states (see table 3).

In spite of the improved racial climate of the South, Asians still encountered discrimination and occasionally met with violence. In 1992 the Civil Rights Commission reported a number of attacks on Asians. Sometimes these attacks ended tragically. In 1989 Jim (Ming Hai) Loo, who had emigrated to the United States from China in 1976, ran into trouble in a Raleigh, North Carolina, pool hall; he was taunted with the epithets "gook" and "chink" and was blamed for American deaths in the Vietnam War. When Loo left the pool hall, he was assaulted and killed.[124] In another incident, Vietnamese fishermen along the Texas Gulf Coast came to national attention when violence erupted between them and non-Asian fishermen gathering shrimp. The conflict included an appearance by the Ku Klux Klan and led to the shooting death of one American in 1979 in Seadrift, Texas. The controversy had begun during hard times for the fishermen and involved disagreements over proper rules for shrimp fishing, with both sides claiming that the others were not following legal procedures and cultural practices.[125] Financial prospects from shrimping did not improve after the 1970s, prompting many of the younger generation to avoid the career paths of their mothers and fathers. "Our community is changing dramatically,"

TABLE 3
Selected Nationalities in the South, 2000

State	Asian Indian	Chinese	Filipino	Korean	Vietnamese
Alabama	6,900	6,337	2,727	4,116	4,628
Arkansas	3,104	3,126	2,489	1,550	3,974
Florida	70,740	46,638	54,310	19,139	33,190
Georgia	46,132	27,446	11,038	28,745	29,016
Louisiana	8,280	7,474	4,504	2,876	24,358
Mississippi	3,827	3,099	2,608	1,334	5,387
North Carolina	261,907	18,984	9,592	12,600	15,596
South Carolina	8,356	5,967	6,423	3,665	4,248
Tennessee	12,835	9,426	5,426	7,359	7,007
Texas	129,465	105,829	58,340	45,571	134,961
Virginia	48,851	36,966	47,609	45,279	37,309

Source: The Bureau of the Census, 2000.
Note: These nationalities include both immigrants (about 60 percent of the total) and native-born Asians.

said the daughter of one Vietnamese fisherman. "People are getting out of shrimping. There are just too many rules and regulations, and it doesn't pay." She herself had become a nursing home administrator rather than follow the career path of the women who culled shrimp.[126] These were not the only incidents of violence against Asians, and racial hatred was by no means limited to the South.[127] The worst incident involved African Americans, Latinos, and Koreans and took place in Los Angeles in 1992.

While poll data provides insight into how Americans view immigration, it unfortunately is not usually broken down by region. Most polls reveal outright opposition or at least a good deal of ambivalence about newcomers. Based on the few polls that mention region, southerners appear to be slightly more opposed to immigration than the rest of the nation. Not surprisingly, these polls also reveal that all sections of the nation and all ethnic groups are more opposed to illegal immigrants than to those with proper visas.[128] Asians are generally considered much more acceptable than Middle Easterners and Arabs, especially since the destruction of the World Trade Center on September 11, 2001. A poll conducted by Middle Tennessee State University in 2002 revealed that about 30 percent of Tennesseans believed Latinos were making life worse in Tennessee compared to 39 percent who viewed Middle Eastern residents with the same animosity. Only 15 percent harbored the same beliefs about Asians.[129] These southern views about Middle Easterners and Asians were not much different from those expressed in a midwestern poll conducted by Worldviews, a joint project of the Chicago Council on Foreign Relations and the German Marshall Fund. It discovered that more than "three-fourths of Americans want U.S. immigration laws tightened to allow fewer immigrants from Arab or Muslim nations into the country." The latter would include Asian nations such as Pakistan and Bangladesh, but clearly the respondents based much of their beliefs on the events of September 11, 2001, and the identification of the hijackers as Near Eastern Muslims.[130]

In general, however, southerners gradually have grown more accepting of immigration since the late nineteenth and early twentieth centuries when southern members of Congress supported the Chinese Exclusion Act of 1882 and after 1900 backed tighter immigration restrictions on Europeans. Congressmen and women from all regions expressed little interest in relaxing the tight controls during the 1930s and 1940s, and after World War II southerners continued their opposition to the postwar refugee and displaced persons laws.[131] Only three representatives and three senators from the South voted to uphold President Harry Truman's veto of the McCarran-Walter Act of 1952, which reaffirmed the national origins system favoring northern and western European immigrants. The congressional delegations of the South were often the center of opposition to changing immigration policy. By 1965, however, the time was ripe for the overhaul of the immigration system, and the Hart-Celler Act, as it was called, passed easily. Most of the opposing votes came from the southern states.[132] Since that time, immigrants have found a better welcome in the South, and southerners in Congress have been more willing to receive new immigrants. In the last thirty-five years, southern proponents of immigration have noted that the skills brought to America by Asian immigrants are a positive addition to the labor force, and growers in the South have urged a temporary worker program. Since 1970, the alliances of anti- and pro-immigration advocates have been composed of strange bedfellows and do not precisely follow regional lines.[133]

Few national politicians have run on an anti-immigrant agenda. In 1994, Governor Pete Wilson did strongly attack immigrants, especially illegal ones, in his winning campaign for reelection as governor of California. But when Wilson attempted to use an anti-immigration message as part of a bid for the Republican nomination for the presidency two years later, he failed dramatically. In 1996, Patrick Buchanan tried to win the Republican presidential nomination with an anti-immigrant message and did win many votes in southern primaries, especially among persons who consider themselves conservatives or part of the religious right. Buchanan's most strongly anti-immigration message was contained in his book *The Death of the West: How Dying Populations and Immigrant Invasions Imperil Our Country and Civilization*, not published until 2002, after his poor showing on the Reform party ticket in 2000.[134] In fact, his run as the Reform Party's right-wing candidate in 2000 ultimately "fizzled in Dixie."[135]

The rapid growth of new Asian immigration stands in sharp contrast to the history of limited Asian immigration before the 1960s. As the numbers have grown, in conjunction with a large flow of Latinos, many parts of the South have undergone—and still are experiencing—significant changes in those largely urban and suburban areas where Asians settle. The precise economic impact of these newcomers on American workers and communities is difficult to ascertain. A number of economists and governmental agencies have examined economic issues and have sometimes reached divergent conclusions. The National Research Council pulled together leading economists to probe a variety of issues, including economic ones, related to Asian immigration and in 1997 concluded that, overall, the economic impact was not large and that many previous studies were flawed.[136] A federal governmental report in 1999 reached similar conclusions, at least about wages, stating: "The conclusion of macroeconomic research is that, at the national level, the net impact of immigration on the earnings and the employment of U.S. wages is rather small."[137] Whatever effect immigrants have on wages and employment occurs at the local level where many immigrants, following the networks of their countrymen, have settled. In addition, Asians are generally better educated than Latinos, and as a result those from across the Pacific have little impact upon low-wage American workers. Indeed, by providing highly skilled workers and by opening many small businesses in the South, Asians on the whole have created new jobs in their communities.[138]

As for other economic effects, they too are felt mainly in local communities. Areas with few immigrants do not have to worry about welfare or school costs, but in towns and cities with many immigrants, bilingual teachers are in demand and new schools are needed. At the national level immigrants probably pay their share of taxes, but in local areas they may place disproportionate demands on social services.[139]

As Japanese firms looked to invest in the United States, the South, with its lack of a strong union movement and lower wages, appeared as a promising place.[140] The extent to which Asian populations attracted Asian firms is not known. Nissan located in Tennessee, but the 2000 census revealed that only 4,304 Japanese reside in the state, representing less than ten percent of the Volunteer State's Asian population. However, one can safely assume that Asian firms would not invest in particular locales if Asians were not treated well there. Thus the South's growing acceptance of its Asian population was no doubt a factor in plant location decisions. The Japanese firms do attract Japanese to aid in setting up and running auto factories, but these are usually nonimmigrants who have temporary visas rather than permanent resident aliens.

When the Houston Rockets basketball team signed Chinese Yao Ming to a contract, team officials also decided to hire four Mandarin speakers and planned a TV show in that language. Clearly, even if the team went to China for recruitment of the linguistics experts, the number sponsored would not be large, and these migrants would have little impact on Houston.[141]

The Census Bureau does not ask questions or keep records about religion. But new Asian immigrants are undoubtedly changing the South's culture of and reputation for white, conservative Protestantism. First, they are bringing with them religions not normally associated with southern practices. The appearance of mosques, as well as Sikh, Hindu, and Buddhist temples attest to this change. Asian Indians mostly are Hindus or Sikhs, and when their numbers have become large enough they build houses of worship. By the late 1990s, Atlanta's Indians supported several temples, with the primary one located in the Riverdale section and built at a cost of two million dollars. Sikhs built a house of worship about the same time, opening its doors in 1991.[142]

Immigrants from Bangladesh and Pakistan are likely to be Muslims, and like Indians they have built their own houses of worship. Estimates of Islam in the United States vary greatly and range between 1.1 and 8 million. A 2001 report from the Council on American-Islamic Relations said the national figure was six million and noted that 26 percent of Muslims lived in the South.[143] Completed about the same time and based on a telephone survey, a study by the Graduate Center of the City University of New York (CUNY) found that, at most, there were 1.1 million Muslims in the United States.[144] Whatever the precise number, there can be no doubt that Islam is growing in America. African Americans and persons from the Near East constitute the majority of Muslims, with South Asians making up the rest, a sizable 30 percent. In the South mosques have appeared with many Asian members. Of course these relatively new religious groups in the American South are limited to those areas with substantial numbers of immigrants and African Americans.

The impact of the new Asians on religion is not limited to the growing number of Muslims, Hindus, and Sikhs. Many of the newcomers join Christian churches. Most experts believe that when they arrive, fully half of Korean immigrants are Christians, mainly Protestants. In addition, many non-Christian Koreans have joined Protestant churches in their communities once they settle in the United States. In 1999, the *Forth Worth Star-Telegram* estimated that in Texas there were 180 Asian Baptist churches, including 80 Korean houses of worship. The largest Asian church in Texas was Presbyterian, a church in Richardson, which had twelve hundred members.[145] The *Atlanta Journal-Constitution* reported that in 1997 Korean Americans had one hundred churches in the Atlanta region.[146] Christianity has attracted other Asians as well. The banner outside the Shallowford Presbyterian Church in DeKalb County, Georgia, reads "'in Christ,' in four languages: English, Korean, Spanish and Asian Indian [sic]."[147]

Of immigrants, Latinos are making the biggest impact upon American Catholicism, but most Filipinos are also Roman Catholic, and consequently they seek out Catholic churches in America. Of the first wave of Vietnamese refugees a disproportionate number were Catholic. Settled in New Orleans with the aid of the Catholic diocese, Vietnamese flocked to attend mass there.[148] Vietnamese Catholics were also found in Houston.[149]

The impact of southern Asians on American foreign policy generally has not been large. The new immigrants are connected to their land of origin, and they do return to visit and sponsor other relatives to come to America.[150] When disasters strike at home, such as an earthquake in India in 2001, Indians in the United States rallied to give aid to stricken villages in India. In 2001 Atlanta Indian motel owners held a rally at the Super Bowl to collect funds for relief; they held a rally because the quake struck Gujarat, the province from which most of them originated.[151] Indians, and Pakistanis, whose numbers are not large in the South, do pay attention to the conflict between India and Pakistan. They make their wishes known, but they have no representatives in Washington. As for politics, a few Asians have won election in local contests, such as the mayorality of Houston, but Asians elected to Congress hail from either California or Hawaii, and the nation's one Chinese-American governor was elected from the state of Washington.[152]

In the 2002 Democratic primary of the fourth congressional district of Georgia, Indian voters and funds threw their weight behind Denise Majette over Cynthia McKinney, whom they regarded as anti-Indian.[153] McKinney herself blamed Indians for contributing to her defeat, and a writer for *The Times of India* agreed that Indians played a role and "was glad to read that Indian Americans were actively involved in defeating Congresswoman Cynthia McKinney in the state of Georgia."[154]

The district contained only about eight thousand Indians, some of whom could not vote, but this election does point to a growing presence of Indians in the South's politics.[155] Recognizing this political potential, Governor Roy Barnes appointed Indian-born R. K. Sehgal to be the commissioner of the Georgia Department of Industry, Trade, and Tourism. The governor also created a Georgia Commission on Asian-American Affairs.[156]

In spite of their role in the race for Georgia's fourth congressional district, Asians face several difficulties in trying to influence southern life. First, Asians are only two percent of the South's population and are concentrated in several states (and metropolitan areas). By organizing effectively they can increase their impact upon those states not only economically, but also politically—but they will have to work in coalitions with others to be successful.

Another problem remains. The South's Asian population is predominately foreign born, and although most Asians become citizens after living in the United States for seven years, a sizable number are not citizens and thus not eligible to vote. As a result, Asians represent less than two percent of the potential voters in the eleven southern states. Finally, it should be kept in mind that Asians are a diverse group with different interests and cannot be counted on to vote overwhelmingly for one political party or candidate.

The role of Asians in southern politics is simply part of the larger issue of New South Asians. They have been significantly on the scene only since 1980, a relatively short period of time. But if Asian immigrants continue to settle in the South, their impact on southern politics, the economy, and religion will grow. This influence will help to move the South further away from the mid-century homogenous culture that Alfred Eckes has described: "The South of the 1950s relied on one party politics, racial segregation, commodity agriculture . . . textile mills, and of course the Piggy Wiggly. In this decade before television harmonized common tastes, the South remained isolated and culturally separate."[157] The civil rights movement, the global economy, and immigration already have altered the region from its 1950s flavor.

Many factors will affect the course of future immigration, which could considerably impact political, social, and economic aspects of southern life. The recession and sluggish economy after 2000 has made some areas unattractive for newcomers. In the wake of the World Trade Center attack, hotels have suffered and airlines have experienced significant economic difficulties. Atlanta, one of the major centers of the New South, was especially hard hit when Delta Air Lines cut its workforce and hotels could not fill their rooms. However, the state of the economy has varied, and some southern states have been able to withstand hard times better than cities such as Atlanta.[158] Many immigrants, Asians included, still want to come to America. Steven A. Camarota, writing in a publication of the Center for Immigration Studies, an organization that advocates tighter restrictions on immigration, said, "There is no evidence that the economic slowdown that began in 2000 or the terrorist attacks in 2001 have significantly slowed the rate of immigrants." He estimated that 3.3 million legal and illegal immigrants came to America from January 2000 to November 2002.[159] If large numbers of Asian immigrants keep heading to the South, their influence will continue to change the southern landscape politically, economically, and culturally.

Notes

1. James C. Cobb, *The Most Southern Place on Earth: The Mississippi Delta and the Roots of Regional Identity* (New York: Oxford University Press, 1992), 110–11.

2. Gavin Wright, *Old South, New South: Revolutions in the Southern Economy since the Civil War* (New York: Basic Books, 1986), chaps. 1–3.

3. John Higham, *Strangers in the Land: Patterns of American Nativism, 1860–1925*, 2nd ed. (New Brunswick: Rutgers University Press, 1988), 167.

4. David J. Tichenor, *Dividing Lines: The Politics of Immigration in America* (Princeton: Princeton University Press, 2002), 119–20.

5. Marina E. Espina, *Filipinos in Louisiana* (New Orleans: A. F. Laborde and Sons, 1988), 1; Suchen Chan, *Asian Americans: An Interpretive History* (New York: Twayne Publishers, 1991), 25. These were the first Asians in the modern era; thousands of years ago "Asians" crossed from Asia to the United States and became "Native Americans."

6. Arlyn Tobias Gajilan, "400 Years of Filipino American History," *The Filipino Express* 10 (May 12, 1996): 15.

7. Espina, *Filipinos*.

8. Espina, *Filipinos*.

9. Raymond A. Mohl, "Asian Immigration to Florida," *Florida Historical Review*, 74 (Winter 1996): 269.

10. Mohl, "Asian Immigration," 269–71.

11. Bruce Glasrud, "Asians in Texas: An Overview, 1870–1990," *East Texas Historical Journal* 39, no. 2 (2001): 14–15.

12. See U.S. Department of Commerce, Bureau of the Census, *Thirteenth Census of the United States*, 1910 (Washington, D.C.: Government Printing Office, 1913).

13. U.S. Immigration Commission, *Immigrants in Industries: Sugar and Tobacco Manufacturing, Furniture, and Sugar Refining* (Washington, D.C.: Government Printing Office, 1911), 15:143.

14. Joan Jensen, *Passage from India: Asian Indian Immigrants in North America* (New Haven: Yale University Press, 1988), 12–13.

15. U.S. Bureau of the Census, 1919, 197, 789, table 14. Koreans were reported under "all others."

16. Roger Daniels, "History of Indian Immigration to the United States: An Interpretive Essay" (paper, "India in America" conference, Asian Society, New York, 1986), 11–12; H. Brett Melendy, *Asians in America: Filipinos, Koreans, and East Indians* (New York: Hippocrene Books, 1981), 184–85.

17. Lucy M. Cohen, *Chinese in the Post–Civil War South: A People without a History* (Baton Rouge: Louisiana State University Press, 1984), 4–11.

18. Cohen, *Chinese in the Post–Civil War South*, 8–17.

19. James W. Loewen, *The Mississippi Chinese: Between Black and White* (Cambridge: Harvard University Press, 1971), 22.

20. Loewen, *Mississippi Chinese*, 29.

21. Loewen, *Mississippi Chinese*; Cohen, *Chinese in the Post–Civil War South*.

22. Somini Sengupta, "Delta Chinese Hang On to Vanishing Way of Life," *New York Times*, November 1, 2000.

23. Cobb, *The Most Southern Place*, 173–75; Loewen, *Mississippi Chinese*, 66.

24. Cohen, *Chinese in the Post–Civil War South*, chap. 4.

25. George Pozzetta, "The Chinese Encounter with Florida, 1865–1920," *Chinese America: History Perspectives* 2 (1989): 43–58.

26. Glasrud, "Asians in Texas," 13–14.

27. Tichenor, *Dividing Lines*, 104.

28. Andrew Gyory, *Closing the Gate: Race, Politics, and the Chinese Exclusion Act* (Chapel Hill: University of North Carolina Press, 1998), chap. 11.

29. Desmond King, *Making Americans: Immigration, Race, and the Origins of Diverse Democracy* (Cambridge: Harvard University Press, 2000), 153–65.

30. King, *Making Americans,* chap. 7.

31. See Numan V. Bartley, *The New South, 1945–80* (Baton Rouge: Louisiana State University Press, 1995).

32. Prior censuses did not have a designation for more than one race, so figures comparing 1980 or 1990 with 2000 are not consistent.

33. INS, *Annual Report,* 2000, 2.

34. INS, *Annual Report,* 2000.

35. U.S. Bureau of the Census, *Profile of the Foreign-Born Population in the United States, 2000,* Current Population Survey (CPS), December 2001.

36. U.S. Bureau of the Census, *Asian Population: 2000.*

37. INS, *Statistical Yearbook,* 2000, 60.

38. A worldwide system came into being in 1978. All nations were granted annual allotments of twenty thousand (not counting immediate family members of United States citizens) based on preferences for family unification, occupations, and refugee status. The family unifications accounted for 74 percent of the slots.

39. The Refugee Act of 1980 allowed fifty thousand as the "normal flow" of refugees, but the president could permit more to arrive, and administrations after 1980 always admitted more than the "normal flow."

40. INS, *Statistical Yearbook,* 2000.

41. The literature on the civil rights movement is vast. A summary can be found in Numan V. Bartley, *The New South, 1945–80* (Baton Rouge: Louisiana University Press, 1995), chaps. 5–6 and 9–10 and Adam Fairclough, *Better Day Coming: Blacks and Equality, 1890–2000* (New York: Viking, 2001).

42. Bartley, *The New South,* chap. 9.

43. Fairclough, *Better Day,* chaps. 12–15.

44. Tichenor, *Divided Lines,* 215. See also Reimers, *Still the Golden Door: The Third World Comes to America,* 2nd ed. (New York: Columbia University Press, 1992), chap. 3.

45. See Hugh Davis Graham, *Collision Course: The Strange Convergence of Affirmative Action and Immigration Policy in America* (New York: Oxford University Press, 2002).

46. Graham, *Collision Course,* chap. 6.

47. See Alfred Eckes, "The South and Economic Globalization, 1950 to the Future," in this volume.

48. James C. Cobb, *The Selling of the South: The Southern Crusade for Industrial Development, 1936–90* (Urbana: University of Illinois Press, 1993). See, generally, the essays in Philip Scranton, ed., *The Second Wave: Southern Industrialization from the 1940s to the 1970s* (Athens: University of Georgia Press, 2001).

49. Karsten Hulsemann, "Greenfields in the Heart of Dixie: How the American Auto Industry Discovered the South," in *The Second Wave,* 228–30. American auto firms also invested in the southern states, the most notable being General Motors's Saturn plant in Tennessee.

50. *New York Times,* December 16, 2002.

51. Bartley, *The New South,* chap. 12. See also Eckes, "South and Economic Globalization."

52. Rogelio Saenz, Sean-Shong Hwang, and Benigno E. Aguirre, "In Search of Asian War Brides," *Demography* 31 (August 1994): 554–55. For the difficulties of Korean women see Ji-Yeon Yuh, Beyond the Shadow of Camptown: Korean Military Brides in America (New York: New York University Press, 2002), and for information on Japanese women, see Elfrieda Berthiaume Shukert and Barbara Smith Scibetta, *War Brides of World War II* (Novato, Calif.: Presidio Press, 1988), chaps. 12–14.

53. Spouses and minor children of United States citizens were not counted in the quotas given to each nation; hence it was relatively easy for them to emigrate to the United States.

54. See Robert J. Scholes, *The "Mail-Order Bride" Industry and Its Impact on U.S. Immigration* (INS, 2001). Such marriages also exacerbated spousal abuse because women risked losing their immigration status if they complained to authorities about domestic violence. Congress finally changed the law to allow an immigrant woman to retain immigration status if she left her husband due to domestic violence.

55. INS, *Statistical Yearbook,* 1998, 65.

56. Data is available for urban settlement of refugees by ethnic group. INS, *Statistical Yearbook,* 1998, 116–18. However, refugees amount to less than twenty percent of all immigrants.

57. *New York Times,* October 3, 1972; November 8, 1972; November 12, 1972.

58. "African-Asians Worldwide" (USA, Canada, South Africa).

59. Roger Ebert, "Mississippi Masala," *Chicago Sun Times,* February 14, 1992.

60. Tunku Varadarajan, "A Patel Motel Cartel?" *New York Times Magazine,* July 4, 1999.

61. Varadarajan, "A Patel Motel Cartel?"

62. Varadarajan, "A Patel Motel Cartel?"

63. Mark Bixler, "Census 2000: Indians State's Largest Asian Group," *Atlanta Journal-Constitution,* May 27, 2001.

64. Bixler, "Census 2000," *Atlanta Journal-Constitution,* May 27, 2001.

65. Varadarajan, "A Patel Motel Cartel?"

66. Kieu-Lin Carolin Valverde, "From Dust to Gold: The Vietnamese Amerasian Experience," in *Racially Mixed People in America,* ed. Maria P. Root (Newberry, Calif.: Sage Publications, 1992), 144–61.

67. INS, *Annual Report,* 2000, 2.

68. *San Jose Mercury News,* March 17, 2002.

69. Ruben G. Rumbaut, "Vietnamese, Laotian, and Cambodian Americans," in *Asian Americans: Contemporary Trends and Issues,* ed. Pyong Gap Min (Thousand Oaks, Calif.: Sage Publications, 1995), 232–44.

70. Rumbaut, "Vietnamese," 245.

71. The Brookings Institute, *The World in a Zip Code: Greater Washington, D.C., as a New Region of Immigration* (Washington, D.C.: Brookings Institution, 2001); "The New Immigrants," *Congressional Quarterly,* January 24, 1997.

72. "Vietnamese Success," *Fort Worth Star-Telegram,* May 8, 2000.

73. *New York Times,* October 2, 2000.

74. *Baton Rouge Advocate,* May 27, 2001.

75. Mark Bixler, "A Handmade Niche in Nails," *Atlanta Journal-Constitution*, June 17, 2001.

76. Associated Press, July 25, 2000.

77. Randolph Smith, "Refugees Pursue Dream: Cambodians Came Here," *Richmond Times-Dispatch*, August 29, 1993.

78. Pauline Agbayani-Siewert and Linda Reville, "Filipino Americans," in *Asian Americans: Contemporary Trends*, 45.

79. *Wall Street Journal*, January 1, 27, 1987.

80. Clifford Pugh, "Pakistani-Americans Blend," *Houston Chronicle*, October 28, 2001.

81. Leon Bouvier and Rosemary Jenks, *Doctors and Nurses: A Demographic Profile* (Washington, D.C.: Center for Immigration Studies, 1998).

82. Bouvier and Jenks, *Doctors and Nurses*.

83. Marjorie Valbruin, "Homeland Security," *Wall Street Journal*, December 30, 2002; "Indian Nurses Come to U.S. Aid," *India Abroad*, December 20, 2002.

84. Katherine Seelye, "U.S. Strikes at Smuggling Ring," *New York Times*, January 15, 1998.

85. *Houston Chronicle*, November 21, 1998.

86. George Borjas, *An Evaluation of the Foreign Student Program* (Washington, D.C.: Center for Immigration Studies, 2002), 4. Some estimates are higher.

87. Jianli Zhao, *Strangers in the City: The Atlanta Chinese, Their Community and Stories of Their Lives* (New York: Routledge, 2002), 76–77.

88. See the discussion in Borjas, *Foreign Student Program*.

89. *Fort Worth Star-Telegram*, April 22, 2001.

90. U.S. Dept. of Justice and U.S. Dept. of Labor, *The Triennial Comprehensive Report on Immigration, 1999* (Washington, D.C.: Government Printing Office, 1999), 118–19.

91. India passed China in the fall of 2002. Karen Aresen, "No Decline in the Number of Students," *New York Times*, November 18, 2002.

92. Laura Secor, "Destination: College, U.S.A.," *New York Times*, January 13, 2002.

93. Aresen, "No Decline," *New York Times*.

94. Laura Secor, "Destination: College, U.S.A."

95. Kevin Miller, "Asian Population Increases," *Roanoke Times*, March 10, 2001.

96. *India West*, June 25, 1999.

97. After the economic downturn in 2001, the number of these visas was cut.

98. *Dallas Morning News*, April 14, 2001; *Atlanta Journal-Constitution*, September 30, 2001.

99. *USA Today*, March 13, 2001.

100. *Austin American-Statesman*, May 15, 2001.

101. Amnesties, diversity visas, and refugees account for many immigrants, but 69 percent of newcomers in 2000 entered under family unification. INS, *Annual Report, 2000*, 2.

102. Steven A. Camarota, *Reconsidering Immigrant Entrepreneurship: An Examination of Self-Employment among Natives and the Foreign Born* (Washington, D.C.: Center for Immigration Studies, 2000). Camarota believes that the degree of immigrant entre-

preneurship has been exaggerated. However, among Asians the ownership of small enterprises is higher than for the native born. In addition, many of those laboring for others are working in the shops of family members and in effect can be counted as part of the category of ethnic entrepreneurs.

103. *Atlanta Journal-Constitution,* May 27, 2001.

104. *Atlanta Journal-Constitution,* Jun 17, 2001; *Baton Rouge Advocate,* May 27, 2001.

105. *Atlanta Journal-Constitution,* May 27, 2001.

106. Brookings, "The World in a Zip Code," 7; U.S. Department of Commerce, news release, "Asia- and Pacific Islander–Owned Businesses," May 22, 2001.

107. Pyong Gap Min, "Korean Americans," in *Asian Americans,* 208–13.

108. For details see, SBA, *Minorities in Businesses, 2001.*

109. Peter Applebome, "Koreans Add to Flavor of Shopping in El Paso," *New York Times,* October 26, 1986.

110. *Richmond Times Dispatch,* April 3, 1989.

111. Rick Badie, "The American Dream: Immigrants Find Niche in Service Industry," *Atlanta Journal-Constitution,* September 13, 1999.

112. Elizabeth Kurylo, "Immigrants Changing the Face of Atlanta," *Atlanta Journal-Constitution,* February 23, 1997.

113. Philip Pan and Peter Pae, "Now Entering Koreatown," *Washington Post,* May 16, 1999.

114. *Washington Post,* July 23, 2002.

115. Graham, *Collision Course,* 146–50; Bureau of the Census, "Asians, 2000."

116. Rochelle Sharpe, "Asian Americans Gain in Affirmative Action Program," *Wall Street Journal,* September 9, 1997. See also the discussion of this issue in Graham, *Collision Course,* 147–50.

117. *Atlanta Journal-Constitution,* July 24, 2002.

118. SBA, *Minorities in Business, 2001,* 10–16.

119. Jim Hopkins, "Asian Business Owners Gaining Clout," *USA Today,* February 27, 2002. For a detailed report on minorities in business, see SBA, *Minorities in Business, 2001.* The SBA study was based on data obtained in 1997.

120. Departments of Justice and Labor, *Triennial Report,* 1999, 58.

121. Peter Kwong, *Forbidden Workers: Illegal Chinese Immigrants and American Labor* (New York: The New Press, 1997); *Washington Post,* October 24, 1998; Ko-Lin Chin, *Smuggled Chinese: Clandestine Immigration to the United States* (Philadelphia: Temple University Press, 2001). Chin's view is more optimistic than Kwong's concerning the likelihood of immigrants getting out of debt and remaining in America.

122. Associated Press, September 23, 1999; John Zebrowski, "For Thousands of Chinese Immigrants, the Journey Here Is Only the First Part of a Long Ordeal," *Savannah Morning News,* August 13, 1999; Morris News Service, September 7, 1999.

123. *New York Times,* November 21, 1998.

124. U.S. Civil Rights Commission, *Civil Rights Issues* (Washington, D.C.: Government Printing Office, 1992), 26–32.

125. Hien Duc Djo, *The Vietnamese Americans* (Westport, Conn.: Greenwood Press, 1999), 51–53.

126. Mary Lea Grant, "Many Shrimpers Leaving Trade," *Houston Chronicle,* March 5, 2000.

127. Southern Poverty Law Center, "Anti-Immigrant Violence Rages Nationwide," *Intelligence Report* (August 1994); Jeremy Hein, *From Vietnam, Laos, and Cambodia: A Refugee Experience in the United States* (New York: Twayne Publishers, 1995), chap. 5; *Asian Week,* October 4, 2001; *Houston Chronicle,* August 2, 2002.

128. David M. Reimers, *Unwanted Strangers: American Identity and the Turn Against Immigration* (New York: Columbia University Press, 1998), 29–31; Steven A. Camarota, *Attitudes toward Amnesty: Zogby Poll Examines Support among Different Constituencies* (Washington, D.C.: Center for Immigration Studies, 2001).

129. *Tennessean,* November 14, 2002.

130. *WorldNetDaily,* online, October 30, 2001.

131. Tichenor, *Dividing Lines,* 176–207.

132. Reimers, *Still the Golden Door,* chap. 3; Tichenor, *Dividing Lines,* 207–18.

133. Reimers, *Unwanted Strangers.*

134. For a discussion of the 1996 election in the South, see Laurence W. Moreland and Robert P. Steed, eds., *The Presidential Election in the South: Southern Party Systems in the 1990s* (Westport, Conn.: Praeger, 1997).

135. John C. Green, "Believers for Bush, Godly for Gore: Religion and the 2000 Election in the South," in *The 2000 Presidential Election in the South : Partisanship and Southern Party Systems in the 21st Century,* ed. Robert Steed and Laurence W. Moreland (Westport, Conn.: Praeger, 2002), 19. After attempting to capture the Republican nomination in 1992 and 1996, Buchanan ran as the Reform party's candidate in 2000.

136. See National Research Council, *The New Americans: Economic, Demographic, and Fiscal Effects of Immigration* (Washington, D.C.: National Research Council, 1997).

137. U.S. Department of Justice, *Triennial Comprehensive Report, 1999* (Washington, D.C., Government Printing Office, 1999), 104.

138. See SBA, *Minorities in Business.*

139. See the discussion in U.S. Department of Justice, *Triennial Comprehensive Report* and the National Research Council, *The New Americans.*

140. See Sayuri Guthrie Shimizu, "From Southeast Asian to the American Southeast: Japanese Business Meets the Sunbelt," unpublished paper; Hulsemann, "Greenfields in the Heart of Dixie," 224–32.

141. *New York Times,* December 15, 2002.

142. Gayle White, "Indian Religions," *Atlanta Journal-Constitution,* August 9, 1997. The newspaper also found evidence of the practice of smaller Indian religions, such as Zoroastrianism and Jainism.

143. See Council on American-Islamic Religion, *The Mosque in America: A National Portrait* (Washington, D.C.: Council on American-Islamic Religion, 2001).

144. "Studies Suggest Lower Count for Number of U.S. Muslims," *New York Times,* October 25, 2001; City University of New York, *American Religious Identification Survey* (2001). See also the comments in Howard Feinberg and Iain Murray, "How Many Muslims?" *Christian Science Monitor,* November 29, 2001. The State Department estimated the number at two million in 2001.

145. Jim Jones, "Asian Americans Flocking to Tarrant County Churches," *Fort Worth Star-Telegram,* April 4, 1999.

146. *Atlanta Journal-Constitution,* February 23, 1997.

147. Jennifer Lee, "Melting Pot Forces Change at Many Southern Churches," *Wall Street Journal,* October 21, 1997.

148. Rick Bragg, "Vietnamese Refugees in New Orleans Find a Little Peace," *New York Times,* October 2, 2000.

149. Gustav Niebuhr, "Vietnam Immigrants Swell Catholic Clergy," *New York Times,* April 24, 2000.

150. *New York Times,* February 29, 2000.

151. Somini Sengupta, "Indian-Americans Mobilize to Send Money Home," *New York Times,* January 29, 2001.

152. Gary Locke's grandfather was born in China.

153. Moni Basu, "Pro-Indian Lobby," *Atlanta Journal-Constitution,* August 23, 2002.

154. "Indian-Americans Help Unseat U.S. Lawmaker," *The Times of India,* August 23, 2002.

155. William Welch, "Crossover Vote," *USA Today,* August 22, 20.

156. *Atlanta Journal-Constitution,* November 20, 2002.

157. Eckes, "South and Economic Globalization," 38.

158. *New York Times,* December 16, 2002.

159. Steven A. Camarota, *Immigrants in the United States—2002: A Snapshot of America's Foreign-Born Population* (Washington, D.C.: Center for Immigration Studies, 2002), 1.

From Southeast Asia to the American Southeast: Japanese Business Meets the Sun Belt South

Sayuri Guthrie-Shimizu

In 1959, the Japan External Trade Organization (JETRO), established a year earlier with partial government funding as a nonprofit institute for market research and trade promotion,[1] surveyed the current state and future prospects for Japanese exports to the United States. The authors of the report marveled at the robust growth and dizzying diversity of the consumer markets in post–World War II America. After noting the vitality of the U.S. economy and Japan's recent gains in industrial capacity, they expressed unabashed hopes that Japanese goods would make further inroads into the markets of America's industrial North and Midwest and those of the Pacific coastal states. Singularly absent from this sanguine assessment was the South, which the analysts at the quasi-government development agency rated "by far the remotest and most underdeveloped" American regional market and one saddled with a formidable array of structural impediments to Japanese commercial penetration.[2]

Government officials and businessmen who studied this widely circulated report had little reason to question its grim view of Japan's future role in this backwater of the world's greatest industrial economy. They needed only to recall their recent brush with "southern inhospitality." Three years before, the South Carolina and Alabama state legislatures had enacted discriminatory local requirements regarding the sale of Japanese textile goods, a development that deeply wounded Japan's national pride, so recently restored by postwar reconstruction and industrial growth. Reports of turmoil rocking southern society over desegregation further tarnished the region's image in the eyes of the Japanese, whose racial anxieties had always conditioned their attitudes toward the Euro-American world. It would have stretched the imagination of the most conceited among them to contemplate that the South would someday come looking for their business.[3]

Yet in the twenty-first century, the American South is home to myriad Japanese business enterprises.[4] Although precise figures are hard to determine, just the five states under the jurisdiction of the Japanese General Consulate Office in Atlanta (Alabama, Georgia, North Carolina, South Carolina, and Virginia) reported the operation of 740 Japanese businesses and their affiliates in 2001. Every southern state except Louisiana has a trade office in Tokyo for the purposes of investment recruitment and export promotion.[5] The Japanese also appear intent on fortifying the commercial pipeline with Dixie. In 1985, JETRO opened a branch office in Atlanta. When it instituted the Office of Senior Trade Advisers in 1990 and placed full-time staffs in key locations around the globe to help local industry export to Japan, it assigned two positions to the U.S. South (in North Carolina and Tennessee).[6] Indeed, the mutual discovery and embrace between the industrial boosterism of "the new New South" of the Sun Belt era and an export reliant Japan in the period after World War II represents a stunning transformation that reflects late-twentieth-century economic globalization.[7]

This connection between Japan and the Sun Belt South was decidedly a product of metamorphosis, not a sudden mutation. Many of the changes that swept across these two distinct societies in the last forty years or so—and some of their unchanging characteristics—have prepared the way for this unlikely transregional partnership in industrial development. This essay will highlight some of the historical forces that coalesced in the postwar period to create this amalgam of political and economic interests stretching across national boundaries. This process of mutual gravitation will be framed in a larger canvas of the restructuring post–World War II international economic order. The essay will conclude with a reflection on the ambiguous promise of the Japan-Dixie connection and its multiple implications for southern society in the age of globalization.

Japan's limited commercial contact with Dixie in the early postwar years stemmed from the uneven development of interhemisphere trade in the previous half century. Since the advent of the commercial steamship in trans-Pacific oceanic traffic in the latter half of the nineteenth century, the termini of Japan's shipping routes to the United States had been heavily concentrated in the upper Atlantic seaboard, with New York serving as the unlikely hub of the pan-Pacific transport system. This transnational industrial structure remained basically unaltered through the first half of the twentieth century.[8] After the sweeping reorganization of industry carried out by the Allied occupation authorities following World War II, Japanese maritime shippers began incrementally to reopen the routes and replace the commercial tonnage lost during the war, beginning with the all-important New York route. A worldwide shipping boom triggered by the Korean War created a political environment serendipitous for Japan's merchant marine, which was readying itself to reenter the world's oceanic transport network. Shortly after the outbreak of the military conflict in the Far East, the Japanese secured blanket clearance to ports in twenty-three noncommunist nations and the right of passage through the Panama Canal, a privilege the United States had withheld since the outbreak of World War II.[9]

At the end of the 1950s, however, 70 percent of Japanese goods entering the United States were still unloaded at locations along the upper Atlantic seaboard, and only 25 percent were routed through Pacific coastal ports. At the time JETRO's influential 1959 report was written, about $6.7 million worth of goods, a meager 3 percent of Japan's total exports to the United States that year, entered through eight southern ports (Charleston, Savannah, Miami, Tampa, Mobile, New Orleans, Galveston, Houston). In a legacy of the Gulf Coast ports' historic development as part of the Caribbean and inter-American trading network, no steamship service originating there reached Japan directly until the late 1950s. The underdeveloped trade infrastructure added to the freight costs and turnaround time borne by Japanese shipments to the U.S. South.[10]

When Japanese manufacturers did eye the southern tier of the U.S. market for the labor-intensive, low-value-added products in which they held comparative advantage in the early postwar period, they faced the burden of Dixie's stunted distribution system and its dependence on northern commercial capital. Only a minuscule number of southern traders had the resources or inclination to import directly from a far-off and unfamiliar land in Asia. Southern importers were generally unacquainted with the administrative procedures involved in commercial transactions with Japan, such as the use of yen-denominated letters of credit. Even the larger southern distributors and retailers usually worked through buying agents in New York and other major cities. Generally better capitalized, the export-import firms in the U.S. commercial metropolis were prone to dumping overstocks, often acquired as a result of price-cutting wars among cash-strapped and overeager Japanese exporters, on these southern buying agents. This structural problem contributed to the notoriously wild price fluctuations of Japanese merchandise sold in southern retail outlets. The so-called one-dollar blouses that provoked an anti-Japan campaign by the Southern Garment Workers' Union and the enactment of discriminatory state laws in the late 1950s illustrates the frequent market disruptions born of the asymmetrical interregional and transnational distribution system of the time. Under these circumstances, Japanese manufacturers were commonly advised that southern retailers, mindful of the public perception of Japanese goods as shoddy (unlike Western European goods), preferred generic "Imported" markings to "Made in Japan."[11]

Less than a decade after the economic takeoff sparked by the Korean War, the Japanese did not yet possess the wherewithal to remove the distributional barriers that were consequent to the South's historic dependence on northern capital. Save for government-subsidized cotton-purchasing agents stationed in Dallas, no Japanese private enterprise had the ability to maintain permanent offices in southern states. Only one out of twenty-seven Japanese trading companies operating in the New York area in the late 1950s had employees stationed in the South (in New Orleans). Unlike in the West Coast and New York, the South had no sizable Japanese immigrant communities that homeland businesses could tap into to establish footholds in the local economy. Starting in 1958, the government and big business began jointly to send annual trade missions to the United States, but their yearly commercial expeditions did not reach a southern location until 1963. Against these grim realities imposed by geography and history, the Japanese had no choice but to let the Western Europeans preempt the choice southern capital goods and consumer markets in the 1960s.[12]

Only when their country's economic standing improved dramatically after the high-speed growth of the 1960s did Japanese industrialists and businessmen begin to reassess what the U.S. South had to offer and, in turn, what they might accomplish there. This change in interest first came in response to marked improvements in the infrastructure of Japan-Dixie trade. By the mid-1960s, Japan's maritime shipping industry had completed the restoration of its fleet and surpassed the prewar tonnage high of 6.3 million. It also went through a period of consolidation in the mid-1950s as key shippers struggled to weather the doldrums in the wake of the Korean War and reversed the basic tenets of the occupation-era deconcentration program. A second wave of government-promoted mergers came a decade later. In 1960, the Japanese government launched a ten-year plan to restructure Japan's merchant marine. Designed to supplement other elements of Prime Minister Hayato Ikeda's "Income-Doubling" policy, a legislative package passed by the Diet between 1960 and 1962 opened the way for strategic allocations of the Japan Development Bank's shipbuilding loans. A result of this "guided" lending was that ninety-five shipping companies consolidated into six moguls and a handful of independents in response to the implied government preference for larger shippers. The increased resources giants like Nippon Yusen and Mitsui Senpaku amassed in these corporate mergers enabled them to begin regular eastbound direct service to the Gulf Coast and the lower Atlantic seaboard.[13]

Through the 1960s, the importance of Gulf Coast ports to Japan's growing procurements of raw cotton, scrap iron, and Florida's phosphorite and exports of low-end metal products, lumber, and plywood furnished strong commercial incentives for the southbound route expansion and the separation of the North American and the Caribbean/Central American sectors for Japanese shippers. In these interregional route reconfigurations, Houston and New Orleans emerged as the twin hubs of the growing southern tier of the U.S.-Japan maritime trade network. According to Japanese estimates, about ten million square feet of Japanese plywood, one of the key items of U.S.-Japanese trade dispute following Japanese accession to the General Agreement on Tariffs and Trade (GATT), entered the U.S. distribution system through the port of New Orleans in 1958. Within three years, the figure doubled. About 80 percent of raw cotton and 60 percent of scrap iron, fodder of the early phases of the Japanese economic miracle, passed through these two southern ports through much of the 1960s. Technological innovations, particularly the introduction of container vessels, sustained the proliferation of Japan's oceanic transport routes. Later in the decade, Japanese shippers came to see the added values of southern ports as they partook in the growth in automobile exports to the United States. Now better connected through the interstate highway networks with the nation's key metropolitan markets, the Gulf Coast ports became principle destinations of Japan's automobile transport vessels.[14]

In the meantime, Japanese trading firms (*Sogo Shosha*) made it their priority to expand North American operations to support the rapidly growing U.S.-Japan trade. As they did so, they typically opened regional offices in southern metropolitan locations such as Atlanta, Dallas, and Houston. The Sun Belt South's vaunted population growth and increasing purchasing power proved a powerful draw. The prospect of federally mandated racial integration lightened, if not completely removed, the psychological inhibitions of those Japanese firms contemplating southward expansion. As gauged by opinions articulated in leading trade publications, Japan's business leaders contented themselves with the idea that Japanese nationals could probably expect "honorary white" status in the post–Jim Crow South, akin to that being accorded to the Japanese business community in South Africa under apartheid. Japanese traders thus strategically embedded themselves in midcentury America's increasingly integrated national distribution system characterized by chain stores and franchises. By the early 1970s, the emergent corporate Japan had constructed beachheads along this commercial perimeter, geared for "selling to the South" and tapping the resources and manpower of the region.[15]

While Japan's dependency on the United States in interstate relations obscured from view the incubation of this subtly colonial subnational coupling, the South continued to rise in the estimation of Japanese industrialists and businessmen. This southern ascent paralleled Japan's rise in the ranks of the world's leading players in foreign direct investment in the 1970s. The nation's overseas capital transfer resumed in 1951 with the end of the Allied occupation, but it initially remained strictly controlled by the Finance Ministry in the name of safeguarding the nation's precarious foreign-exchange reserves. A series of piecemeal deregulations took place after the mid-1960s under accumulating pressures from the U.S. government, the Organization for Economic Cooperation and Development (OECD), and other external entities. Between 1969 and 1971 the liberalization of Japan's foreign direct investment was completed, with only the Finance Ministry's licensing system, now premised on automatic approval, remaining. What students of Japan's political economy call the nation's first postwar foreign investment boom began soon after.[16]

Initially, Japanese investments in the United States did not approach the amounts expended on industrial production and resource extraction in Southeast Asia—the nearby "underdeveloped" world. In the early postoccupation years, Japan lost no time in initiating capital transfer to Southeast Asia in an act benignly cloaked as reparation payments to the former victims of its recent military aggressions. Between 1954 and 1959, the government in Tokyo reached bilateral reparations agreements with four claimants (Burma, the Philippines, Indonesia, and South Vietnam) under the terms of the San Francisco peace treaty. The acrimonious and wrenching negotiations marred Japan's already strained relationships with these countries, but the infusion of Japanese public funds into these nascent national economies delivered a fully intended boon to Japanese business, which profited handsomely from providing the goods and services the World War II reparation agreements called for in lieu of cash settlements. Minimally, the Japanese public capital invested through this "public" avenue profoundly shaped the face of infrastructure and industrial development in the receiving countries. Arguably, it laid the foundation upon which the Japanese could build their private-sector investments in postcolonial Southeast Asia in the subsequent decades.[17]

Compared to this early engagement with Southeast Asia, Japan came late to the business of investing in the United States, trailing far behind the British, Canadians, and Western Europeans. But the catch-up was swift. Upon lifting the residual restrictions on foreign direct investment in mid-1971, the Finance Ministry approved 156 applications for business ventures in the United States. The number of permits issued almost doubled to 274 in 1972 and then jumped spectacularly to 1,057 in 1973. The 1973 Arab oil embargo dampened Japan's foreign investment fervor, but international macroeconomic forces, including the yen's further appreciation, generated another spike in Japanese capital transfer to the United States in 1978.[18]

The exponential increase in Japanese direct investment in the United States was accompanied by a marked change in its composition. Until the early 1970s, Japanese investment in the United States had concentrated in the commercial and service sectors, with less than a quarter going into manufacturing. This pattern contrasted sharply with the Canadians and Western Europeans, who directed more than half of their capital invested in the United States to manufacturing enterprises.[19] Japan's distinct slant toward commercial and service ventures reflected an overall trade strategy that emphasized exports to the United States to overcome the chronic dollar shortage of the early postwar period. Since Japan's trading firms and manufacturing companies found America's distribution systems pleasantly uncomplicated and easy for newcomers to enter, they opened subsidiaries with relative ease and expanded marketing and service headquarters devoted to the sales of goods manufactured in Japan or at production sites elsewhere in Asia and in Latin America. Financial and insurance services that catered to those operations quickly followed.[20]

Japanese investment in the United States began to expand into the manufacturing sector around the mid-1970s. This shift from export support to import substitution occurred in the gravitational pull of macroeconomic forces and political considerations. The shrinking difference in the costs of production in the United States and Japan was one important impulse. In the summer of 1971, President Richard Nixon imposed a 10 percent surcharge on all dutiable imports, unpegged the dollar from gold, and forced a revaluation of America's key rivals' currencies. By the year's end, the Smithsonian agreement among the Western industrial nations put the value of the Japanese currency at 308 yen to the dollar. As the yen's value continued to float on an upward trajectory through the 1970s, Japanese business had to come to terms with the mixed blessings of a stronger yen. Although the new monetary situation made exporting more difficult, Japanese industrialists now saw the costs of manufacturing in the United States, most critically labor costs, go down significantly on paper. Fluctuating yen-dollar exchange rates led some manufacturers to move part of their operations to the United States as a way to minimize risks.[21]

Political circumstances also made manufacturing in the United States increasingly attractive. Conflict over Japan's mounting exports and trade surpluses, by then a staple of U.S.-Japanese relations, contributed to the rise of protectionism in the United States. In this changed environment, Japanese business was forced to adopt measures to calm American industries fretting over their loss of competitive edge in the international marketplace and/or asking for time for internal structural adjustments. The Japanese government entered into a series of "voluntary export restrictions" (VER) or "orderly marketing agreements" (OMA) with Washington in disputed areas. Made outside the framework of GATT, these bilateral arrangements limited Japanese exports of textiles, steel, and consumer durables, among other products, to the United States at negotiated levels.[22]

Looking at these long-term trends, many in Japanese business circles concluded that offshore production had become a more viable market defense strategy vis-à-vis the United States and began to look for manufacturing facilities. The mass media's portrayals of the United States as a society saturated with violent crime and counterculture upheavals notwithstanding, reasoned evaluations of criteria for "country risk" assessment convinced Japanese big business that the United States was actually by far the safest place in the world to invest. The ultimate champion of private property, Washington would never nationalize foreign enterprises; the Japanese were no stranger to the bitter experience of nationalization in countries like Peru and Ethiopia. Boasting a stable and unquestionably nonrevolutionary polity with the world's oldest functioning written constitution, the United States promised immunity from the kind of political uncertainty that plagued many hosts to Japan's industrial investment in Southeast Asia and elsewhere in the Third World. Additionally, the United States had inexpensive energy sources and abundant supplies of raw materials accessible by well-developed extractive facilities. At a time when the trend among Third World countries toward assertions of control over subsoil materials was ominous to resource-poor Japan, America's lack of nationalism-inspired possessiveness—of oil and other lifebloods of industrial production—was particularly appealing. The business infrastructure was highly sophisticated, and land and real estate were affordable, especially in rural areas. Furthermore, America's capital markets imposed few restrictions on foreigners. But could the United States offer a skilled and yet reasonably pliant labor force not hostile to foreign capital? [23]

This last point was particularly important to Japanese government officials, state bureaucrats, and business leaders looking at the United States as a new focus of their overseas investment strategies. The animosity toward Japan's economic saturation manifested throughout Southeast Asia profoundly affected their thinking. In Thailand, where the Sarit Thanarat regime's recruitment of foreign capital in the 1960s had resulted in the most concentrated Japanese investment, student-organized boycotts of Japanese goods had taken place periodically since the fall of 1972. In October 1973, General Thanom Kittikachorn's military rule collapsed amid a popular uprising, delivering a disorienting blow to Japanese commercial interests that had thrived on close and often venal connections with the toppled military regime. But in the immediate wake of the Thanom regime's overthrow, a majority of Japanese corporations in Thailand still did not fully grasp their own role in the political upheaval in a nation long considered relatively pro-Japanese among the Southeast Asians.

Thailand's anti-Japanese sentiment was given dramatic vent when Prime Minister Tanaka Kakuei visited five nations of the Association of Southeast Asian Nations (ASEAN) three months later. Tanaka and his entourage were besieged by violent anti-Japan demonstrations that even threatened the security of the Japanese Embassy in Bangkok. The Thais decried the Japanese colonial attitudes toward the local populace, labor exploitation, predatory resource extraction, and the environmental degradation caused by Japanese manufacturing plants. Similarly intense displays of hatred toward "the ugly Japanese" [24] awaited the Japanese delegation in Indonesia. Only in the Philippines, then under martial law, was local reception cordial. Southeast Asia's hostility sent shock waves through the Japanese establishment. Leading business organizations had adopted voluntary codes of conduct six months earlier to improve the standing of Japanese enterprises in the developing world, but the outbursts during Tanaka's tour exposed the inadequacy of private-sector self-regulation. This realization generated calls within Tokyo's elite circles for a comprehensive government-business review of corporate behavior overseas.[25]

Japanese direct investment in the United States took off in this atmosphere of purposeful reorientation. Against the unmasked hostility Japanese business encountered in Southeast Asia, Americans, while unhappy about their trade deficits with Japan and rising national unemployment, appeared earnest in courting Japanese capital. In the spring of 1973, the U.S. Department of Commerce and the industrial development agencies of thirty-four states held joint investment seminars in Tokyo and Osaka. All twelve southern states sent high-ranking officials headed by state governors to this marketing endeavor. Blazingly bannered "Invest in U.S.A.," the events were a huge success, bringing together the 170-member American delegation and representatives from more than three hundred Japanese companies in Tokyo and over two hundred in Osaka.[26]

In a follow-up to the American overture, Japanese big business sent a survey team in the fall to gauge the investment climate in the United States. The business community's changed geographical focus was already apparent in the delegation's itinerary. After landing in Los Angeles, it headed South, visiting Dallas, Atlanta, Macon, Savannah, Columbia, and several cities in Florida. The group's posttour report candidly explained why the formerly neglected U.S. South now held so much allure for Japanese industry. First and foremost, the southern state governments had invited Japanese business to come and offered incentive packages consisting of tax breaks and exemptions, subsidized or free infrastructure improvements, and other privileges. Second, since there was little room left in Japan for large-scale plant constructions, the South's abundant space and cheap land were enticing, especially to those interested in "greenfield" sites. Plant constructions and business starts supported by state and local governments, such as the YKK Industries (a clothes fastener manufacturer) in Macon, received special mention in the report as examples of early successes.[27]

The Japanese business scouts found the characteristics of the southern labor market particularly attractive. Southern wages were noticeably lower than the national average, and unions were rare. Workers took a bread-and-butter approach that would make them amenable to paternalistic appeasement, at least relative to the more ideologically driven union activism in Europe or the nationalist labor revolts against foreign capital in the Third World. All southern states except Kentucky had right-to-work laws on the books. Compared to the loaded packages commonly provided to the Japanese workforce, the bare-bones expectations of nonunion American labor regarding fringe benefits meant significant savings for prospective Japanese employers. Other attributes of the southern political economy also put Japanese businessmen at ease. Like procapitalist authoritarian regimes in the developing world, Dixie officeholders appeared accommodating to industry and disinclined to regulate it. But unlike other "underdeveloped" regions that the Japanese were accustomed to doing business with, the U.S. South was not devoid of local capital markets. Foreigners had equal access to the area's credit facilities; state, county, and municipal politicians and industrial recruiters eagerly offered assistance in Industrial Revenue Bond issues (IRB). A second survey team dispatched three years later produced a similarly positive report about the South's "growth potential" and "good business climate."[28]

These Japanese appraisals validated years of efforts by southern industrial promoters and political elites to lure outside investors. As historians of the New South have shown, subsidized industrial hunting had many precedents in the region, with Mississippi's Balance Agriculture with Industry (BAWI) program of 1936 the modern-day trendsetter. In the postwar era, growth-oriented state and local leaders actively solicited outside capital to modernize the area's economy and adopted a variety of de facto industrial policies in the absence of a consciously coordinated and politically disciplined industrial policy at the federal level.[29] In the 1960s, southern governments created development agencies through which they launched a variety of promotional efforts. Inspired by Florida's successful experimentation in state-funded vocational training, all of the southern states instituted similar programs at the secondary and postsecondary levels to make local workforces attractive to outside investors. For instance, in 1961 South Carolina's State Board for Technical and Comprehensive Education began offering free or subsidized industrial training and technical assistance to employees of newly locating or expanding businesses. Georgia launched a comparable program, Quick Start, in 1967. At a time when some Japanese businesses felt hounded by developing countries to funnel corporate resources into technical training to benefit the local workforce, the offer by state governments to foot the bill did not escape notice.[30]

The Sun Belt South's endogenous drive for change also warranted the positive Japanese assessment of the region's future. The transformation of southern politics after the desegregation crises of the late 1950s and 1960s accelerated the region's opening to the wider world. More cosmopolitan southern politicians rose to prominence and aligned themselves with industrial recruiters and business leaders seeking outside capital. This new political coalition came to accept, with varying degrees of alacrity, greater conformity with national norms. One manifestation of this evolutionary process was the election of several moderate state governors in the 1970s. Largely freed from the yoke of the polarizing desegregation issue, the new generation of southern governors was able to build a broader interracial coalition and devote most of their energies to economic growth and expanding opportunity. These "New South governors" included Reubin Askew of Florida, Jimmy Carter of Georgia, Dale Bumpers of Arkansas, James Hunt Jr. of North Carolina, and John West of South Carolina.[31]

Reflecting this general sociopolitical trend, the horizon of the South's industrial recruitment naturally began to expand beyond the U.S. borders. In the late 1960s, the term *reverse investment* came into common use among southern officeholders and business leaders to describe the then-novel concept of recruiting investment capital from overseas. In March 1969, North Carolina led Dixie by dispatching a reverse investment mission to a location other than Western Europe to size up a rising star in foreign direct investment: Japan. Within a year, South Carolina and Georgia followed suit.[32] With the advent of affordable jet travel and innovations in communications technology adding to the ease of international business travel, southern governors' job descriptions seemed to include frequent trips abroad as their states' chief advertising officers. Carter was representative of the probusiness southern moderates who seized the moment to go global. In 1972, as Georgia governor, he spearheaded a campaign to recruit Japanese capital to his home state. Working with the city of Macon, the local chamber of commerce, and Bibb County, Carter persuaded YKK, a target of several GATT "escape clause" and federal antidumping investigations, that it would find in this southern location a safe haven. An inceptive package featuring the sale of a two-hundred-thousand-square-meter plant site at twenty-five cents per square meter—one eighth of the going land price—sealed the deal. The following year, Carter leaped to the forefront of Dixie's pursuit of Japanese investment by opening a permanent trade office in the heart of Tokyo.[33] Hunt followed five years later by setting up the Japan Office of the North Carolina Department of Commerce's Division of International Trade, a second Dixie outpost in Japan. By that time, as a president battling post-Vietnam America's economic distress, Carter was exhorting state governors to "go to Japan. Persuade them to make in the United States what they sell in the U.S. Bring their plants and those jobs to your states."[34]

One of the second generation of "New South governors" who drew inspiration from Carter's call to "go West" in search of business was Tennessee's Lamar Alexander, a Republican who followed the path set by his Democratic predecessor, Ray Blanton. In 1980, consummating Blanton's aggressive pursuit of Japanese business, Alexander emerged victorious from a contest with Georgia and landed Nissan Motors' first manufacturing operation in North America. It was the largest Japanese overseas manufacturing investment ever. Alexander won this coveted prize after personal lobbying in Tokyo with Nissan president Ishihara Takashi and key government officials. In 1985, Kentucky governor Martha

Layne Collins (later appointed by the Japanese government as honorary consul general of Japan in Kentucky) launched similar hands-on marketing campaigns, including eight lobbying trips to Tokyo. Her efforts were rewarded by Toyota's decision to locate its first solely owned U.S. manufacturing facility in her state.[35]

In the 1970s, these entrepreneurial southern governors were able to ride the crest of global macroeconomic forces. As the postwar world predicated on American industrial supremacy underwent a tectonic shift, key segments of the Japanese manufacturing economy were gravitating toward the U.S. Sun Belt. Television sets, at the forefront of trade disputes in the late 1960s and emblematic of Japan's advance into more capital-intensive, value-added manufacturing sectors, illustrate this drift. In 1972, Sony broke from the industry's norm of shifting production sites to Southeast Asia or Taiwan and instead built a plant in San Diego. The company's primary aim was to stop the charges of dumping and other unfair trade practices by its U.S. rivals, most notably Zenith, and safeguard its share in the prized American consumer electronics market. San Diego was chosen for its supply of nonunion labor and proximity to Mexico, from which the company planned to procure cheaper subassemblies. Sony was also the first Japanese consumer electronics manufacturer to set up shop in the Deep South. In 1977, Dothan, Alabama, became home to Sony's magnetic goods (vcrs and recording devices) plant.[36]

Emulating Sony's retooled market defense strategy, Matsushita (Panasonic) acquired Motorola's television division (Quasar) in Franklin Park, Illinois, in 1974. Sanyo acquired Warwick, a subsidiary of Whirlpool, and built a new manufacturing facility in Forrest City, Arkansas, in 1977 and another in San Diego the following year to produce a variety of household electrical appliances. After an oma was reached on color televisions in May 1977, two more leading Japanese manufacturers, Toshiba and Sharp, opened greenfield plants in Tennessee (Lebanon and Memphis). Mitsubishi also shifted part of its tv production to a nonunion plant in Los Angeles in 1978.[37]

Japanese automobile manufacturers duplicated the pattern of trans-Pacific industrial migration with greater fanfare.[38] After the 1973 oil crunch increased the appeal of Japanese compact cars among American consumers, Japanese manufacturers encountered rising protectionism in the United States. Although the industry's key players began considering "local" production in North America in the wake of the Arab oil embargo, the not-so-encouraging results of initial feasibility studies, particularly the magnitude of estimated start-up costs, kept Japan's top two automakers, Nissan and Toyota, famously reluctant to "go east" for a long time.[39] In 1978, the more enterprising industry upstart, Honda, took the plunge and began manufacturing less capital-demanding motorcycles in a greenfield plant near Marysville, Ohio. Governor

James Rhodes's recruitment efforts helped bring about Honda's decision to build the $61 million facility in central western Ohio, at a safe distance from the United Auto Workers' citadel in Michigan. Two years later, the company announced the construction of a $250 million automobile production facility next to the Marysville motorcycle plant.[40]

In the late 1970s, Nissan and Toyota shifted to a higher gear in their hunt for U.S. manufacturing sites, albeit reluctantly. The yen's further rise in value, the accelerated sales of Japanese compact cars in the United States after the second oil shock, and the prospect of U.S. automakers producing fuel-efficient cars in the 1980s made the move imperative. The VER agreement reached between Washington and Tokyo in May 1981 simply provided added rationale for what industry insiders by then considered the inevitable. Once word spread of Nissan's stepped-up search for a U.S. plant location, a phalanx of southern governors including Alexander, Georgia's George Busbee, and Kentucky's John Brown entered what escalated into interstate bidding wars waged under the combined pressures of high national unemployment and media-fueled public expectations.[41]

In 1980, Nissan announced the selection of Smyrna, Tennessee, out of thirty-four locations across the United States, as the site for its third production headquarters outside Japan (following those in Australia and Mexico). The incentive package Tennessee offered was estimated to total $33 million. From the perspective of the state's political leadership and industrial recruiters, it was a worthwhile investment of state and local funds made to entice an enterprise that promised multiple spin-offs. The initial $300 million Nissan poured into the truck assembly plant was in fact the largest foreign manufacturing investment in Tennessee's history. In five years, that investment ballooned to $745 million, sustaining a business employing three thousand workers and building 180,000 trucks and automobiles each year.[42] Toyota took five more years to announce its move across the Pacific. After comparing forty or so states, the company negotiated an estimated $149 million incentive package with Kentucky. Amid lingering local outcries against the perceived giveaway, Toyota's $800 million plant in Georgetown began production in 1988. Without so much media hype, Subaru-Isuzu built a $500 million plant in Lafayette, Indiana, on the basis of $83 million in state inducements.[43]

The southern governors and industrial recruiters' anticipation of spin-off effects was vindicated to some measure. In the case of Tennessee, Bridgestone, the number one Japanese tire manufacturer, acquired and resuscitated a dying Firestone plant in LaVergne near Nissan's Smyrna plant in 1982. The more significant benefits, however, came from the migration of small- to medium-sized, or "second tier," Japanese enterprises to southern locations after the mid-1980s. Although the trans-Pacific production strategy was initially adopted by mostly large Japanese manufacturers of consumer end-products, the just-in-time production/inventory system (JIT) employed by many of them generated a delayed wave of relocation of parts producers and related enterprises to the South. Dubbed the Toyota system, or the "24-hour inventory system," the JIT method requires suppliers to make and deliver only what is needed by manufacturers when it is needed. Japan's automotive industry was the most prominent example of this general pattern of industrial migration shaped by this production/inventory model. Less vertically integrated than their American counterparts, Japanese automakers are more reliant on outside parts and material supplies that tend to come from smaller manufacturers employing less automated production systems. This industrial structure, once projected to its transplant locations in the United States, led component suppliers subcontracting to the moguls to relocate from Japan and Southeast Asia to areas close to the new Japanese auto assembly and engine plants.[44]

This secondary Japanese industrial migration throughout the 1980s and 1990s was a major factor in the emergence of America's "automobile corridor" cutting through the nation's midsection. This new industrial belt stretched from the lower Midwest (Ohio and Indiana), through the upper South (Tennessee and Kentucky), to the Deep South (Georgia and South Carolina) by the close of the twentieth century. In the new millennium, with the ongoing and planned plant constructions by the Japanese Big Three and South Korean manufacturer Hyundai, the automobile corridor now cuts across Alabama and Mississippi. As the Japanese economy languishes in a decade-long recession, the automotive companies now see these production sites as key to their strategies for industrial rejuvenation in the race for a lion's share of a new American middle-class consumer fascination: minivans, light trucks, and sports utility vehicles.[45]

Dixie officeholders paved the automobile corridor's southward extension with a new layer of large-scale state incentives. In May 1999, Honda announced plans to build a $400 million assembly and engine plant in Lincoln, Alabama, the second coup in the state's automotive industry recruitment since a Mercedes plant in 1993. What lured Honda away from competing sites (Tolono, Illinois; Richmond, Virginia; and Commerce, Georgia) was a $158 million incentive package put together by Governor Don Siegelman and the executive of the state's $23 billion pension fund. In November 2000, Mississippi brought Nissan's projected $950 million, four-thousand-employee assembly plant to Canton with a package worth $295 million and the personal involvement of Senate Majority Leader Trent Lott. In February 2001, Huntsville, Alabama, secured Toyota's $220 million, 350-job engine plant with a $29 million package. The recruitment of Hyundai's Montgomery, Alabama, plant cost the state $252 million.[46]

While southern governors jostled each other to attract investment, especially as the political stakes grew in the unemployment-plagued 1980s,[47] they also pursued a common regional development strategy. In December 1971, nine governors signed executive orders creating the Southern Growth Policies Board (SGPB), later to be headquartered in Research Triangle Park in North Carolina. By 1978, twelve states (Alabama, Arkansas, Florida, Georgia, Kentucky, Louisiana, Mississippi, the Carolinas, Oklahoma, Tennessee, Virginia) came under the SGPB's organizational umbrella. Governors of member states share a yearly revolving chairmanship. Each state also has its own SGPB.[48]

This mode of public-private collaboration set in regional unity, a key feature of American corporatism identified by some political scientists,[49] was applied also to the solicitation of Japanese investment. In 1975, political and business leaders of Japan and seven southeastern states congregated in Tokyo to formalize their political and economic ties. One outcome of the much-heralded Tokyo conference was the chartering of the Southeast U.S./Japan Association. Parties to this mix of public- and private-sector elites agreed to meet annually, alternating sites between Japan and a location in the Southeast. They also designated the association as the central repository of resources and information related to trade and investment between Japan and Dixie. Georgia's Governor Busbee—who obviously knew how to win Japanese businessmen's hearts—was instrumental in this institution-building effort. The idea of a permanent government-business forum linking Japan and the U.S. Southeast was given specific form in a conversation he and Coca-Cola senior executive Sam Ayoub had with the chairman of Sumitomo Chemical (an avid golfer), Hasegawa Norishige. Hasegawa had been invited to the 1974 Masters Golf Tournament in Augusta, Georgia, as Governor Busbee's special guest. Befitting the Peachtree State's particularly ardent courting of Japanese investment and Busbee's SGPB chairmanship that year, its capital played host to the association's first annual meeting in 1976, cosponsored by the Japanese Consular General Office established there just two years before.[50]

In the official investment guides the association has circulated in Japan, sales pitches conjure up the image of Dixie as a safe haven for Japanese capital while Japanese officials and industrialists lock horns with their American competition and organized labor ensconced in the northern industrial metropolises. Dixie's key spokesman in Japan's elite circles, Hasegawa harped on the South-as-refuge theme first as a corporate executive credited with a successful joint venture in Mount Pleasant, Tennessee, in 1975, and then as vice chairman of the influential *Keidanren* (the Japan Association of Economic Organizations) in the early 1980s.[51] The South's chief executives displayed striking regional solidarity in emphasizing cheap and cooperative labor, low taxes, probusiness state legislatures, and judicious and efficient (i.e., minimal) government regulation—the features scholars often refer to as the very markers of the South's backwardness. On the other hand, marketing tracts hasten to add that the South has attained some of the key characteristics of the industrial North: quality education, industrial training and other social services, improved infrastructure, and increasing social and cultural diversity. Of paramount importance, the governors do not neglect to remind the Japanese, the South is a constituent part of a nation unsurpassed in its technological prowess, political stability, commitment to private property and free enterprise, material abundance, and lifestyle amenities. The South is thus presented as Japanese capital's conduit to the benefits of America's modernity.[52]

Not so obvious in these southern business manifestos, however, is an acknowledgment of who is left untouched by such recently acquired "progressive" attributes of southern government and society. Are the South's "modern" aspects readily accessible only to outside industrial investors and their coteries, who may come and leave as the global economy dictates? Are they equally open to the locals whose existence is not so footloose? Quick Start, Georgia's industrial training program hailed in many business magazines as the most effective among the South's industrial recruitment tools,[53] serves as an illuminating example. The program that "promises to deliver success, not just training," as described in the state's official investment promotion brochure, has been offered to businesses that locate in Georgia or significantly expand existing in-state operations. Benefits of this state-financed service include free and customized employee training by certified economic development trainers (CEDT) at thirty-two state facilities or sponsoring educational institutions. But these "public" services can only be rendered to those employed or about to be employed by qualifying businesses, and other residents not associated with such "private" entities are denied access to this chance at economic and social advancement. Regardless of the crafter's original intent, standby incentives like Quick Start, a form of public policy, afford a mechanism for exclusion in the public domain on the basis of private criteria. The state government in effect anoints nonelectoral entities, such as out-of-state investors, to be arbiters of this weeding-out process.[54]

Other incentives, such as infrastructure improvements and energy provision, gifts of land and property, which often involve the invocation of eminent domain, and "efficient" regulatory practices (for instance, Georgia's One-Stop Environmental Permitting that guarantees environmental screening within ninety days and Alabama's similar permit system) have been woven into the South's administrative regimes. These allocations of resources and privileges that are geared primarily to the needs of locating industry have lasting impacts, often irreparable, on local economic development and physical topography.[55] The conveniences accorded to newcomers also draw the institutional boundaries within which benefits of the South's "progressive" life get disseminated to local citizenry. The solicited entries of outside industry thus may, rather than effecting progressive change in southern institutions, simply reconfigure the status quo.

This contradiction in the South's industrial recruitment is magnified when one examines the privileges tucked into big-ticket incentive packages. Tennessee, now one of the hubs of Japanese investment in the South along with Georgia, won the Nissan plant in Smyrna on the basis of inducements estimated at $33 million. One of the "public" services earmarked for private corporations, employee training, entailed the outlay of $7.4 million in state funds and $2.5 million diverted from the federally funded Comprehensive Employment Training program. The state and Rutherford County pledged funds (an estimated sixty to eighty thousand dollars annually) exclusively for Nissan's employees and their families. They agreed to provide tutors for advanced math instruction (a subject in which the company feared American public education was deficient), Saturday school for the youth (classroom instruction in Japanese to keep the Nissan children abreast of their peers in the homeland), and English-language classes for adults.

The Kentucky-Toyota deal also came with a pledge of special disbursements not intrinsic to automobile production to benefit employers and family members. The state made a twenty-year commitment to provide a Saturday school program for the children of Toyota employees and to pay for English-language classes for the Toyota adult contingent for ten years. According to one estimate, $5.2 million was needed to effect these alterations to the local educational system. In an asymmetrical bargaining setting, Japanese industrialists were not required to disclose information regarding their site selection criteria and procedures. Shielded behind the protective barrier built in the name of "private" corporate decisions, the Japanese giants were free to pit one state government against another. This advantage enabled them to broaden the parameters of concessions beyond the generics in the South's recruitment toolbox and made the hosting locales share the cost of their "Japanese" corporate paternalism. These additional inducements showed just how eager these state governments were to accommodate the large-scale investors, so much so that they became complicit in the creation of a separate category of people whose right to education was more equal than that of others.[56]

The Japan-Dixie bonding has numerous other faces as well. The continual influx and enduring presence of foreign businesses in the South have irrevocably altered the fabric of local life, at least in urban and suburban counties where they tend to locate.[57] Unlike absentee outside capital of the past, many foreigners transplanted into the South today create vibrant sojourners' communities not entirely dissimilar in function to foreign settlements in nineteenth-century treaty ports. Such enclaves of outside influences within southern society are characterized by the relatively high turnover of constituent members and porous boundaries shared with the host society. For example, in present-day Georgia, six thousand Japanese nationals are on some type of residency (nontourist) visa. The thriving expatriate community resulting from Japan's growing economic presence has produced a wide spectrum of civic organizations. Such institutions are notable for being supported, financially and otherwise, by the locals, who are far more accepting of nonsouthern ways of life than were their Jim Crow forebears.

The Japan-America Society of Georgia, cosponsored by homegrown businesses, including global and marketing-conscious Coca-Cola, has close to fifteen hundred dues-paying members. Since its inception in 1980 under the leadership of businessmen like Robert Broadwater, a former Japanese POW who helped introduce Coca-Cola to postwar Japan, the group has provided a variety of venues for cultural exchange. The first was the Tomadachi (Friend) Club of Georgia, which brings together Japanese corporate spouses and members of local women's clubs.[58] The Japan Chamber of Commerce of Georgia, with nearly two hundred corporations on its membership roster,[59] is one of several outposts of Japanese business through which Japanese industrial practices and managerial ideas have been introduced locally. These groups diversify local civic life and contribute to the multiplicity of nonformal organizations that aggregate and articulate social interests.[60] This increasing social plurality provides the impetus toward the kind of desirable, albeit gradual, political evolution that political scientist Jeane Kirkpatrick identified in Iran under the Shah and Anastasio Somoza's Nicaragua. In her agenda-setting 1979 article in *Commentary*, the critic of the Carter administration's foreign policy lamented that liberals' moralistic and reflexive rejection of these authoritarian rulers killed the chance for nurturing in these countries social and political change ever more congruent with "American" democratic values. Kirkpatrick need not have looked that far afield in search of a successful laboratory for her model of social change; she would have found it within America's own borders, in the Sun Belt South.[61]

Kirkpatrick's prescription was also put to more successful test by Asians. Aspiring to be more "American," Japanese business and government agencies began to channel significant amounts of resources into building bridges with the host society in the mid-1970s. This self-conscious practicing of corporate citizenship bears the mark of Japanese business's collective self-reflection at the time. In the wake of Southeast Asia's anti-Japan backlash, Japanese big business came to espouse global corporate citizenship as a key to lessening the disruptive impact of its overseas presence. Under this conceptual umbrella, a number of Japanese corporations have stepped into the unfamiliar terrain of social responsibility to foreign citizenry. Many of them initially sought a model in the philanthropic activities undertaken by American multinational corporations operating in Japan. Mobil Oil's support of the neglected Japanese arts and Pepsi-Cola's sponsorship of Japan's perennially underfunded youth sports, for instance, were frequently cited as successful cases of global corporate citizenship and inspired similar Japanese programs designed to project a benevolent image overseas.

Sony's charismatic founder Morita Akio, who had imbibed the notion of corporate citizenship during his tenure in New York in the 1960s, played a central role in coordinating Japanese private-sector activities in the United States. In 1989, Morita became the inaugural chairman of the Council for Better Corporate Citizenship (CBCC) and lobbied successfully for government designation as a "public-benefit organization." As such the council became the mechanism through which Japanese business enterprises could receive exemption from domestic corporate taxes for their CBCC-approved philanthropic programs administered overseas. In their metamorphosis into entities with global reach, Japanese multinationals reproduced the ideology and practices of American big business by staking out a social space where the state, the market, or private charity intersected, thus reinforcing global capital's capacity to reconfigure itself adaptively.[62]

Many of today's business-born Japanese communities in the South are constituted primarily by families, a pattern that holds a special potential to transform the cultures of host society and expatriates alike.[63] In the mid-1970s, just as Japanese investment in the South began to grow significantly, many Japanese corporations reversed their earlier policy and allowed (or required) employees to take their families to overseas posts. The sources of this shift were many. The lifting of the Foreign Ministry's residual restrictions on foreign exchange was one. Embarrassment over the behaviors of the quasi-bachelor communities of Japanese businessmen overseas, especially in the developing world in the 1960s and early 1970s, was another. Perhaps most important was the perceived need to project a family-friendly image. To conform to mainstream American expectations, Japanese businesses in the United States came to see the presence of women and children in their charitable activities as indispensable. They began to urge, and in some cases require, the wives of their Japanese employees to participate in company-sponsored social events and local programs—a practice extremely rare in the gender-segregated world of homeland business.[64] Japanese corporate spouses in the United States, whose visa status precludes paid employment, are expected to donate their time to community outreach and charities, particularly church-sponsored ones in the case of business operations in the Bible Belt, as part of their spousal duties. They are also strongly urged to involve themselves actively in volunteer youth groups such as the Boy/Girl Scouts to help project a good-citizen image through their parenting. Although some companies offer material incentives for such work, the appropriation of women's unpaid labor has become essential to the construction of Japanese multinationals' "American" corporate identity.[65]

Family-based migration also means the presence of a growing number of Japanese school-age children in Dixie. Since 1975, four Japanese schools have been launched in Georgia for the dependents of businessmen. These arms of the expatriate community have led to new seasonal rituals (the Atlanta-based JapanFest and Macon's Cherry Blossom Festival, for instance) and tourist attractions (such as festivities in Stone Mountain Park) that give local residents easier exposure to things foreign.[66] Metro Atlanta is now speckled with more than forty Japanese restaurants and at least five specialty grocery stores to satisfy the consumerist wants of the relatively affluent sojourners. These spin-off commercial establishments contribute to the diversification of culinary culture, in which, a few decades ago, sushi was probably as unfamiliar to the local palate as bagels and lox. Two Japanese TV news programs (the semipublic NHK and the 100 percent commercial Fuji network) are broadcast daily, delivering images and information suggesting life's alternative possibilities to local audiences. Georgia Public Television has continued, despite cuts in state funding, its broadcast of a Japanese language program (Irasshai—"Welcome") targeting high school students. Combined, these institutions flowing out of the sojourner communities contribute to what historian Warren Cohen calls the "Asianization of the U.S." even in a region once known for its fierce resistance to outside influences.[67]

But just how southern society will evolve under the influences of this imported diversity will depend on the way the local power structure and its challengers incorporate these external elements into their visions for the future. Similarly, transnational agents who respond to the beckoning of southern industrial recruiters have the capacity to induce in the host both forward-looking change and regressive backsliding, or a mixture of both. This ambiguous potential can be symbolically glimpsed from a short article that appeared in the Georgia Japanese community's bimonthly newsletter recently. A profile of a local law firm specializing in labor management quotes the firm's representatives (an American and a Japanese national) as listing among their shining accomplishments the defeat of the UAW-instigated unionization elections in the Nissan Smyrna plant in 1989 and 2001.[68]

This candid profession by a binational team of urban professionals leaves one with a familiar catechism about the South's industrial development in the age of globalization. If one posits that labor activism is an inexorable outcome of the South's approximation to the North, advances of traditional industrial unions such as the UAW arguably are a measure of the distance Dixie has traveled toward becoming a more egalitarian and pluralistic society by virtue of economic development. This model of southern industrialization and social change opens up a corollary that is not entirely comforting about the South's trajectory into the twenty-first century: the South's globalization and the alliances of insiders and outsiders generated by it require constant vigilance and policing. Or does the Japan-Dixie connection celebrated in this antiunion self-evaluation provide another piece of evidence that there is nothing inherently liberalizing or democratizing about industrial development? The corollary, then, is equally somber: the Jim Crow South would have been too reactionary and repressive to entice Japanese capital, but when Japanese industrial capital readied itself to cross the Pacific, the Sun Belt South, also angling to go global, was just conservative, oligarchical, and hierarchical enough to attract it.

Notes

I wish to thank James C. Cobb, William Stueck, John Coogan, Joseph Fry, and Thomas Zeiler for their helpful comments on earlier drafts of this essay. Akiko Kano of the National Graduate Institute for Policy Studies and Maki Okabe of Tokyo University helped me gather Japanese language sources and brought some neglected materials to my attention. I was also ably assisted by my undergraduate student Melissa Krause in collecting information. Throughout this essay, Asian (Japanese, Korean, and Thai) names are given family name first followed by given name.

1. *JETRO 20 Nen no Ayumi* [JETRO's first twenty years] (Tokyo: Nippon Boeki Shinkokai, 1973), 54–55.

2. "Tokushu: Nanbu Shijo no Kaitakuni Tsuite" [Special report: Development of the southern regional market], *Kaigai Shijo* [Overseas market survey] (hereafter *KS*), March 1959. In this report, the South is defined as a region covered by nine federal customs districts (North Carolina, South Carolina, Georgia, Florida, Mobile [Alabama], New Orleans, Sabine [Texas], Galveston-Houston, Laredo [Texas]). This report was reprinted with additional statistical data as Nippon Boeki Shinkokai, *Beikoku Chiiki Shijyo to Ryutsu Kiko* [America's regional markets and distribution networks] (Tokyo: JETRO Press, 1961).

3. The Japanese government and public reacted strongly when the South Carolina and Alabama legislatures instituted laws in 1956 requiring retailers carrying Japan textile products to display a storefront sign saying "Japanese Goods Sold Here." Failure to do so constituted a misdemeanor, carrying a penalty of one hundred dollars or up to thirty days in prison. The government of Prime Minister Hatoyama Ichiro officially protested to the Eisenhower administration about these state requirements. Similar posting requirements were considered (but not enacted) by other southern state legislatures. *KS*, May 1956, 35–36, December 1956, 19–20. Interestingly, the South Carolina law remained on the books as of the 2000 legislative session as Title 39, Section 39-1-30 of the State Codes of Law. For this early Japan-Dixie encounter, see Sayuri Shimizu, *Creating People of Plenty: The United States and Japan's Economic Alternatives, 1950–60* (Kent, Ohio: Kent State University Press, 2001), 148–60.

4. The South as designated in this essay includes the eleven states of the old Confed-

eracy plus Kentucky. It corresponds (minus Oklahoma) to the area covered by the 1938 *Report on Economic Conditions of the South*. This famous report prompted President Franklin Roosevelt to declare the South to be "the nation's no. 1 economic problem." Japanese sources published since the 1980s generally include in the designation *U.S. Southeast* the six states in the Federal Reserve Board's Sixth District (Alabama, Florida, Georgia, Louisiana, Mississippi, Tennessee) plus the Carolinas. A more expansive Japanese designation of the South seems to correspond to the thirteen-state group plus southern Ohio and south central Illinois. For a useful discussion of various criteria used to define the South as a regional unit, see John Shelton Reed, *My Tears Spoiled My Aim and Other Reflections on Southern Culture* (Columbia: University of Missouri Press, 1993).

5. *SouthWind* 15, no. 11 (March 2002).

6. North Carolina Department of Economic and Community Development, news release, February 13, 1991.

7. The periodization of the Sun Belt era used in this essay comes from Bruce J. Schulman's *From Cotton Belt to Sunbelt* (Durham, N.C.: Duke University Press, 1994). Kevin P. Phillips's classic "discovery" of the Sun Belt is in *The Emerging Republican Majority* (New Rochelle, N.Y.: Arlington House, 1969).

8. For the emergence of trans-Pacific maritime shipping routes in the late nineteenth century, see David M. Pletcher, *The Diplomacy of Involvement: American Economic Expansion across the Pacific, 1784–1900*, especially part 1.

9. Nippon Yusen Kabushikigaisha, *Nippon Yusen Kabushikigaisha Hyakunenshi* [One-hundred-year history of the Nippon Mail Steamship Company] (Tokyo: Nippon Yusen Co., 1988), 459–60, 501–17; Yamashita Shin Nippon Kisen, *Shashi* [Corporate history] (Tokyo: Yamashita Shin Nippon Kisen Co., 1980), 454, 489–533.

10. *Chiiki Shijo*, 19; Two commercial shippers, Lykes Brothers Co. and Shin Nippon Kisen, opened direct Japan–Gulf Coast routes in 1958. Nippon Yusen, *Hyakunenshi*, 517–18.

11. *KS*, August 1957, 3–21; March 1959, 2–12; see also *JETRO Trade Manual* (Tokyo: Nippon Boeki Shinkokai, 1983), 15–16.

12. *Sengoni Okeru Wagakuni Kaigai Toshi no Jisseki* [Cumulative records of Japan's overseas direct investments in the postwar period] (Tokyo: Kokusai Gijutsu Kyoryoku Kyokai, 1965), 1–16.

13. Takashi Ryu, *Sekaino Umiwo Nettosuru Nippon Yusen* [Nippon Yusen in the global oceans] (Tokyo: Asahi Sonorama, 1980), 80–86, 124–36, 146–49. Yamashita Shin Nihon Kisen, *Shashi*, 533; Nippon Yusen, *Hyakunenshi*, 606–9; Taiheiyo Kisen, *Junenshi* [The ten-year history] (Tokyo: Taiheiyo Kisen Co., 1966), 55–56.

14. *Juneshi*, 110–14; Yamashita Shin Nihon Kisen, *Shashi*, 533; Nippon Yusen, *Hyakunenshi*, 606–9; Taiheiyo Kisen, *Junenshi*, 55–56; JETRO, *Chiiki Shijo*, 175–86.

15. Nomura Shoken Research Division, *Nippon no Daikigyo* [Japan's big corporations] (Tokyo: Nomura Securities Co., 1960), 94–112; Mitsui Bussan, *Chosen to Sozo: Mitsui Bussan 100-nen no Ayumi* [Challenge and resourcefulness: One-hundred-year history of Mitsui Bussan] (Tokyo: Mitsui Bussan Co., 1976), 352, 400; Sumitomo Shoji Shashi Hensan Iinkai, *Sumitomo Shoji Kabushiki Kaishashi* [The official history of Sumitomo Trading Company] (Osaka: Sumitomo Shoji Co., 1972), 714–77; Ishii Kazuo, *Nip-

pon no Boeki 55 Nen [Fifty-five years of postwar Japanese trade] (Tokyo: JETRO Press, 2000), 94–98.

16. Shishido Toshio, *Nippon Kigyo in USA* [Japanese corporations in the USA] (Tokyo: Nikko Research Center Press, 1980), 20–22.

17. Yamamoto Mitsuru, *Sengo Nippon no Keizai Gaiko* [Postwar Japan's economic diplomacy] (Tokyo: Nippon Keizai Shinbunsha, 1974), 47–65; Kobayashi Hideo, *Sengo Ajia to Nippon Kigyo* [Postwar Asia and Japanese corporations] (Tokyo: Iwanami Shoten, 2001), chaps. 2–3.

18. Japan Export-Import Bank Research Division, *Wagakuni Kaigai Toshino Genjyo* [Statistical data pertaining to permits by the Ministry of Finance] (Tokyo: Japan Export-Import Bank Printing Office, 1972), 28–62; Shishido, *Nippon Kigyo in USA,* 20–34.

19. Shishido, *Nippon Kigyo in USA,* 20.

20. Masaoka Mitsuhiro, "Taibei Shinshutsu Nippon Kigyo no Genjo to Kadai" [The current state and future challenge of Japanese enterprises in the United States] in *Japanese Americans,* ed. Togami Soken (Kyoto: Mineruva Shobo, 1986), 412–13. Early cases of successful Japanese manufacturing investment in the United States were food-processing ventures targeting niche markets. Nissin, for instance, began producing "Cup o' Noodles" in California in 1970 and gained acceptance of ramen noodles as a snack/light meal among American consumers. In 1973, Kikkoman began manufacturing naturally brewed soy sauce and related products in Wisconsin. These corporations are widely credited with increasing the market appeal of Asian food among middle-class, nonethnic Americans. See Masaoka, "Taibei Shinshutsu," 418–19; *Essentials of Nissin* (Osaka: Nisshin Shokuhin Kabushiki Kaisha, 1998), 40–41; Ronald Yates, *The Kikkoman Chronicle* (New York: McGraw Hill, 1988), chap. 6.

21. Ministry of International Trade and Industry (MITI), *Keizaikyoryoku no Genjo to Mondaiten* [Status and problems of economic cooperation] (Tokyo: Government Printing Office, 1973); JETRO, *Kaigai Shijyo Hakusho* [White paper on overseas markets], vol. 2, 1974.

22. Takura Nobuaki, ed., *Taibei Toshi no Jittai to Kankyo* [Report on investment and business climate in the United States] (Tokyo: Daiyamondosha, 1978), 204–10.

23. Shishido, *Nippon Kigyo in USA,* 11–24, 29–33. For a useful analysis of American attitudes toward energy sources, see Martin Melosi, *Coping with Abundance: Energy and Environment in Industrial America* (New York: Alfred A. Knopf, 1985).

24. "Nippon Seihin Boykotto Undo," *KS* 23, no. 257 (March 1973): 110–12. The term "Ugly Japanese" was popularized by a *Wall Street Journal* article (May 2, 1975) on Japanese corporate behavior in Southeast Asia. See also "Japan's Foreign Investment Machine," *BusinessWeek,* March 24, 1973; Hozumi Goichi, "Ajia ni Okeru Hannichi Undo" [Anti-Japanese movements in Asia], special issue, *Keidanren Geppo* (hereafter *KG*), July 1973, 28–29.

25. Kobayashi, *Sengo Ajia to Nippon Kigyo,* 75–86; Tanokura, *Taibei Toshi no Jittai to Kankyo,* 146–47; *KG,* no. 3 (1973). For the text of the guidelines in June 1972, see *GP's* special issue, July 1973.

26. Charles Oaroak, "Nippon Kigyono Beikoku Shinsutsuwo Nozomu," *KG,* no. 7 (1973): 42–25. "Shuyoukoku no Tainichi Kigyo Yuchikatsudo no Jokyo," *KG,* no. 10 (1973): 47–48.

27. Yoshida Kogyo Kabushiki Kaisha, *YKK Gojunenshi* [Fifty-year history of YKK] (Tokyo: Yoshida Kogyo, 1984) 114–23. When a company making foreign direct investment builds a new facility rather than acquiring an existing one, it is called "greenfield investment." See Geoffrey Jones, *The Evolution of International Business* (London: Routledge, 1996), 319. A broader definition of greenfield strategy refers to starting a business from scratch, in part to avoid old, unionized employees, expensive land, and entrenched political interests. A manufacturer's production system and managerial ideology have a significant impact on the location decision and the spatial arrangement between the main plant and its suppliers. This symbiotic relationship had important ramifications for the geographical patterns of southern industrial development in the Sun Belt era when foreign manufacturing investment played a key role. For this point, see Kim Choong Soon, *Japanese Industry in the American South* (London: Routledge, 1995), especially chaps. 4–5; Karsten Hulsemann, "Greenfields in the Heart of Dixie," in *The Second Wave: Southern Industrialization from the 1940s to the 1970s* (Athens: University of Georgia Press, 2001), 219–54. For an analysis of the reasons why Japanese enterprises in North America prefer greenfield investment, see Okamoto Yasuo, "Hokubei Nikkei Kigyo and Keiei Senryaku" [The business strategies of Japanese corporations in North America], in *Hokubei Nikkei Kigyo no Keiei* [Managing Japanese corporations in North America], ed. Okamoto Yasuo (Tokyo: Dobunkan, 2000), 13–39.

28. *Taibei Toshi Chosadan Hokokusho* [Report by the U.S. Investment Research Mission] (Osaka: Osaka Chamber of Commerce, 1974, 1976); *Beikoku Nantoubuni Okeru Gaikokukarano Chokusetsu Toshi* [Foreign direct investments in the U.S. Southeast], JETRO report, September 1985. For a comprehensive list of the incentive packages the southern states offered to Japanese industry, see Chogin Keiei Keinkyusho, ed., *Kaigai Shinshutsu Deta Manual: Beikokuhn* [Foreign investment data and manual: USA] (Tokyo: Sogo Kohan, 1978); Roundtable Discussion, "Nichibei Keizai Kankei no Tenbo wo Kataru," *KG*, no. 12 (1978): 26–28.

29. I use political scientist David Lowery's definition of industrial policy: "the total set of governmental actions that influence private economic development, including both a wide array of micrcoeconomic policies and strategies of macroeconomic intervention." David Lowery, "The National Level Roots of the Failure of State Industrial Policy," in *The Politics of Industrial Recruitment*, ed. Ernest J. Yanarella and William C. Green (Westport, Conn.: Greenwood Press, 1990), 191.

30. For the history of southern industrial recruitment, especially its red-carpet treatment of foreign business in the Sun Belt era, see James C. Cobb, *The Selling of the South: The Southern Crusade for Industrial Development, 1936–90* (Lexington: University of Kentucky Press, 1983), 169–77; Kawaide Ryo, *Sunberuto* [The Sun Belt] (Tokyo: Nippon Keizai Shinbunsha, 1974), 5–43; Kim, *Japanese Industry*, 38. For the South's de facto industrial policies and their downsides, see Thomas A. Lyson, *Two Sides to the Sunbelt* (New York: Praeger, 1989), 1–24.

31. Dewey W. Gratham, *The South in Modern America: A Region at Odds* (New York: HarperPerennial, 1995), 210; Gratham, *The Life and Death of the Solid South: A Social History* (Lexington: University of Kentucky Press, 1988), 181–84; Larry Sabato, "New South Governors and the Governorship," in *Contemporary Southern Politics*, ed. James F. Lea

(Baton Rouge: Louisiana State University Press, 1988), 83–106; Gordon E. Harvey, *A Question of Justice: New South Governors and Education, 1968–76* (Tuscaloosa: University of Alabama Press, 2002), 1–14.

32. Ushijima Hiromi (director of the State of Tennessee Development Office in Tokyo), letter to author, August 15, 2002. For a "view from within" of South Carolina's reverse investment recruitment, see Marko Maunula, "From Mill Town to Euroville: Economic Change and the Arrival of Foreign Corporations in Spartanburg, South Carolina," *Business and Economic History* 28, no. 2 (1999): 145–52.

33. Gojunenshi Hensanshitsu, *YKK 50 Nenshi* (Tokyo: Yoshia Kogyo, 1984), 123. The collaboration in this business start-up in Macon led to Carter's close personal friendship with YKK president Tadao Yoshida. Yoshida was invited to Carter's presidential swearing-in ceremony in 1977 as a special guest. The presence of a Japanese zipper company president at the presidential inaugural attracted considerable media attention in Japan at the time.

34. Lamar Alexander, *Friends: Japanese and Tennesseeans* (New York: Kodansha International, 1986), 14–16.

35. U.S. Department of Commerce, Bureau of International Commerce, *Kokusai Shokusetsu Toshi: Zentaiteki na Keiko to Beikoku no Yakuwari* [Foreign direct investment], 1984; South Carolina Department of Industry, *Beikoku Shubetsu Toshi Gaido Bukku: South Carolina* [U.S. state-by-state investment guidebook] (Tokyo: JETRO, 1988), 15, 32–34; Miyauchi Takeo, "Toyota Beikoku Shinshutsu wo Enshutsushita Otoko" [The man who masterminded Toyota's location to the United States], *Bungeishunju*, December 1986, 148–64; *Think Kentucky* 3, flyer produced by the Kentucky State Development Office in Tokyo, October 1999.

36. John Nathan, *SONY: The Private Life* (Boston: Houghton Mifflin, 1999), 102–3. Sony's charismatic founder Akio Morita helped Alabama governor Fob James establish a state development office in Tokyo in 1980. Makiko Nakajima (State of Alabama Japan Office), letter to author, July 24, 2002.

37. Shishido, *Nippon Kigyo*, 73–79; MITI, Tanokura Takeshi, *Taibei Toshino Jittai to Kankyo* (Tokyo: Daiamondosha, 1978), 77–83; *Nippon Keizai Shinbun*, August 4, 1979; Masushita Denki Sangyo, *Gekido no Junen* [A turbulent decade] (Osaka: Matsushita Denki Shashishitsu, 1978), 491, 555–58; Sanyo Denki Kabushikigaisha, *Sanyo Denki Sanjunenno Ayumi* [Sanyo's thirty-year history] (Osaka: Sanyo Denki Co, 1980), 478–81. Under the 1977 OMA, Japan limited the number of exports of finished color television sets to 1.56 million units per annum. Unassembled color televisions were restricted to nineteen thousand units. Mori Yasuhiro, "Kara Terebi Mondai" [The color TV problem], *Kogin Chosa* 207, no. 2 (1981): 67–84.

38. The relocation of production sites by Japanese automobile manufacturers in the South from the late 1970s on should be viewed as part of the "southern drift" of the international auto industry. Hulsemann, "Greenfields," 231–34.

39. For example, see remarks by Katsuji Kawamata (Nissan chairman) at roundtable discussions sponsored by *Keidanren* (Japan Federation of Economic Organizations); "Nichibei Keizai Kankei no Tenbo wo Kataru," *KG*, no. 12 (1978): 20–21; "Aratana Nichibeikakei no Kochikuni Mukete," *KG*, no. 9 (1984): 9–10. See also, Suzuki Naotsugu,

Amerika Shakai no Nakano Nikkei Kigyo: Jidosha Sangyo no Genchi Keiei [Japanese corporations in American society: The automobile industry's overseas operations] (Tokyo: Toyo Keizai Shinposha, 1991), especially chaps. 1 and 2.

40. David Gelsanliter, *Jump Start: Japan Comes to the Heartland* (New York: Farrar, Straus and Giroux, 1990), 20–21. For a comprehensive study of Honda's North American operations, see Inabetsu Masaharu, ed., *Honda no Beikoku Genchi Keiei: HAM no Sogoteki Kenkyu* [Honda's local management in North America] (Tokyo: Bunshindo, 1998).

41. For a useful survey of the U.S.-Japan automobile trade disputes up to 1981, see *Kogin Chosa* 208, no. 3 (1981). Nishiyara Haruhiko, "80-nendai no Wagakuni Sangyono Kadai-Jidosha Sangyo," *KG*, no. 5 (1980): 66–71; Nissan Jidosha Kabushikigaisha, *Nissan Jidoshashi* [Corporate history of Nissan Motors] (Tokyo: Nissan Jidosha Shashi Iinkai, 1985), 187–200; Toyota Jidosha Kabushikigaisha, *Sozo Kagirinaku: Toyota Jidosha 50-Nenshi* [Unlimited creativity: Fifty-year history of Toyota Motors] (Toyota: Toyota Jidosha, 1987), 1:693–702, 711–18, 795–805.

42. William Fox, "Japanese Investment in Tennessee: The Economic Effects of Nissan's Location in Smyrna," in *The Politics of Industrial Recruitment*, 176–87.

43. H. Brinton Milward and Heidi Hosbach Newman, "State Incentive Packages and the Industrial Location Decision," in *The Politics of Industrial Recruitment*, 23–51. A useful list of incentives offered in the six major automotive site decisions in the 1980s is on pp. 34–35.

44. Dorinne Kondo, *Crafting Selves* (Chicago: University of Chicago Press, 1990), chap. 2; Fox, "Japanese Investment in Tennessee," 183–85; Kobayashi, *Sengo Ajiato Nippon Kigyo*, 94–97; "Nissan Expanding Smyrna Operations," *Nashville Banner*, April 7, 1988; "Nissan Supply Firms Move to Midstate," *Nashville Tennessean*, September 22, 1987; Kim, *Japanese Industry*, 44–49; Hulsemann, "Greenfields," 233–34; Gelsanlitter, *Jump Start*, 213–23; Toyota Jidosha, *Sozo Kagirinaku*, 804–5; *Ward's Auto World* 35, no. 5 (May 1999); Ide Takamichi, "Jidosha no Beikoku Genchiseisan to Chusho Jidosha Gyokai," *Kikan Keizai Kenkyu* 11, no. 2 (September 1988): 85–97.

45. "Beikoku Nantobu: Sekai Yusu no Jidosha Kairotaru Yuen," *Nikkei Bizinesu*, September 3, 2001; *Nippon Keizai Shimbun*, June 4, 2002. Lists of Japanese businesses and their affiliates in Kentucky and Alabama clearly point to the secondary migration of small manufacturers involved in automobile production following the moguls in the 1980s and 1990s. "Kentakkishu Shinshutsu Nipponkigyo Risuto," record of the Kentucky Far East Representative Office; "Japanese-Based Manufacturing Investments in Alabama," a list distributed by the Alabama Development Office in Tokyo; John Paul Mac-Duffie and Susan Helper, "Creating Lean Suppliers: Diffusing Lean Production through the Supply Chain," in *Remade in America: Transplanting and Transforming Japanese Management Systems*, ed. Jeffrey K. Liker, W. Mark Fruin, and Paul S. Adler (New York: Oxford University Press, 1999), 154–200; Okubo Yoshito, "Kansei Dankai wo Mukaeta Nipponsha no Hokubei Genchi Seisan Taisai" [Final stages of local production of Japanese automobiles in North America], *Sekai Shuho*, 77, no. 47 (December 1996).

46. Blockbuster Deal of the Week, November 13, 2000, http://conway.com/ssinsider/bbdeal/bd 001113.htm; *Clarion-Ledger*, August 3, 2001; *Automotive News*, June 21, 2002.

Site Selection 45, no. 1 (January 2000); 44, no. 5 (September 1999); *Automotive News*, May 10, 1999; *Montgomery Advertiser*, April 5, 2002; Chang Se-moon, "Incentive Packages for Hyundai's Plant in Alabama," *Korea Times*, April 2, 2002.

47. David Lowery, "The National Level Roots of the Failure of State Industrial Policy," in *The Politics of Industrial Recruitment*, 197–201.

48. These boards include the governor, a state senator, a state representative, and two private citizens appointed by the governor. Cobb, *Selling of the South*, 201.

49. Lowery, "The National Level Roots."

50. *Toshi no Chishiki* [An investment guide], Southeast-Japan America Society of Georgia, 1988. *History of the SEUS/JAPAN and the Japan-USSE Association*, 1985, a pamphlet in author's possession. See also the *SEUA/JAPAN Steering Committee Report* (B-3123 XI-U ER-99/2000) in the JETRO Resource Library, Tokyo.

51. Sumitomo Kagaku Kogyo Kabushiki Kaisha, *Shashi* (Oosaka: Sumitomo Kagaku, 1981), 703–4.

52. Norishige Hasegawa, "Yakushin suru Beikoku Nantoubu," *KG*, no. 3 (1979): 41–45, "Amerika wo Homonshite," *KG*, no. 5 (1975): 40, "Dou Taiousuru Nichibei Keizai Masatsu," *KG*, no. 4 (1982): 5–6; "Tooshi no Chishiki; Roundtable Discussion," "Wagakuni Keizeino Kadaito Taiosaku," *KG*, no. 1 (1982), 14–15.

53. Translation is the author's based on the Japanese-language text of a pamphlet titled *Georgia Power*, 2000 edition.

54. For a discussion of Japanese manufacturers' recruitment practices and their implications for the race issue in American southern states, see Robert E. Cole and Donald R. Deskins Jr., "Racial Factors in Site Location and Employment Patterns of Japanese Auto Firms in America," *California Management Review*, Fall 1988, 1–31; Koushiro Kazutoshi, "Kaigai Genchi Seisan to Roshi Kankei" [Overseas production and labor-management relations], *Economia* 100 (March 1989): 83–86.

55. For environmental impacts of the Japanese manufacturing presence in Kentucky since the 1980s, see Miranda Schreurs, "Japanese Corporate Environmental Practices in Kentucky" and Gary A. O'Dell, "Assessing Environmental Performance of Japanese Industrial Facilities in Kentucky," in *Japan in the Bluegrass*, ed. P. P. Karan (Lexington: University Press of Kentucky, 2001).

56. Milward and Newman, "State Incentive Packages and the Industrial Location Decision," 45–46; Miyauchi Takeo, "The Man Who Lured Toyota to Kentucky," *Economic Eye*, March 1987, 23–27. In endorsing incentive packages, many state legislatures required that a fixed amount of funds for the incentive package be spent on setting up automobile-related technical training courses at local community colleges. For example, in the case of Kentucky, the initial legislative resolution mandated a minimum $10 million for new community college courses. Senate Joint Resolution No. 7, General Assembly, Commonwealth of Kentucky, Regular Session (January 24, 1986). For an impact of Japanese auto production on offerings at community colleges in the United States, see Muto Rokuzaburo and Sato Kazuo, "Beikokuni Okeru Jidosha Kogyo Kyoiku no Genjo" [Current situation in automobile technical training in the United States], *Chunippon Jidosha Tanki Daigaku Ronso* 10 (1980): 25–33; Sakuraya Okimichi and Nakajima Yasunori, "Amerika no Komyuniti Karejji niokeru Jidoshagijutsu Kyoiku no Hokoku" [A report

on automobile vocational training in U.S. community colleges], *Chunippon Jidosha Tanki Daigaku Ronso* 14 (1984): 155–66. These Japanese automakers and other major manufacturers take care to recruit the vast majority of their workforce from the local population. For instance, the percentage of local recruitment was 95 percent for Toyota during its first ten years of operation in Kentucky. A breakdown of white-blue collar jobs, however, reveals a distinct pattern where Japanese "imports" are preferred. See for example, Besser, *Toyotano Beikoku Kojo Keiei*, 55–57. For a report on Japanese corporations providing different "retention" incentives to blue-collar and white-collar employees in the United States, see Shinji Hideo, "Genchikoyo Maneja no Ikusei Toyo" [Training and promotion of locally hired managers], *Sekai no Rodo* 40, no. 9, 32–41.

57. Lyson, *Two Sides to the Sunbelt*, passim.

58. John R. McIntyre and Robert H. Hart, "Georgia," in *The Survey Reports on Japan-Related Regional Activities in the U.S.*, The Japan Foundation Center for Global Partnership (Tokyo: Japan Foundation, 1993), 1:212–15.

59. Japanese expatriate communities in the South by no means constitute an undifferentiated collectivity. Georgia's Japanese community is the largest and most pluralistic, with no single corporation shaping its tenor. The existence of governmental (Consular General Office) and quasi-governmental (JETRO) offices in Atlanta also contributes to the Georgia Japanese community's greater functional diversity and capacity for civic engagement.

60. Yukio Yotsumoto, "Social Impacts of Japanese Businesses in Small Communities of Kentucky," in *Japan in the Bluegrass*, 167–200.

61. *Atlanta no Nipponjin Shakai* [The japanese community in Atlanta], booklet distributed by the Tokyo Office of the Georgia State Office of Development, Trade, and Tourism, n.d.; Fumie Kumagai, *Nipponteki Seisan Shisutemu In USA* (Tokyo: JETRO Press, 1985); Jeane Kirkpatrick, "Dictatorships and Double Standards," *Commentary* 68, no. 5 (1979): 34–45.

62. "Ima Kigyo wa Nanio Nasubekika," *KS* 24, no. 268 (February 1974): 24–52; Sakurai Kiyohiko, "Wagakuni Kaigai Shinshutsu Kigyo no Kadai," *KG*, no. 5 (1975): 58–59; "Shimin no Genchi Yuwarei," *KS* 25, no. 280 (February 1975): 39–41; Kobayashi Naoya, "Matsushita Denki no Kokusaika Kyoiku Puroguramu," *Gendai no Esupuri* 299, 160–71. Shikata Hiroshi, *Amerika Firansoropii Kikou: Nikkei Kigyou no shakai Kouken Katsudou* (Tokyo: TBS Britanica, 1992); Akira Oshikawa, *Toyota Nissan Honda no Ikinokoriwokaketa Sekaisenryaku* [Toyota, Nissan, Honda's global survival strategies] (Tokyo: Sanno Daigaku Shuppankai, 1992), 13–14, 143–44, 205–6; Council for Better Corporate Citizenship, *Report, 2002: Corporate Citizenship in Action*, n.d., a manual compiled by Sadami Wada of Sony Corporation of America. The author thanks Maya Shimamoto, Reiko Wada, and Miwa Kojima for making various corporate citizenship manuals and pamphlets available.

63. In 1987, a group of Japanese businessmen who had returned to Japan from assignments in Georgia formed a fraternal group called the Georgia Kai. Its quarterly newsletter, *Georgia on My Mind*, offers a fascinating glimpse into how the experience of living in the South transformed the lives and worldviews of these Japanese white-collar workers.

64. Anne Allison, *Nightwork: Sexuality, Pleasure, and Corporate Masculinity in a Tokyo Hostess Club* (Chicago: University of Chicago Press, 1994), chap. 5.

65. Sawa Kurotani Becker, "Transnational Home-Making and the Construction of Gender and Cultural Identities among Expatriate Japanese Wives in the United States," (Ph.D. diss., Department of Anthropology, University of Colorado at Boulder, 1999), 102–3; Oshikawa, *Toyota Nissan Honda,* 13–14, 143–44, 205–6; Terry L. Vesser, *Toyotano Beikoku Kojo Keiei* [Toyota's management of North American plants], trans. Suzuki Yoshiji (Sapporo: Hokkaido Daigaku Tosho Kankokai, 1999), 271–81.

66. In a similar vein, Marko Maunula has reported the infusion of Western Europe's cultural influences in South Carolina. Maunula, "From Mill Town to Euroville," 151.

67. Warren Cohen, *The Asian American Century* (Cambridge: Harvard University Press, 2002), chap. 3. There is one "public" school in Atlanta supported by the Japanese government, another in Columbus funded mostly by the local chamber of commerce and the development office, and two private schools run by Japanese corporations in DeKalb and Sumter counties.

68. *SouthWind* 15, no. 11 (March 2002). For Japanese major manufacturing companies' contorted attitude towards American industrial unions, see Kawakita Takashi, "Amerika ni Okeru Genchi Romu Kanri no Jitsujo to Shorai Tenbo" [Current conditions and future prospects for labor-management relations in the United States], *Rosei Jiho* 2840 (July 1987): 38–43; JETRO Atlanta Center, *Beikoku Nantobu niokeru Nikkei Seizogyo no Romu Mondai* [Labor management problems for Japanese manufacturers in the U.S. Southeast] (Atlanta: JETRO, 1991).

Another Southern Paradox: The Arrival of Foreign Corporations— Change and Continuity in Spartanburg, South Carolina

Marko Maunula

For the past three decades, Spartanburg has been the mantelpiece of South Carolina's economic progress. Both academic and journalistic observers have periodically descended upon this once-placid old community of forty-three thousand in the South Carolina Piedmont to document the impressive success story of a mill town that refused to wither away with the decline of its textile industries. Public commentators, consisting mostly of those with favorable attitudes toward globalization and deregulation, have celebrated Spartanburg as a prime example of a locality that embraced the challenge of open markets and globalization, turning these often ominous forces to its advantage.

In the 1960s, when most American businesses and community leaders understood the global economy as merely a matter of exports and imports, Spartanburg's forward-looking boosters geared their recruitment efforts toward attracting foreign investors and corporations to their town. Rather than focusing on moving goods, these boosters were interested in transferring capital, production, and technology across borders. Spartanburg's leaders took an open-minded and aggressive outlook on economic globalization, endearing themselves to some of the most noteworthy economic gurus of the day.

No less an authority than Milton Friedman came to Spartanburg in 1980 to use the community as one of the case studies in his TV series *Free to Choose*, a ten-episode celebration of free enterprise and laissez-faire economics. According to Friedman, by implementing right-to-work laws and cutting corporate taxes to the bare minimum, the leaders of Spartanburg successfully had sold their town to outsiders as a solid business investment. "By any standards, let alone Spartanburg's, the results were revolutionary," Friedman commented. "Industrialists came from Germany, Switzerland and all over the world to build factories, to set up plants." As far as economic attitudes are concerned, Friedman expressed his hope that the entire United States would become Spartanburg writ large.[1]

A decade and a half later, Rosabeth Moss Kanter, a distinguished professor of business administration at the Harvard Business School, also admired Spartanburg's business culture in her book *World Class: Thriving Locally in the Global Economy*. Although she shared Friedman's enthusiasm about Spartanburg's optimistic business culture, her account of the town's transformation paid more attention to the role of the visible hand in the community's transformation. While Friedman celebrated the town's free-market ethos, Kanter credited Spartanburg's good work ethic, farsighted leadership, and excellent technical training program for the town's success.[2]

Both Friedman's and Kanter's fundamental premises were correct. For the last few decades, the town's economy has benefited from the increasingly unobstructed flow of capital among nations. Perhaps even more, it has benefited from local- and state-level boosters' efforts to attract industries to the region, including South Carolina's technical training program and Spartanburg's highly effective machinery for industrial recruitment, refined by decades of experience in recruiting northern corporations.[3] Indeed, the town's economic progress has been remarkable, making it in many aspects a true southern success story. By recruiting foreign companies and taking a decidedly global perspective on economic development, Spartanburg secured its economic survival during a time when most other southern textile towns were facing increasingly intense competition from abroad. As far as employment and new business activity are concerned, Spartanburg has not only survived, it has thrived.

While Spartanburg's economic progress and transformation have been obvious to most casual observers, the town's leadership has managed to control the process, preserving intact the fundamental character and power structures of the community. Globalization and the ensuing economic transformation in Spartanburg have been directed from the top. The decision to recruit foreign corporations was born within the town's existing leadership, and, by and large, incoming foreign companies and individuals have been incorporated into Spartanburg's old social and economic power structure. Spartanburg's revolution has been economic, not social or political. In the classic southern tradition, this one, too, has been a "revolution from above."

In many ways, Spartanburg is almost a caricature of a southern Piedmont textile town. In its commercial fervor, openness to outside investors, and orderly industriousness, Spartanburg epitomizes the factors and culture behind the Piedmont's largely successful transition from the Old to the New South and beyond. In Spartanburg, southern cultural conservatism has merged with doses of outside talent and money, creating a community that has kept itself open to business but successfully maintained the social and political status quo.

The character of Spartanburg is rooted in its inhabitants. Promoted initially both by scholars of progressive persuasion and chamber of commerce types, the public image of the area's residents for decades has consisted of assertive portrayals of industrious, independent, and individualistic men and women accustomed to life and labor in paternal mills and mill villages. Local bosses have worked to transform the potentially dangerous individualism of the Piedmont's working class into dislike of the unions. Additionally, evangelical churches that dominated the mill village social life lent their emotionalism to the antiunion cause. Although the mill villages are long gone and paternalism has either reformed itself or even disappeared, the stereotype of the Piedmont's working class has been durable and persistent, substantially modernized but with its fundamental character intact.[4]

On the other side of the proverbial desk sits another Spartanburg icon: the urban, professionally educated middle-class booster, with often intertwined views of personal success and community welfare. Spartanburg's post–Civil War emergence as an industrial town was largely controlled and directed by middle-class professionals, who sat firmly in charge of local commerce, credit, and investment capital. As Spartanburg grew and matured as a textile town during the decades after the Civil War, it willed its way to prosperity under the commercial and communal fervor of the town's professional classes.[5]

As the New South was ready to take off in the South Carolina Piedmont, the movement was hindered by the region's severely underdeveloped markets for capital. The solution was to rely extensively on small, local investors. Spartanburg's boosters, like their colleagues around the South Carolina Piedmont, worked hard to pool meager local capital to back up investments in mills and railroads.[6] The extensive roles of local, small scale investors offered additional benefits by creating and enforcing a widely shared, communal vision of Spartanburg's prosperity among the town's middle class. The roots of Spartanburg's contemporary conservatism lie in a persistent sense of community and a nearly obsessive desire for order and control among its middle classes, and they reach deep into multiple layers of the town's economic history.

The result has been a largely successful and productive union of labor and capital, Protestant ethic and bourgeois individualism. Spartanburg has clearly evolved from its emergence as a textile town in the postbellum decades, but its fundamental character has remained surprisingly constant. Through the challenges and pressures of two world wars, economic crises, and the civil rights movement and other social transitions, Spartanburg has nevertheless remained a cohesive and controlled community, where challenges are muted and social structures enforced by careful and partial amalgamation of new elements into the decision making. By reputation, Spartanburg does not believe in violence or conflict. Instead, the town's leadership has learned to face labor challenges, African American discontent, and other challenges to the preestablished order with conciliatory negotiation and even preventive measures intended to ensure conflict-free community and workplaces.

Contemporary Spartanburg began to take shape during the first two decades after World War II. The town's economy in the early 1960s was on the move, and both the population and industrial base of the town had been growing consistently since the 1940s. In the twenty years leading to 1960, Spartanburg's population jumped from 32,249 to 44,352.[7] The surrounding county was growing equally rapidly, with the population shooting from 127,733 in 1940 to 156,830 in 1960. The improved mobility of the region's car-owning working class was increasingly turning parts of the surrounding Spartanburg County into the town's extension.[8]

Improvements in Spartanburg's urban character, services, and economic opportunities accompanied this growth. New and more sophisticated fields of industrial production, such as machinery manufacturing, grew to complement the county's old textile industries. The number of Spartanburg's professional and technical workers—including the town's engineers, doctors, teachers, and the like—more than doubled from 1,676 to 4,478 during the 1950s. Between 1947 and 1958, the total number of business establishments grew from 124 to 177, with a combined annual payroll jumping from $50,422,000 to $77,749,000.[9]

Spartanburg's economic boom was but a subplot in the master narrative of the U.S. postwar prosperity. While the entire nation's per capita income skyrocketed during the 1950s, the South's and South Carolina's growth rates surpassed even the rest of the nation, especially in services.[10] South Carolina's rapid progress in fields such as finance, insurance, and real estate offered solid, quantifiable evidence of a maturing economy that was responding positively to the postwar challenges. While the nation's finance, insurance, and real estate markets expanded approximately 36 percent during the 1950s, in the Palmetto State the growth rate climbed over 133 percent. In construction, retail, and manufacturing, South Carolina nearly doubled the national growth rates.[11]

This growth and prosperity did not come with the promise of security, and, in fact, Spartanburg's progress was tainted with a foreboding sense of uncertainty. While textiles, the entire South Carolina Piedmont's economic foundation and the reason for Spartanburg's success, were faring reasonably well, the culture associated with it was rapidly transforming. Mill villages were disappearing, as mill owners, hoping to liquidate capital and reduce their operational responsibilities, were selling the company-owned houses to their workers.[12] In the mills themselves, the "wringing out" process was underway, as factories with antiquated machinery were either closing down or replacing their workers with new, more sophisticated, and increasingly automated machines.[13]

Throughout the Piedmont's history, a desire for security had tempered its commercial impulses. Starting with its antebellum "safety-first farmers," locals had tried to pursue growth without losing their traditional republican independence, to participate in a speculative economy without submitting their fortunes completely to its whims.[14] While thoroughly capitalistic, the commercial *mentalité* of the region had also appreciated stability. Spartanburg had held on to cotton and, later, to textiles with a dogged determination, seeking security and solace in the cultural and commercial predictability they had offered for so many decades. Now, whatever promises of prosperity the postwar era had brought, its unpredictability made it an occasionally portentous force.

The worst hit against the status quo came from abroad. In July 1955, using economic carrots to help keep Japan in the western Cold War camp, American trade negotiators had allowed the Japanese to export their cotton textiles to the United States.[15] Despite their relatively modest quantities, these imports were enough to push South Carolina into a near hysteria against unfair foreign competition. By early the next year, the South Carolina legislature had pushed through, without a debate, the Hart-Arthur Act, which required all establishments selling foreign textiles in the state to hang up a sign stating "Foreign Textiles Sold Here."[16]

During the same legislative session, the legislature's Fiscal Survey Commission delivered its report on economic conditions before the House of Representatives. After celebrating the impressive economic advances of the past decades and demonstrating how the last twenty-five years had formed possibly the most prosperous quarter century in the state's entire history, the committee nevertheless concluded its report with a gloomy assessment: "[U]ntil there is some effective handling of the textile import situation, the future of the textile industry will remain under a cloud of uncertainty as will the future economy of South Carolina."[17]

A few years later, the new global economy began to show its more alluring side to South Carolina, and especially to Spartanburg. The origins of Spartanburg's large-scale economic globalization date back to 1961. Roger Milliken, the town's New York–born textile magnate, was looking for new machinery for his rapidly growing Spartanburg operations, and his search focused on Swiss and German machinery producers. Because Europeans had started the double-knit production technique years before their American competitors, the quality of European machinery surpassed anything produced on this side of the Atlantic. Milliken purchased his equipment from the Rieter Company and Sulzer Brothers of Winterthur, Switzerland.[18]

During the purchase negotiations, Milliken convinced his suppliers that the interests of both parties would be served if the Swiss would open sales and service centers in Spartanburg. Milliken was a large customer, and his ideas received a careful hearing from the management of both companies. Spartanburg's location in the heart of the American textile industry provided the Swiss manufacturers with another incentive, and in 1961, Rieter moved its American operations from New Jersey to Spartanburg. The same year, Sulzer Brothers moved in directly from Switzerland.[19] In 1965, yet another textile machinery corporation, Karl Mentzel Maschinenfabrik, opened a machinery plant in Spartanburg, becoming the first German company to start manufacturing in the town.[20]

The arrival of Rieter and Sulzer caught the attention of the Spartanburg Chamber of Commerce and its executive vice president, Dick Tukey, another transplanted New Yorker. Faced with steadily growing foreign competition in textiles, Tukey and other boosters began to view international recruitment as a potential method to bring industrial diversification to the community. Since the arrival of cheap Japanese textile imports, Spartanburg, as well as the entire state of South Carolina, had grown increasingly aware of the dangers its narrow industrial base posed for the community's economic future. The time appeared right and the risks worth taking for Tukey to recruit foreign investors.

When Hoechst, the German chemical giant, was scouting locations in 1965 for a polyester fiber factory the company had decided to build in America, Tukey launched a four-week campaign to convince Hoechst to come to Spartanburg.[21] When meeting with the Hoechst representatives, Tukey showed the Germans how cheaply they could acquire all the necessary land, water, energy, and cheap labor in the South Carolina Piedmont. In addition to touting the town's economic advantages, Spartans involved in the recruitment effort worked to ease a variety of the German's concerns, ranging from the quality of Spartanburg's schools to the availability of dark bread at local grocery stores.[22] One delegation after another shuttled between the continents, distributing information and taking care of problems ranging from arranging housing for the company executives to giving crash courses in American shopping culture to the wives of the Hoechst executives.[23] Spartanburg's boosters' effort made a distinct impression on German managers. When comparing Tukey's barrage to the sales pitches of other American communities, a high-ranking Hoechst executive described Spartanburg's presentation as being "in a league of its own."[24]

The successful campaign to lure Hoechst became a model for Tukey's and the Spartanburg Chamber of Commerce's future recruitment efforts. Their recruitment strategy concentrated on a far-reaching commitment to the economic and emotional well-being of the newcomers, a strategy designed to lure additional firms to their Piedmont town. Tukey's motto was straightforward and simple: "I'll do anything to get them here and help 'em get in the black. Then word of mouth does the rest."[25] International recruitment became a community-wide effort. Chamber representatives convinced local grocery stores to carry foreign sausages and cheeses to please newcomers. Local real estate agents received a stern warning from the chamber not to overcharge the incoming foreigners. Spartanburg's media were downright zealous in their embrace of the gospel of international recruitment. Bringing foreign investment to the town was a widely approved goal for the local booster elite and a personal crusade for Tukey.[26]

The Spartanburg recruitment machine was well oiled. Tukey and the chamber used their decades of experience in recruiting, complementing it with some new tricks aimed specifically to foreign bosses. The message they spread to the foreigners was built upon the same foundation of cheap and docile labor, natural resources, low unionization, and growing markets that they had used for decades to draw in northern investors.[27] Spartanburg's salesmen recognized the need to sell the entire community to their international visitors, realizing that some of the recruits might possess limited knowledge of the region and even some suspicions about southern quality of life. When potential foreign investors came to town, they received thorough tours of community hospitals, schools, country clubs, and neighborhoods. Entertainment took place at the hosts' private homes, where the recruits had a chance to rub elbows with Spartanburg's economic and social elites.[28]

Spartanburg's savvy salesmanship, human factors, and other quality-of-life issues were, undoubtedly, important, but in the final analysis business is about numbers. In Hoechst's case, the deciding factor was Spartanburg's location at the heart of the American textile industry. According to one Hoechst executive's calculations, approximately 80 percent of American textile manufacturing took place within a 250-mile radius of Spartanburg.[29] Additionally, the available land, water, and transportation networks, combined with the region's peaceful labor environment, helped to convince Hoechst and those who followed that Spartanburg and the South Carolina Piedmont were good places for business.[30]

Another of South Carolina's, and especially the Piedmont's, main selling points was its workforce. Several state-level industrial location studies of the era repeatedly emphasized the importance of large, nonunionized, and skilled labor in attracting outside corporations.[31] A 1962 Clemson University survey of nineteen companies that had recently built facilities in the rural South Carolina Piedmont found that labor-related issues dominated their location decision. Amicable labor relations (or, more bluntly, low level of unionization) and availability of workers, combined with community attitudes, higher productivity, South Carolina's labor laws, and the region's lower wages were the most important factors behind the location decisions of these companies.[32]

When the Spartanburg campaign to recruit foreign corporations began, labor in the region was cheap and unorganized, if not yet particularly skilled. An intra-South regional comparison found that wage rates and fringe benefits in the South Carolina Piedmont were substantially below already low southern and South Carolina averages. In 1960, a typical Greenville payroll clerk made $56 per week, while her colleagues elsewhere in the South averaged $74.35. A Greenville electrician earned on average $2.09 per hour, while electricians in Charleston could expect more than $2.70 for an hour's work. Even unskilled Myrtle Beach laborers made $2.35 more per day than an unskilled man could get in Greenville.[33] Researchers concluded their findings by stating that, with a very few exceptions, Greenville-area nonmanagerial workers made less, worked longer hours, received fewer paid holidays and vacations, and earned smaller shift differentials than their colleagues elsewhere in the South.[34]

The Piedmont's workers rarely looked to unionization as a way to improve their lot. The region was, and is, a notoriously difficult target for the labor unions, who often have found their entries hindered by both the communities and corporations. Union agents working in the region faced police officers and other public servants who were exceptionally zealous in protecting local workers from "harassment" by outside agitators. Responding to a set of trumped-up charges against a visiting field agent in Spartanburg, a local representative of the American Federation of Hosiery Workers informed his union boss about regional realities: "This is typical of most industrial communities in the two Carolinas and certainly is representative of the general attitude in Spartanburg."[35]

In addition to hostile corporations and civic officials, unions faced additional challenges in persuading reluctant workers, who resisted unionization either out of fear of consequences or because of their tacit acceptance of the region's patriarchal industrial traditions. When the International Ladies Garment Workers' Union got bargaining rights for 165 workers at JaLog Industries in Spartanburg, ILGWU had difficulty getting the workers' signatures for the union cards, despite the company's cooperation. Some of the workers went to management, expressing their desire to remain "neutral" from unionization. "Even though a union is given to them on a silver platter, they are still reluctant to accept it," commented a frustrated AFL-CIO representative.[36]

The region's labor was indisputably cheap and unorganized, but South Carolina's leaders wanted to increase its quality by expanding the state's technical training program. Since the system's conception in 1947, the state's two technical schools, one for whites in West Columbia and the other for blacks in Denmark, had produced skilled technicians with an impressive 95 percent employment rate. In 1960, young Governor Ernest "Fritz" Hollings asked the legislature to expand the program, and in May of the following year, the state legislature authorized the opening of nine regional technical schools, including one in Spartanburg.[37]

Successful continuation of industrial recruitment required improvements in the state's labor force. A statewide technical education program helped to convert unemployed farmhands and technologically misplaced "lintheads" into welders, machinists, and electricians, skilled and willing to serve the state's new industrial residents. Increasingly, South Carolina perfected its industrial training programs by tailoring them to the specific labor needs of incoming corporations, training their future workers in state facilities with state-provided funds.[38]

The state-level focus on improved industrial recruitment and the technical training program complemented Spartanburg's own recruitment efforts. European corporations continued to flow into the community throughout the 1960s and 1970s. Tukey's theory about the wonders of word of mouth advertising was validated, as local Germans, eager to expand their ranks, enthusiastically participated in their adopted community's foreign recruitment efforts. Europeans might ignore a paid recruiter's pitch for the community, but a compatriot's description of how well he or she had been treated in Spartanburg was harder to disregard. "The word has spread that Hoechst has been treated well here," said the company president, Guenther I. O. Ruebcke, in 1975. "Since our arrival, a number of multinational companies engaged in highly specialized fields decided to locate in Spartanburg area."[39]

South Carolina's state-level officials also noticed the developments in Spartanburg and joined the fray in recruiting foreign industries. In 1967, Tukey had shared his "reverse investment plan" with then–Lieutenant Governor John C. West, who later admitted taking Tukey's plan and using it as a platform for his successful run for governor in 1970.[40] South Carolina's state-level industrial boosters adopted Spartanburg's recruitment plan down to the most minute detail. State officials' strategies emphasized the same devoted attention to potential foreign investors' smallest problems and personal contact with the target companies. This "red-carpet, kid-glove treatment" for potential investors also included personal attention from the state's governor to the most interesting recruits and, if concerns or questions arose, easy access to other high-level officials.[41]

Developments in South Carolina were intimately linked to larger developments in the global economy. Revamped tariffs, technological improvements in transatlantic communication, managerial advances, and internal political developments of both the United States and the home countries of South Carolina–bound companies contributed to the rapid globalization in Spartanburg County. The county's economy was tied to the global developments with new, intricate strings. International agreements, changes in the U.S. trade balance, and even European election returns all had an impact on Spartanburg.

When Spartanburg's international recruitment campaign began, the federal government was already committed to the swift but gradual liberalization of global trade, as agreed upon at the Bretton Woods Conference in June 1944 and various GATT Trade Round negotiations, beginning in 1946. Since the end of the war, Washington had consistently fought off protectionist impulses, such as the one emerging from the textile states during the mid-1950s dispute concerning Japanese imports. Even after the industrial recovery of Asia and Europe made their products more competitive in international markets, both Congress and the White House administrations remained true to the principles of lowering tariffs and fostering international trade.[42]

Spartanburg's path toward globalization began with textile machinery producers' need to be closer to their customers. Later, however, sudden turns in American trade policies, and, to a lesser extent, the European domestic situation fostered a larger surge of foreign corporations to the area, even in industrial sectors that had no vested interests in the community's textile traditions.

Ironically, the turning point that cemented Spartanburg's globalized future turned out to be President Nixon's controversial, protectionist decision to unilaterally overturn parts of the Bretton Woods contract. Throughout the 1960s, the Vietnam War and other U.S. military commitments, combined with increased foreign imports and heavy American investments abroad, had contributed to the rapidly escalating flow of dollars out of the country. As the decade approached its end, signs of discord started to emerge between America and its close allies. European Economic Community's price supports and import levies were building a protective wall around their agriculture, and the Japanese were dumping their cheap textiles on foreign markets.[43] Frustrated with the growing U.S. deficits and lack of international cooperation, President Nixon announced on August 15, 1971, that the USD was no longer tied to the gold standard and that the country would impose a ten percent surcharge on imports.

Shocked by the announcement, the Group of Ten, an advisory board of the capitalist world's major economic powers, met at the Smithsonian in Washington, D.C., to negotiate a new monetary system for much of the noncommunist world. The United States agreed to limit its devaluation to 10 percent, and the rest of the participants agreed not to retaliate against the American import surcharge.[44] The meeting rescued the international economic system by acknowledging the legitimacy of American grievances and actions, therefore preventing a major international trade war. The agreement also provided a major boost for Spartanburg's globalized economy.

A devalued dollar and increased duties made investing in the United States more profitable, even necessary. Currency flows turned back toward the United States as foreign investors decided to bypass the tariff wall by moving some of their manufacturing operations to the United States. The domestic situations in their home countries provided an additional incentive for European corporations to move production to America. Inflation, tightened labor markets, saturated markets, increased regulation, and occasionally even fear of socialism led some European corporations to seek a more nurturing business climate in the United States.[45] A series of remarkable socialist election victories beginning in the mid-1960s and a rapid radicalization of the European left began to shape many European corporations' plans for the future, and in many cases, these plans included expanding their operations in the United States. "We have had company after company come over here and say: 'We look at the United States as the last great capitalistic country in the world'," said one Citibank executive used to dealing with foreign investors, a sentiment echoed widely in articles and discussions about the foreign investment invasion of the 1970s.[46]

Investing in the United States reached almost a fever pitch during the early 1970s. During the years of negative American balance of payments, European central banks had steadily increased their dollar holdings. After the U.S. devaluation, the enormous dollar assets of European central banks were ready to return to the United States with gusto. Undervalued U.S. corporations and the availability of cheap and educated labor led many Europeans to view the United States as the latest Xanadu. "It's a joke, isn't it," marveled one young British investment banker in a 1973 Forbes interview. "Europe is flooded with all those Euro-dollars that you paid for our businesses. Billions and billions. The answer for us is to lap up those dollars and buy into America. I am in El Dorado. It's like getting Harrod's at half price."[47]

While European and other foreign investors were overcome by the rapidly rising American fever, neither the Congress nor the White House displayed noticeable, active interest in attracting foreign investments. When Representative John C. Culver, the chairman of the Subcommittee on Foreign Economic Policy of the House Foreign Affairs Committee, held hearings in 1972 on the adjustment assistance program to ease the pressures towards protectionism, "no one even mentioned the possibility of encouraging foreign investors as a way to increase domestic employment."[48] Rather than planning and preparing for the influx of foreign companies and investors, the federal government stuck mainly to the role of observer or regulator, leading some commentators to perceive it even as a hostile force toward foreign investments.[49]

States displayed a much more active and positive approach toward globalization. Once the investment flows to the United States started, southern states, especially South Carolina, were at an obvious recruiting advantage. The southern advantages of cheap labor and probusiness political culture had successfully penetrated northern business consciousness, as southern states started to pull in even some high-tech companies and headquarters of several Fortune 500 companies. The manufacturing employment in the Southeast had grown from

1.68 million jobs in 1950 to 3.05 million in 1981, while jobs of the same type in the North had either declined or experienced only minimal growth.[50]

Foreign corporations were well aware of the industrial shift toward the Sun Belt, and they were eager to join the movement. The South's growing markets, low unionization, and cheap labor enticed executive boards in Munich, Frankfurt, and Paris just as much as they had attracted their counterparts in Chicago and Boston. Foreign companies joined the march toward the Sun Belt with such vigor that it occasionally puzzled even some American industrialists, who publicly questioned the wisdom behind tire company Michelin's decision to concentrate its U.S. operations in the South Carolina Piedmont rather than in the vicinity of American automobile manufacturers.[51]

The Palmetto State and Spartanburg were experienced international recruiters, and Spartanburg's existing base of foreign corporations and nationals provided an additional lure for the incoming companies. While the competition for foreign investments was heating up between the states, the Southeast attracted 26.3 percent of all foreign investments in the United States between 1976 and 1983, making it the biggest recipient of international investors in the United States.[52] In its convincing analysis of international investments in the United States, *The Economist* applauded southern efforts and success in foreign industrial recruitment, nominating South Carolina in particular as "the most skilled angler for foreign investment" and complemented its salesmen's "blend of Southern charm and northern hucksterism," which had helped the state to pull ahead in the tight competition over foreign corporations.[53]

As the competition for international corporations intensified, the companies found themselves in an outstanding bargaining position. While the states hustled to put together increasingly generous subsidy packages, companies soon learned to prolong their location decisions until, in the words of Governor Wallace Wilkinson of Kentucky, "[T]hey were sure they had squeezed every drop of blood out of every turnip."[54] The industrial location game developed into a high-level combination of poker and extortion, where the corporations skillfully pushed the locations to outbid each other in tax breaks, free land, and other subsidies.

In the 1960s, during the early days of Spartanburg's and South Carolina's international recruitment efforts, the state of South Carolina did not give direct concessions to the incoming corporations. The most important state-level contribution consisted of creating business legislation conducive for investing in the state, such as right-to-work laws and low corporate taxes. Most of the direct subsidies were provided by individual communities.[55] However, as the competition intensified and stakes got higher, South Carolina, like most states engaged in this level of industrial recruitment, felt forced to put together subsidy packages that were beyond the scope of anything a single community could offer. Successful bids for large industrial immigrants often entailed relief from state taxes, free land, labor educated at the state's expense, improved transportation infrastructure, cooperative media, and substantial lobbying from the state's senators and governor and community representatives, as was the case in Spartanburg's and South Carolina's recruitment of BMW.[56]

BMW's search for the site for its first car factory outside Germany started with a list of 250 places around the world. Eventually, the list shrank to ten locations. Until only a few weeks preceding the announcement, a rumored list of potential locations included the South Carolina Piedmont, North Carolina, Georgia, and Nebraska, but on June 23, 1992, BMW announced its decision to ecstatically happy Spartans. At the time of the announcement, the factory was estimated to represent a billion dollar investment, providing directly three to four thousand jobs in the South Carolina Piedmont.[57] Additionally, bringing in an international quality car manufacturer was a huge achievement for the region's decades-long campaign to shake off its reputation as the center of low-cost, low-tech industries.

Throughout the process, both BMW and public officials controlled the flow of information carefully. The bidding process went forward in increments, with state representatives responding rapidly to BMW's whims and requests. After the company announced its choice, both the state of South Carolina and BMW remained mum about the price tag of its subsidy package, but media estimates put its value at $130–145 million.[58] The subsidies included free and prepared land, road improvements, fifty-five free apartments, state-funded labor training at BMW's site, and even an extension of the Greenville-Spartanburg Airport's runway to accommodate 747 jets.[59]

The actual investment proved to be an even bigger jackpot than expected. BMW's decision led to an investment flow of three billion dollars to South Carolina and Spartanburg, with two billion coming from BMW and one from its South Carolina suppliers. The factory and its suppliers grew to employ directly almost ten thousand Carolinians. By the same date, BMW also had paid $5.1 million in use taxes, $35.52 million in county property taxes, and $221.8 million in U.S. import fees. However, the state had to wait for its cut. By the end of the year 2000, BMW had not paid any income tax in South Carolina, claiming, in fact, $710 million in losses during its first eight years in the state.[60]

The economic impact of globalization in South Carolina and especially Spartanburg is indisputable. Foreign corporations helped to reshape Spartanburg's economy. The arrival of large-scale international manufacturers to the region pushed up wages, modernized the community's economy, and provided much-needed commercial diversity to ease Spartanburg's dangerous dependence on textiles. In November 1973, more than fifty foreign-owned companies were either operating in or building plants around the state, totaling approximately $432 million in capital input. In 1974 alone, foreigners invested a total of $313,053,000 in South Carolina industries, meaning that almost 47 percent of all industrial investments in the state that year came from outside the United States. By 1977, South Carolina had attracted some $1.7 billion in foreign investments, of which 40 percent was located in Spartanburg. As for their impact on local labor markets, foreign-owned corporations directly employed 1,500 foreigners and 4,500 Americans in Spartanburg, contributing more than $30 million in annual payrolls to the local economy. By 1980, Spartanburg's average annual salary of $8,002 was more than ten percent above the state average of $7,265.[61] With the arrival of BMW, international manufacturing had established itself as an integral part of South Carolina's economic landscape.

In addition to their economic impact, arriving foreign corporations and individuals helped to revitalize Spartanburg's cultural and community life. The community became host to one of the liveliest Octoberfests and Bastille Days in the Southeast, if not the entire country. A local Swiss-German delicatessen and a hangout for European expatriates, Deli Korner, serves some of the best sausages and beer in the American South. In Spartanburg's shops and cafés, French and German languages resonate among the Piedmont accents. Its public schools, thanks partially to the community's response to the foreign executives' concern over their own children's schooling, are widely touted to be among the best in South Carolina.

Despite the economic magnitude and culturally invigorating effects of globalization in the South Carolina Piedmont and in Spartanburg in particular, the community's existing elites have effectively protected their positions and the fundamental character of their town. The town's decision to focus its development efforts on international recruitment was conceived and developed by people who occupied the leading economic decision-making positions in Spartanburg, including its richest and most powerful man, Roger Milliken, and the CEO of its chamber of commerce, Dick Tukey. With the rest of the town's economic leaders, they successfully shaped the goals and methods of the community's recruitment efforts.

Spartanburg, like any other community in the South Carolina Piedmont, is a resolutely antiunion town. Since 1960, major local employers have worked through the Spartanburg Development Association to direct the community's economic development. A substantial part of this stewardship has focused on preventing the arrival of unions through personnel management training and by participating in the shaping of the community's recruitment policies.[62] The association exerts substantial influence in determining the future direction of Spartanburg's recruitment efforts. Rumors, urban legends, and verified stories alike circulate among Spartanburg's dissidents and workers about unionized

American and international companies that found their entry to the town effectively blocked. According to William W. Falk and Thomas Lyson, Spartanburg's gatekeepers were less than enthusiastic about Mazda corporation's possible arrival to the community; as one development association representative admitted, "It is our considered view that the Mazda plant would have a long-term chilling effect on Spartanburg's orderly industrial growth. An auto plant, employing over 3,000 card-carrying, hymn-singing members of the UAW would, in our opinion, bring to an abrupt halt future desirable industrial prospects."[63] Some of the stories are better documented than others, but it is obvious that Spartanburg's recruitment efforts and successes have focused on non-unionized, conservative corporations from overseas.

Although France and Germany enjoy higher unionization rates than the USA and possess more vigorous and powerful labor movements, executives of most incoming foreign corporations have either proven that they share the region's values before their arrival or adapted rapidly once in the area. In many cases, foreign corporations considering relocation or expanding their operations to the United States were extremely concerned about unionization, seeking determinedly to steer away from the areas of labor activism.[64] In South Carolina and Spartanburg, they found a community relatively free from organized labor and determined to keep things that way.

When Michelin, the French tire manufacturing giant, was eyeing the South Carolina Piedmont as a possible location for a new factory during the mid-1970s, it faced a relatively cold reception until local boosters learned about the Michelin family's staunch conservatism and hostility toward unions.[65] Family patriarch François Michelin's ardent capitalism and dislike of unions rivaled that of Roger Milliken himself. Michelin would be likely to attract similarly minded companies to follow the tire giant to the region; as one prospective French investor said in the *Columbia Record:* "If Michelin . . . chose South Carolina, there was no need for other smaller French companies to scour the nation looking for a better business climate. If it is good enough for Michelin, it is good enough for them."[66]

Michelin's paternalistic welfare capitalism has been a near-perfect fit for Spartanburg and the entire South Carolina Piedmont. Michelin's bosses joined Dr. Paul Foerster of Hoechst, one of the first Germans to arrive in Spartanburg, in blaming poor management rather than greedy workers and outside agitators for unionization. The company fights unionization with relentless vigor, while, like any good welfare capitalist, using more carrot than stick. Local workers learned quickly that Michelin paid better salaries than other local factories and rewarded its most favored workers with good pay and other incentives.[67]

Such modern welfare capitalist practices worked well in a community whose history is built largely around mill villages and patriarchal textile barons. Mill owners and European bosses understood each other. Europeans learned also to adapt their ways to correspond to the American form of welfare capitalism. For example, corporate donations for good causes in their host communities was an alien concept to Europeans, who were more accustomed to generous government funding for various pro bono projects. After a few years in town, Hoechst's Spartanburg-based executives started to propagate corporate giving in the company headquarters in Frankfurt, eventually managing to convince the company's leaders of the importance of voluntary giving.[68] By participating in fundraising for various benevolent projects in the community, Hoechst and other European corporations became even more rooted in the local community and traditions.

True to Spartanburg's traditions of avoiding conflict and evaluating cultural issues mainly through their effects on business, foreign corporations joined the moderates in the Confederate flag debate that resurfaced in the Palmetto State at the turn of the millennium. As the NAACP threatened to put South Carolina in a costly economic boycott unless it removed the Stars and Bars from the top of its legislative building, representatives of BMW and Michelin joined Governor Jim Hodges in supporting a compromise that would remove the flag and display it on another building on the state premises.[69] They, like most South Carolina businesspeople and corporations, wanted to acknowledge regional traditions without endangering their business interests. Rather than emphasizing their global and placeless nature, these foreign corporations paid homage to the Palmetto State's history and culture.

Spartanburg's experience with economic globalization has been largely a success story. The community secured its economic survival with the help of international recruitment, and foreign nationals have brought new dollars, foods, and languages into the town. Foreign corporations have played key roles in economic diversification in Spartanburg, by bringing in new jobs and optimism to replace the lost textile industries. In 1997, textiles brought in less than 20 percent of Spartanburg County's annual manufacturing payroll of $1.1 billion. While textile mills continued to be the county's biggest industrial field, the sovereign rule of King Cloth was over. Textile products, the second pillar of the region's old industrial order, paled in comparison to the county's upstart auto industry. Transportation equipment manufacturing employed almost twice as many people as textile product factories and brought in almost three times more money.[70]

However, the emergence of globalization has not radically altered Spartanburg's cultural foundation, its values, or the region's economic thinking. Foreigners have influenced but not radically changed the region's culture. The same forces—even individuals—that controlled the community before the 1960s are still in charge, ranging from old textile families to local chamber of commerce types. Their ranks have been reinforced by a few leading industrial immigrants who have been successfully introduced to the regional social traditions and Spartanburg's centers of power, such as its chamber of commerce and country clubs.

No community in the American South—maybe the entire United States—may have benefited more from economic globalization than Spartanburg. Yet, its workers today are almost as protectionist as their fathers were in the 1950s, when Japanese "one dollar blouses" shocked South Carolinians into a protectionist frenzy to secure the future of their local textile industry. The protectionist crusade has crossed class lines, uniting textile bosses and their floor-level workers to rally behind the same banner for tariff increases and other protectionist measures. The spiritual leader for these rank-and-file protectionists has been Roger Milliken, the same man who brought the first foreign corporations to town. He has shifted from laissez-faire capitalism toward Pat Buchanan–style isolationism, endearing him even more to the town's remaining textile workers and to some Greens, Naderites, and other antiglobalists.[71]

Spartanburg's selective recruiting, combined with the protectionist attitudes of substantial segments of the town's corporations and individuals, has proven that Spartanburg's decision makers have chosen a carefully managed strategy for growth. As a result, Spartans have witnessed their neighbor and friendly rival, Greenville, surpass Spartanburg in size. By adapting themselves to the global economy, controlling it, and introducing incoming global corporations and their foreign managers to local traditions and social customs, Spartanburg's leaders have managed to maintain tight control over their community. Foreign corporations have willingly embraced local business values, appreciating the conservatism, stability, low levels of unionization, and individualistic work ethic of the South Carolina Piedmont.[72] Some of these regional characteristics they had sought consciously, others they learned to know and appreciate after putting down new roots in Spartanburg County.

The newcomers' obvious embrace of southern business culture demonstrates the power of determined localities to shape and influence globalization in their neighborhoods. In Spartanburg, globalization has triggered an economic revolution but not a political or social one. Here community leaders have incorporated foreign companies and individuals into the local culture and values. This has not been a hard sell by any stretch of imagination, as the southern Piedmont's individualistic work ethic and probusiness mindset have liberated foreign corporations from much of the baggage associated with operating in their unionized, usually more regulated home countries. Globalization in Spartanburg has been a conservative and controlled movement—a classic revolution from above.

Notes

I wish to thank Professors James C. Cobb, Peter A. Coclanis, Andy Fry, William Stueck, and Thomas Zeiler for their intelligent support and criticism, regarding both the style and content of my paper. Additionally, Professor Dave Anderson improved this paper with his sharp comments and analytical clarity. Any possible mistakes that might have crept into the final work are my responsibility.

1. Milton Friedman, *Free to Choose, Episode Eight: Who Protects the Worker?* (TV series, 1980).

2. Rosabeth Moss Kanter, *World Class: Thriving Locally in the Global Economy* (New York: Simon and Schuster, 1995), 282.

3. For a good early description of the functions and goals of South Carolina's industrial training program, see Steven J. Shaw, "Special Education for Industrial Expansion," *University of South Carolina Business and Economic Review* 10, no. 1 (October 1963): 1–5.

4. For a seminal progressive interpretation of the South's emergence as a textile region, see Broadus Mitchell, *The Rise of the Cotton Mills in the South* (Baltimore: Johns Hopkins University Press, 1921); Walter Edgar, *South Carolina: A History* (Columbia: University of South Carolina Press, 1998), 182–86; WPA, *A History of Spartanburg County* (Spartanburg: The Reprint Company, 1976), 1–18.

5. David L. Carlton, *Mill and Town in South Carolina, 1880–1920* (Baton Rouge: Louisiana State University Press, 1982), 13, 40–81.

6. For a good discussion about the nature of postbellum southern capital markets, see David L. Carlton and Peter A. Coclanis, "Capital Mobilization and Southern Industry," in *The South, The Nation, The World* (Charlottesville: University of Virginia Press, 2003), 99–114.

7. U.S. Census of Population, 1940 (Washington, D.C.: U.S. Government Printing Office, 1943), 429; U.S. Census of Population, 1960 (Washington, D.C.: U.S. Government Printing Office, 1963), 42-13.

8. U.S. Census of Population, 1940, 418; U.S. Census of Population, 1960, 42–73.

9. U.S. Census of Manufacturers, 1947 (Washington, D.C.: U.S. Government Printing Office, 1950), 557; U.S. Census of Manufacturers, 1958 (Washington, D.C.: U.S. Government Printing Office, 1961), 39–9; U.S. Census of Population, 1950 (Washington, D.C.: U.S. Government Printing Office, 1952), 40–49; U.S. Census of Population, 1960, 42–157.

10. A. C. Flora, "The Dynamic Economy of South Carolina since 1958," *The University of South Carolina Business and Economic Review* 8, no. 2 (November 1961): 1.

11. Charles E. Edwards, "The South Carolina Economy in Perspective," *University of South Carolina Bureau of Business and Economic Research: Essays in Economics,* no. 15 (June 1967): 45.

12. Harriet L. Herring, *Passing of the Mill Village: Revolution in a Southern Institution* (Chapel Hill: University of North Carolina Press, 1949); Toby Moore, "Discourses of Work and Consumption in the Demise of the Southern Cotton Mill Village System," *Journal of Business and Economic History* 28, no. 2 (Winter 1999): 163–72.

13. Ralph McGill, *The South and the Southerner* (Athens: University of Georgia Press, 1992), 227.

14. Lacy K. Ford, *Origins of Southern Radicalism: The South Carolina Upcountry, 1800–1860* (New York: Oxford University Press, 1988), 73–74.

15. Alfred E. Eckes Jr., *Opening America's Market: U.S. Foreign Trade Policy since 1776* (Chapel Hill: University of North Carolina Press, 1995), 157, 169.

16. David Cohn, *Life and Times of King Cotton* (New York: Oxford University Press, 1956), 225–27; *Journal of the Senate of the 2nd Session of the 91st General Assembly of the State of South Carolina*, 865.

17. *Journal of the House of Representatives of the 2nd Session of the 91st General Assembly of the State of South Carolina*, 377.

18. "European Business People Like Carolina—and It's Mutual," *U.S. News and World Report*, June 26 1972, 62; Frank Vogl, "The Spartanburg Example: How an Old Southern Town Became 'Euroville'," *Europe*, May–June 1979, 26; Lou Parris, "South Carolina's 'Secret Weapon'," *South Carolina Business*, November 1988, 43.

19. Vogl, "The Spartanburg Example," 26; Roul Tunley, "In Spartanburg, the Accent Is on Business," *Readers' Digest*, January 1974, 166.

20. Vogl, "The Spartanburg Example," 26.

21. *Independent*, May 8, 1993, 16; *Sunday Times*, November 1, 1970, 1.

22. *Richard E. Tukey*, a promotional video in possession of the Spartanburg Chamber of Commerce; "European Business People Like Carolina—and It's Mutual," 62.

23. *Spartanburg Herald-Journal*, October 23, 1966, 1.

24. Dr. Paul Foerster (retired Hoechst executive), interview with the author, January 30, 1998.

25. Parris, "South Carolina's 'Secret Weapon'," 42

26. *Spartanburg Journal*, July 26, 1979, A1, A4.

27. "Investing in the U.S.: Let's Go Where the Unions Aren't," *Economist*, June 4, 1977, 101–2; For a thorough study of the southern industrial recruitment strategies, see James C. Cobb, *The Selling of the South: The Southern Crusade for Industrial Development, 1936–80* (Baton Rouge: Louisiana State University Press, 1982). Additionally, Bernard L. Weinstein, Harold T. Gross, and John Rees, *Regional Growth and Decline in the United States*, 2nd ed. (New York: Praeger Publishers, 1985) summarizes the size and scope of America's industrial shift to the South and West thoroughly and conclusively.

28. Dr. G. B. Hodge (long-term Chamber of Commerce activist and civic leader), interview with the author, September 24, 2002.

29. Foerster, interview; Vogl, "The Spartanburg Example," 26.

30. Foerster, interview.

31. Steven J. Shaw, "Special Education for Industrial Expansion," *University of South Carolina Business and Economic Review* 10, no. 1 (October 1963): 1–5; A.C. Flora, "Industrial Location in South Carolina," *University of South Carolina Business and Economic Review* 10, no. 10 (January 1964): 1–4;

32. Clinton H. Whitehurst Jr., "Industrialization in South Carolina's Rural Piedmont Counties: The Plant Location Decision," *University of South Carolina Business and Economic Review* 10, no. 10 (January 1964): 4–6.

33. David R. Pender and Ronald O. Clark, "Wage Rates and Fringe Benefits in the Manufacturing Industries of South Carolina," *University of South Carolina Bureau of Business and Economic Research: Essays in Economics*, no. 9 (February 1964): 19–28.

34. Ibid., 33–34.

35. AFL-CIO Region 5/8, Records, 1940–74, box 2772, folder 3: American Federation of Hosiery Workers, 1956–65. Southern Labor History Archives, Georgia State University, Atlanta.

36. AFL-CIO Region 5/8, Records, 1940–74, box 2771, folder 8: United Garment Workers of America, 1956–60. Southern Labor History Archives, Georgia State University, Atlanta.

37. Steven J. Shaw, "Special Education for Industrial Expansion," *University of South Carolina Business and Economic Review* 10, nos. 1, 2; "South Carolina's New Plant Boom," BusinessWeek, March 26, 1960, 128.

38. "Special Education for Industrial Expansion," 3; Cobb, *The Selling of the South,* 166–70.

39. Foerster, interview; "Southern Hospitality," *Trends,* Winter 1975, 17.

40. Parris, "South Carolina's 'Secret Weapon'," 40; *Spartanburg Herald-Journal,* August 5, 1979, 4

41. Spero C. Peppas, *A Comparative Study of Promotional Activities to Attract Foreign Investment: An Application of Marketing Theory to the Efforts of Southeastern States* (Ph.D. diss., Georgia State University, 1979), 124–25; "South Carolina Mission Sparks Brisk Interest by Europeans," *International Commerce* 75 (November 24, 1969): 22; "Remarks by Caleb C. Whitaker Regarding South Carolina's Foreign Investment Program. SCIDA Meeting—Hilton Head Island, May 1979," Vertical Files: International Relations. South Caroliniana Library, University of South Carolina, Columbia, South Carolina; Cobb, *The Selling of the South,* 189–90.

42. Robert A. Pastor, *Congress and the Politics of U.S. Foreign Economic Policy, 1929–76* (Berkeley: University of California Press, 1980), 4–5.

43. Harald B. Malmgren, "Coming Trade Wars? (Neo-Mercantilism and Foreign Policy)," *Foreign Policy* 1 (Winter 1970–71): 116–22.

44. Joan Spero, *The Politics of International Economic Relations,* 3rd ed. (New York: St. Martin's Press, 1985), 55.

45. "Why Foreign Corporations are Betting on the U.S.," *BusinessWeek,* April 12, 1976, 50; *New York Times,* January 29, 1978, 9.

46. "The New Immigration," *Forbes,* 116, November 1, 1975, 31; "Challenge in Reverse," *Economist,* October 25, 1980, 1–14; "Michelin Goes American," *Economist,* July 26, 1975, 56–64.

47. "Foreigners Are Coming: Should We Cheer or Should We Blench?," *Forbes,* 112, July 15, 1973, 28.

48. Pastor, *Congress and the Politics of U.S. Economic Policy,* 222.

49. "America's Welcome to Foreign Companies: Trip on the Mat," *Economist,* 260, July 17, 1976, 77–78.

50. Weinstein et al., *Regional Growth and Decline in the United States,* 15–18

51. "Investing in the United States: Let's Go Where the Unions Aren't," 101–2.

52. *Foreign Direct Investment in the United States, Completed Transactions, 1974–83, Volume 3: State Location* (U.S. Department of Commerce: Office of Trade and Investment Analysis, June 1985), 20.

53. "Investing in the United States," 101–2.

54. Douglas J. Watson, *The New Civil War: Government Competition for Economic Development* (Westport, Conn.: Praeger Publishers, 1995), 9.

55. "South Carolina's New Plant Boom," 128.

56. *Spartanburg Herald-Journal,* April 3, 1992, 1, 4; *New York Times,* June 23, 1992, D-6; *Wall Street Journal,* July 6, 1992.

57. *Spartanburg Herald-Journal,* April 3, 1992, 1.

58. *New York Times,* June 23, 1992, D6; "BMW's American Affair," *Economist,* June 27, 1992, 80.

59. Ibid.; *Wall Street Journal,* July 6, 1992.

60. *Spartanburg Herald-Journal,* May 11, 2001.

61. *Wall Street Journal,* November 5, 1973, 6; *Columbia Record,* August 23, 1977, 2; "Oompah in the Bible Belt," *Time,* July 25, 1977, 50; Vogl, "The Spartanburg Example," 26; U.S. Department of Commerce, *Local Area Personal Income, 1975–80* (Washington, D.C.: U.S. Government Printing Office, 1982), 1:3; U.S. Department of Commerce, *Local Area Personal Income, 1975–80* (Washington D.C.: U.S. Government Printing Office, 1982), 6:234–45.

62. *Spartanburg Herald-Journal,* January 9, 1960, 5; Hodge, interview; Foerster, interview; William W. Falk and Thomas A. Lyson, *High Tech, Low Tech, No Tech: Recent Industrial and Occupational Change in the South* (Albany, N.Y.: SUNY Press, 1988), 84–85.

63. Falk and Lyson, *High Tech, Low Tech, No Tech,* 84–85.

64. "Investing in the United States: Let's Go Where the Unions Aren't," *Economist,* 101.

65. *New York Times,* January 29, 1978, 1, 7.

66. *Columbia Record,* May 19, 1981, C6.

67. *New York Times,* January 29, 1978, 1, 7; Foerster, interview.

68. An undated *USA Today* article, found at the University of South Carolina, South Caroliniana Library, Vertical Files, Spartanburg County.

69. *Spartanburg Herald-Journal,* February 18, 2000, A1.

70. U.S. Department of Commerce's 1997 Economic Census, http://www.census.gov/prod/ec97/97m31-sc.pdf. In 1997, 4,170 workers in transportation equipment manufacturing in Spartanburg County made $156,541,000, while 2,184 Spartans in textile product mills brought in $58,255,000.

71. For a good article about Roger Milliken's anti–free trade activities, see Ryan Lizza, "Silent Partner," *New Republic,* January 10, 2000, 22–25. Dana Frank also provides an informative discussion about Milliken's campaigns for encouraging consumers to practice economic nationalism in *Buy American: The Untold Story of Economic Nationalism* (Boston: Beacon Press, 1999), 192–99.

72. "Investing in the United States: Let's Go Where the Unions Aren't," *Economist,* 101.

Andrew Young and Africa: From the Civil Rights Movement to the Atlanta Olympics

Andy DeRoche

At the National Summit on Africa in Washington, D.C., in February 2000, President Bill Clinton declared: "Africa never had a better friend in America than Andrew Young."[1] Although Young's advocacy of nonviolence and capitalism has not been embraced by all Africans, from the 1960s until the present day he has succeeded remarkably well in building bridges between the United States and Africa.[2] Moreover, he played a key role in overhauling the image of the South. Indeed, Young's career may be seen at once as a reflection of internal change in the South and the impact of that change on its relationship to the world beyond the nation's boundaries.

Young's life exemplifies at least two key aspects of the latest stage in the South's globalization, namely the importance of individuals and the centrality of race. He belongs in the ranks of solo contributors with Muhammad Ali, Ted Turner, and Michael Jordan.[3] Young worked through established American political institutions and embraced the traditional American values of democracy and capitalism. In promoting racial change in the South, he followed the path set out by Martin Luther King Jr., in contrast to the more radical alternatives of Stokely Carmichael and Malcolm X. More than most African Americans, he transcended his early career in the civil rights movement with a major presence on the international stage. Yet he did so without abandoning his roots in the South or his commitment to integration. While his contributions to the civil rights movement at home made him relevant to the contemporaneous struggle for freedom in Africa, his continuing international ventures, which focused on that continent, gave him unique stature in the South's evolving engagement with the outside world. As James Cobb reminds us, the region's development over the last two generations includes "pervasive national and international influences."[4]

Young's work from the 1960s to the 1990s tells us much about the evolution of the South in both foreign relations and economics. In the first aspect, Young's emphases contrasted dramatically with southern traditions. Historically, the

South's greatest influences on U.S. foreign relations had included a strong dose of white supremacy. The nineteenth century actions of Thomas Jefferson and Andrew Jackson brought about the conquest and subjugation of Native Americans. In the early twentieth century Woodrow Wilson, although an idealist and a progressive in some respects, championed segregation in the federal government and vetoed a Japanese resolution against racism at Versailles. His diplomatic appointments included an inordinate number of southerners, who staunchly opposed any move toward racial equality.[5]

The less savory aspects of Wilson's legacy received support from a multitude of southern politicians throughout the 1950s and 1960s. Led by the likes of George Wallace, Orval Faubus, John Stennis, Harry Byrd, Richard Russell, and Strom Thurmond, influential white southerners resisted the civil rights movement and rejected any notion that it should be linked to decolonization in Asia and Africa. They opposed internationalism, criticized the United Nations, and denounced foreign aid. According to Joseph Fry, these southerners were "more pessimistic than other Americans about the long-term prospects for international peace and the ability of Third World, nonwhite countries to function successfully."[6] They warned of communist subversives under every rock, both at home in Martin Luther King Jr.'s Southern Christian Leadership Conference and abroad in Nelson Mandela's African National Congress.

The foreign relations approach of leading southerners in the 1950s and 1960s also included support for unilateral intervention and a strong military. During the Eisenhower administration, Senate Majority Leader Lyndon Johnson coordinated southern support for operations in Guatemala, Asia, and the Middle East. Southerners in Congress backed President John F. Kennedy's attempts to oust Castro. Many of the key architects of U.S. policy in Vietnam were southern: Johnson, Dean Rusk, William Westmoreland, and Stennis. Meanwhile, southerners successfully transformed their region into "Fortress Dixie." Led by Russell, the South acquired seven of the ten largest defense contractors in the country. By 1970 the South held 25 percent of the nation's best defense contracts, up from just 7 percent in 1950. Not surprisingly, as their economy increasingly depended on contracts with the Pentagon, leading southerners opposed arms control.[7] Southern senators' militarism and their opposition to internationalism continued into the 1970s, anchored by another Byrd (Harry Byrd Jr.), Thurmond, Stennis, and Jesse Helms.

Andrew Young and others in the civil rights movement, on the other hand, criticized both U.S. intervention in Vietnam and the massive military budgets. Young fought both tendencies while in Congress from 1973 through 1976. The battle was truly joined in 1977 when Young took center stage in the den of iniquity itself, the United Nations. Young championed foreign aid, befriended Marxist guerrilla leaders, and crafted policies that contributed to racial progress in southern Africa. After some successes at the United Nations, he brought his vision back to the South and helped make Atlanta a center of internationalism. As mayor from 1982 to 1990 he fought apartheid and criticized President Ronald Reagan's policies in Nicaragua and Angola as promoting senseless violence justified by archaic cold war logic. The fact that someone with Young's views on foreign relations could be politically successful in the South in the 1970s and 1980s illustrated how much had changed there in the wake of the civil rights movement.

Young's support for economic development, on the other hand, represented a continuation of an approach championed by key members of Atlanta's white leadership since the early 1950s. In the aftermath of World War II, white businessmen such as Ivan Allen Jr. hoped to build Atlanta into a "national city" by promoting economic growth. Allen's goal received important support from William Hartsfield, the city's mayor from 1942 to 1962. When Allen became mayor in 1962, he continued Hartsfield's support for business with his "Forward Atlanta" program. Their philosophy expanded to the state level when Georgia Governor Carl Sanders championed a "New Georgia" during his tenure from 1963 to 1967.[8] The approach of Allen, Hartsfield, and Sanders in the 1950s and 1960s provided a blueprint for Young's close cooperation with business in the 1980s. Young's success in winning the Olympics for Atlanta took the older generation's boosterism onto a higher plane, helping transform the city from a national to an international one. Fittingly, Allen's son Ivan III played a key role in fundraising for the games, soliciting donations of three hundred thousand dollars from each of the fifteen largest corporations in the city.[9] Both Allens had been longtime supporters of Young's career and shared his vision of Atlanta as a center of international business.

Andrew Young's remarkable ability to contribute to the globalization of the South by emphasizing progress in race relations and building bridges, symbolized by the 1996 Olympics, developed gradually over several decades. His interest in Africa began during the early 1950s. As a student at Howard University and the Hartford Theological Seminary, he met several Africans who impressed him with their intelligence and determination. At Christian summer camps he met future African leaders such as Eduardo Mondlane of Mozambique and was inspired by a white American who had volunteered to be a missionary in Rhodesia.[10] Although Young's attempt to serve in Angola was denied by the Portuguese government, he followed events in Africa closely and encountered many African leaders while working for the National Council of Churches in New York City. In the late 1950s leading African Americans such as Martin Luther King Jr. expressed increased interest in Africa, as the civil rights movement and decolonization progressed simultaneously.[11]

In 1961 Young returned to the South and became directly involved in the civil rights movement. Over the next few years his vision for multiracial democracy and economic development really began to grow. As executive assistant to King, Young was a central figure in the events at Birmingham, St. Augustine, and Selma. He helped bring about passage of the Civil Rights Act of 1964 and the Voting Rights Act of 1965.[12] These accomplishments earned him national recognition and later helped open doors in politics and business, which afforded him more prominent positions from which to promote his ideas about foreign relations and economic development. His successful transition into both fields was undoubtedly made easier by his reputation as a logical and moderate reformer.

Although the civil rights movement was in some ways a revolution, leaders such as Young did not seek to overturn national institutions. On the contrary, they endeavored to solidify the principles in the U.S. Constitution, as amended in the Reconstruction era, by seeing that fundamental rights were enjoyed by all Americans and then by extending them to people in Africa. In addition to Young and King, many other southern black leaders, such as John Lewis and Thurgood Marshall, championed this moderate approach, though black leaders from the north, including W. E. B. Du Bois and Malcolm X, offered more radical visions.

Young's years in the movement also shaped his philosophy regarding foreign relations, which was inspired by King's ideals, his international vision to end institutionalized racism everywhere, with South Africa a particular focus. Young began incorporating ideas similar to King's into his own talks and writings.[13] At the Southern Christian Leadership Conference (SCLC) convention in August 1965, Young proposed gradually expanding the assault on injustice. He contended: "We must see that our work extends beyond the South and into the North, and when we have completed our work there we must go from New York to London and Paris and from there to Brazzaville and Johannesburg until the rights of man are secure the world over."[14] In early 1967 Young commented: "I am especially concerned about our relationship to South Africa, Angola, and Rhodesia. . . . We are beginning to see a role in relation to the African nationalists and we must have a nonviolent alternative—mainly because the countries are prepared to thwart violence and the U.S. will keep them supplied with arms."[15] Working with King refined Young's view that the civil rights movement was an integral part of the larger global movement for freedom and justice.[16]

The effort by King, Young, and other southern black leaders to equate their struggle with similar movements in Africa and Asia constituted a key departure from the traditional foreign policy stance of most leading southerners. Since the end of World War II influential southern policy makers had emphasized military intervention, opposed foreign aid, and rejected any efforts to connect civil rights at home to foreign relations.[17] These entrenched views would not be easy to overcome, but Young was determined to try. Throughout 1967 Young closely assisted King as he spoke more forcefully against the war in Vietnam, and as the tumultuous decade came to a close, Young and other southern blacks such as Julian Bond and John Lewis concluded that the next step was to challenge traditional white southern politicians directly.

After consulting with Lewis and Bond, Young opted to run in 1970 for a seat representing Georgia's Fifth District in the U.S. Congress. His decision reflected how much things had changed in the South since the 1950s. In Georgia the percentage of voting age blacks who were registered had increased from 27 percent in 1963 to 56 percent in 1968, clearly indicating the impact of the 1965 Voting Rights Act, which Young had helped get passed.[18] Young's entrance into politics also reflected his qualifications as a black candidate who could conceivably win in a predominantly white district. As a key negotiator and mediator during the civil rights struggles, Young had proven that he could get along with whites, and this crossover appeal helped him secure wide-ranging support. He lost his first bid but tried again in 1972 and won. Young received virtually the entire black vote, but the Fifth District was only 44 percent black. He also secured 25 percent of the white vote, which made the difference. These white voters did not consider him a threat to their well-being and were comforted by his association with King's nonviolence and integrationist goals. Many of them also could identify with his status as a well-educated member of the middle class. His victory in 1972 represented the only time a black candidate was elected to Congress from a majority-white district in the Deep South until 1996.[19]

Upon his arrival in Washington Young joined the Congressional Black Caucus (CBC), which had been organized in 1971 to address issues of special concern to African American legislators; he was one of the first members from the Deep South.[20] In July 1973, in his first real foreign policy initiative in Congress, Young proposed an amendment that would prohibit Portugal from using U.S. funds to support its military operations in southern Africa. Portugal's attempts to maintain colonial rule were to him just plain wrong. "Instead of ceding to the vast majority of the people of Mozambique, Angola, and Guinea-Bissau their legitimate rights to control of those African lands," he declared, "the Portuguese colonialist government to this day pursues a policy of terror, massacre, torture, and violence."[21] Young concluded his case by putting U.S. policy toward Portugal into the broader context of his international vision: "I consider it my duty to speak out against the repression of human rights, wherever it is found."[22] His amendment passed in the House, sixty-nine to fifty-seven.

As Portugal withdrew from fighting in Angola and Mozambique, Young's attention turned increasingly to South Africa. In December 1974 Young visited that country for the first time, and he decided to meet with Robert Sobukwe, a black antiapartheid activist who was confined in Kimberley. Sobukwe asked Young to facilitate an education in the United States for his two oldest children. Young invited them to live in his home in Atlanta and attend college there, and Sobukwe gladly accepted. His daughter Miliswa and son Dini flew to Atlanta in June 1975, moved into the Youngs' house, and started their higher education at Atlanta Junior College.[23]

Young's help evidenced his personal generosity and southern hospitality. But it also revealed much about Young's potential as a new voice in U.S. foreign relations. He was among a growing group of African Americans who began to directly influence foreign policy in the 1970s, a direct result of the civil rights movement of the 1960s. Black policy makers who had been influenced by King acted in unprecedented ways. Walter Fauntroy (D-D.C.) and Ronald Dellums (D-Calif.) called for American actions against apartheid, and Barbara Jordan (D-Tex.) eloquently criticized Richard Nixon's immoral conduct. Young personified this increasing demand for moral policy and actions, which echoed the dreams of King. Not only did he speak out against racial injustice throughout the world, but he had actually opened his home to the children of one of black Africa's best-known activists. This new reality spoke volumes about the kinds of relationships that Young could forge with world leaders of color. It also manifested the changes that had occurred in the South and their implications for developing the region's connections with Africa.

In November 1975, Young visited Zambia, Kenya, and Nigeria. Leaders of those countries talked enthusiastically of their growing economic power, both as suppliers of resources and as markets for American goods. Many developed nations were working hard to get a slice of the economic pie in Africa. For example, both Germany and Japan had already joined the African Development Fund (ADF). Upon returning to Washington in early December, Young urged his colleagues in Congress to approve U.S. membership in that organization. He contended that the entrance fee of $25 million was a bargain and that membership was necessary in order to compete with other nations. For example, a Michigan manufacturer was bidding against Germans and Japanese for a contract to supply $125 million in trucks to Nigeria. Another deal was pending in which Nigeria would purchase 200,000 pairs of combat boots from a Tennessee firm.[24]

Young emphasized that joining the ADF would increase American contacts with economic decision makers in countries such as Nigeria and put Americans on an equal footing with competitors. Young insisted that fellow members of Congress not view the ADF as another form of international aid, but rather as an investment of American capital that would reap large profits in the long run. He harbored reservations about advocating the involvement of U.S. corporations in less-developed countries, but he concluded: "I think American multinational corporations are probably better than German and Japanese, and it is a very relative thing."[25]

Young's appraisal of the ADF and its potential benefits for U.S. companies helped win the day, and the House voted 249 to 166 in favor of American participation. The bill then went to the Senate, which debated it on March 30, 1976. Senators Hubert Humphrey (D-Minn.) and Edmund Muskie (D-Maine) strongly advocated American participation in the ADF, while Senators Harry Byrd Jr. (I-Va.) and Jesse Helms (R-N.C.) staunchly opposed it. Helms decried African governments as corrupt and socialist. He initially proposed that the United States not support the fund at all, but then settled for an amendment prohibiting any ADF dollars from reaching Uganda and its notorious dictator Idi Amin. The Senate approved the amended measure and the United States joined the ADF. The triumph of Young's position on the ADF over that of Helms and Byrd demonstrated the influence of a new southern voice in Congress, a voice that sought to build bridges with Africa.

While the decision to support the ADF pleased Young, revelations regarding Angola certainly did not. During the debate over American membership in the ADF, Young complained that "we have got another CIA-run war in Angola matched with equal brutality by the influx of the Soviet Union."[26] He contended that the harm done to America's reputation in Africa by CIA activities in Angola was all the more reason why the United States should support economic development in other African nations. He presciently predicted that even Angola would turn eventually to Americans for technical assistance for drilling oil and mining uranium, and the sooner the United States stopped inciting war, the sooner such development could begin.

In December 1975 Young denounced Secretary of State Henry Kissinger's policy toward Angola as a "dangerous course" and proposed that Congress stop the U.S. intervention.[27] Many other members of Congress agreed, and the Senate passed an amendment blocking all covert aid to Angola. In January 1976, the House considered similar legislation. Young again spoke forcefully, contending that war was not the answer and that "the only thing we are doing is putting more weapons in to kill more people."[28] The amendment passed easily, and covert U.S. involvement in Angola ended.[29] Southern conservatives such as Jesse Helms did not give up, however, and would lead the move to support Jonas Savimbi's forces in the 1980s.[30]

Soon afterward, the eyes of the world once again focused on South Africa. In June 1976 some fifteen thousand school children in Soweto staged a peaceful demonstration against apartheid education policies, only to be met by police bullets that killed fifty-eight of them. In late August, Young excoriated the apartheid regime and its security forces for this outrageous conduct. He exclaimed: "South Africa should be made to face the reality that the interests of the United States are not coterminous nor reconcilable with those of the present Vorster government." He urged U.S. bankers and businessmen to cease their dealings with such an oppressive state, whose white leaders obviously were afraid of change, and he believed it was time that Americans took a firm stand in support of black South Africans.[31]

In September during the annual Congressional Black Caucus weekend, Young and Charles Diggs (D-Mich.) convened about thirty black leaders to discuss foreign relations. The group decided to form an organization to lobby for progressive policies toward Africa and debated who should head the new entity. They selected Randall Robinson, a young black member of Diggs's staff, who had a Harvard law degree and experience as an activist.[32] The working group evolved into TransAfrica, which officially opened its doors in 1978. Helping to found TransAfrica proved to be one of Young's most important contributions to foreign relations during his four years in Congress. It goes without saying that traditional southern legislators such as Richard Russell would not have been involved in such an initiative.

Young's primary activity in 1976, however, was to help Jimmy Carter win the presidency. One of his key contributions to Carter's campaign was advising the candidate on controversial African issues, such as the war in Rhodesia. Most importantly, Young attracted African American backing across the South, which was crucial to Carter's win. The civil rights movement, in particular the Voting Rights Act of 1965, made a concrete impact on a presidential election for the first time. Nowhere was this more true than in Mississippi. In the early 1960s virtually no African Americans in Mississippi dared to vote, but in 1976 they won the state for Carter. Young summed up the significance of the Mississippi vote: "When I heard that Mississippi had gone our way, I knew that the hands that picked cotton finally picked the president." Black voters made the difference in several states. They actually provided the margin of victory in North Carolina, South Carolina, Mississippi, and especially Louisiana, where Carter received just 41 percent of white votes but 94 percent of African American votes.[33] The role of blacks, and Young in particular, in the 1976 presidential contest illustrated clearly how much had changed in Dixie.

Young won his own race for reelection to the House, garnering two-thirds of the vote, but was soon faced with the difficult choice between Congress and the cabinet. In December 1976 Carter asked Young to become the U.S. ambassador to the United Nations. Carter told him that the fact that he had been "associated with Martin Luther King would help people take human rights seriously from the United States."[34] Young accepted the offer and was sworn in by Supreme Court Justice Thurgood Marshall in January 1977. Immediately thereafter the president requested that Young "go to Africa and get some sense of what African leadership expected."[35] He did just that, visiting fifteen countries and meeting with seventeen African heads of state. Perhaps most importantly, he spent several days in Nigeria. He talked with General Olusegun Obasanjo, Nigeria's head of state, for several hours, convincing him of U.S. support for majority rule throughout southern Africa. The subsequent improvement in U.S.-Nigerian relations, which had deteriorated drastically with Kissinger in office, was significant for several reasons. Nigeria, Africa's most populous nation, possessed a powerful military and large oil deposits. Resuscitating relations with Nigeria was one of Young's key accomplishments while UN ambassador.[36]

Back in Washington, Young summed up his findings to the cabinet. Carter thanked him for doing an "extraordinarily good job in Africa."[37] Indeed, Young had found out exactly what the key African leaders wanted. Julius Nyerere of Tanzania and others emphasized the importance of repealing the Byrd Amendment, which had been passed in 1971 and allowed the importation of Rhodesian chrome in violation of UN sanctions. Before a House committee in February, Young called repealing this measure a "kind of referendum on American racism," which would demonstrate that the United States did not support the white minority government in Rhodesia and its leader, Ian Smith.[38] In mid-March the Congress voted in favor of repeal.[39] Young, a symbol of the New South, had been central in overturning the effort to support Smith's white regime, which had been championed by Byrd, member of a classic southern white family and longtime defender of segregation.

Young returned to Africa in May. Government officials in South Africa did not roll out the red carpet for Young, who had recently referred to them as "illegitimate."[40] When he arrived in Johannesburg, the customs officers directed the plane to a remote part of the airport to minimize publicity. It was a futile effort. Young waved to the customs police, then enthusiastically shook hands with the black limousine drivers. Soon after arriving he addressed business leaders, emphasizing that it was in their best financial interests to end apartheid. He contended that they could play a key role in finding a solution, just as business leaders had done in Birmingham, Alabama. He praised the potential of capitalism to help end apartheid peacefully. In the short run, opponents of apartheid could use boycotts to put pressure on the system. Eventually, as the economy included more blacks, the likelihood of armed rebellion would diminish.[41] Thus Young compared the battle against apartheid in South Africa to the civil rights movement in the southern United States and emphasized the role of boycotts and economic growth in ending institutionalized racism there.

The next day the ambassador spoke to a racially diverse group of about seventy liberals. His inspirational account of his own experiences in the 1960s drew a standing ovation. Mangosuthu Buthelezi, a powerful Zulu leader, embraced Young and praised his peaceful approach. The crowd sang the black national anthem, "God Bless Africa," and cheered Young again as he departed. During his next stop at the U.S. Information Service office, he admitted that it would be hypocritical of Americans to condemn black South Africans for using violence, considering the extremely violent revolution the United States had fought against Great Britain. Young realized that the problem in South Africa was complex and would not be solved quickly by a few boycotts. He did suggest that if apartheid continued the World Bank might cut off aid to South Africa. Young's conduct and message angered the white leaders. Connie Mulder, the minister of information, criticized the ambassador for breaking his promise not to be provocative or create an embarrassment for the Pretoria regime. An Afrikaner publication labeled Young a "blabbermouth."[42]

Some black South Africans, in contrast, castigated Young as a front man for American capitalism. Steve Biko, whose black consciousness movement was becoming quite influential, declined to meet with Young, in part because he thought the ambassador should instead visit the imprisoned leader of the African National Congress (ANC), Nelson Mandela. He also disliked Young's pro-capitalism philosophy. In Biko's opinion the ambassador had "no program except the furtherance of the American system."[43] Tsietsi Mashinini, a key figure in the 1976 Soweto demonstrations, denounced Young as a "tool of imperialism." The leaders of the Pan-African Congress distrusted Young and contended that the United States used the UN to suppress revolution. Oliver Tambo, president of the ANC-in-exile, believed that Young was acting primarily to advance the interests of the American economy.[44]

In fall 1977, circumstances in South Africa went from bad to worse. Rioting and repression escalated, sparked by the September murder of Biko by the police. In October, forty-nine African nations requested that the UN Security Council consider imposing tough comprehensive sanctions against South Africa. Young announced that he personally favored such measures but added: "The president and the secretary of state will have to decide what sanctions are appropriate."[45] Following their instructions he voted in favor of a mandatory arms embargo, which prohibited sales to Pretoria of weapons, ammunition, and military vehicles. The measure passed, and for the first time the UN imposed mandatory sanctions against a member state.

Early in 1978 British and American diplomats convened talks with Robert Mugabe and Joshua Nkomo, the leaders of the two main guerrilla armies fighting Smith's government in Rhodesia. Mugabe and Nkomo, who had formed a loose coalition called the Patriotic Front (PF), accepted an invitation to meet on the island of Malta. As the final logistics were being arranged, Young insisted that he stay in the Dragonara Hotel with the PF delegation. Much of the progress at Malta resulted from Young's informal personal interactions with them. He established a relationship of mutual respect, swimming in the hotel pool or jogging. He drank orange soda with Mugabe and drank beer with Nkomo, who "clearly felt himself in the presence of a friend in Andy Young." Young's diplomacy at Malta did not end the conflict, but it did help keep the negotiating process alive.[46]

The approach to the conflict championed by Young and the British, known as the Anglo-American plan, bogged down in the fall of 1978 as the war escalated. Young defended the Anglo-American plan and U.S. policy toward southern Africa at a conference in Khartoum, Sudan, in early December. Many Africans challenged Young and accused the United States of being racist in its dealings with southern Africa. They pointed to Smith's recent visit to America as evidence. One PF representative confronted Young and wondered what the United States had ever done to help the liberation forces. Young remained calm, as he did throughout the conference, and spoke to the Zimbabwean in good humor. He apologized for not calling him "doctor," a title he had earned at an American university. Young added that the higher degrees from American colleges held by more than thirty PF leaders could surely be viewed as a contribution to the liberation struggle.

In such lively exchanges, Young's strengths were evident. While Africans argued with him over U.S. policy, they clearly felt comfortable around him, calling him "Andy" and acknowledging that he was among the greatest advocates in America for African rights. Although they liked him personally, many Africans considered him to be a right-winger politically and an apologist for a fundamentally conservative American policy. Being branded a right-wing conservative in Khartoum due to the same positions for which many in Washington called him a radical leftist did not dismay Young, and he clearly articulated the American strategy.

Young maintained his optimism about the work he was doing in Africa and joked with Hal Gulliver of the *Atlanta Constitution* that his greatest concern was how he would get back to Atlanta after his UN job ended. Stephen Rosenfeld of the *Washington Post* summarized Young's performance at Khartoum as "terrific." Gilbert Cranberg, editor of the *Des Moines Register,* also witnessed Young in action in the Sudan and concluded: "America needs to be sophisticated enough to overlook Young's occasional verbal gaffes and to recognize him for the major asset he is for the United States in this part of the world."[47]

In spite of the positive view of some analysts, critics jumped on Young's "verbal gaffes," usually taking brief statements out of context from long interviews. For example, during a lengthy July 1978 discussion of Carter's policies toward Africa, Young alluded to the existence of "political prisoners" in the United States. Representative Dan Quayle (R-Ind.) requested that the White House provide documentation on the political prisoners, and if none could be produced, that Young resign. Southern white legislators echoed Quayles's denunciations of the ambassador. Representative Larry McDonald (R-Ga.) called for

Young's impeachment, but the motion was defeated 293 to 82. Senator Harry Byrd Jr. blamed Young for turning the American policy toward Rhodesia into a "pro-terrorist position."[48]

In spite of such criticism, throughout his tenure as ambassador Young defended his vision for a future Zimbabwe that would feature peace and political rights for all of its people. Carter's decision to maintain sanctions in summer 1979 was one of the high points of Young's service.[49] The president demonstrated a steadfast commitment to the policy that the ambassador had done so much to craft. Young had accepted the job in part because it would allow him to carry the ideals of King onto the international stage, particularly regarding southern Africa. In this case he had succeeded, and the Carter administration contributed to the process, which soon resulted in the independent, majority-ruled nation of Zimbabwe.[50] Any satisfaction Young may have felt about this triumph in the summer of 1979 proved short lived, however. He resigned in mid-August in a cloud of controversy over his meeting with a representative of the Palestinian Liberation Organization.[51]

Young returned to Atlanta in 1979, joining a wave of return migration by blacks to the South. Declining economic opportunity in the North helped encourage this trend, but another factor was an increasing tendency for African Americans to identify themselves as "southerners."[52] Like many blacks Young considered the South his home and anticipated having many opportunities there. He formed a consulting firm called Young Ideas. He was in high demand as a speaker and earned over three hundred thousand dollars in 1980. At the urging of Mayor Maynard Jackson and others in the black community, he decided to run for mayor in 1981. With help from his friend Harry Belafonte, he raised hundreds of thousands of dollars in New York for his campaign, but in Atlanta it was a different story. The white business community almost unanimously backed Sidney Marcus, a white state legislator. The third candidate was Reginald Eaves, a black former police chief. Young edged out Marcus 41 percent to 39 percent in the general election. Most African Americans voted for Young, most whites for Marcus. Eaves finished a distant third. In the runoff against Marcus, Young triumphed with 55 percent of the vote. Nearly all of Young's support came from blacks, who constituted 56 percent of registered voters.[53]

The mayoral election had degenerated into a contest of black against white. Despite having received almost no support from white businessmen, Young met with a group of Atlanta's white elites almost immediately after the balloting and asked for their support. He fully intended to work closely with the private sector in order to attract investment to Atlanta and transform it into an international city. Business leaders shared his vision of economic development and found his approach a welcome change from Maynard Jackson's. According to builder Bob Holder, Jackson's attempts to befriend white leaders with "give-

and-take" sessions had often turned into lectures by Jackson or even "a total ha-
rangue about his discomfort." Jackson's affirmative action initiative during the
expansion of Hartsfield Airport had been challenging and even frustrating for
many white contractors.[54] One businessman remarked, "Andy Young's style is
much easier for a white person to deal with."[55] On January 4, 1982, Young took
the oath of office as Atlanta's mayor. Just as his own work in the civil rights
movement had led him to the international stage at the UN, Young believed that
Atlanta's positive race relations were a key to the city becoming a force in the
global economy.

An embodiment of Atlanta's progressive race relations, Young himself could
do much to generate international interest in the city. In at least one case during his first year in office his influence turned the tide, when a Nigerian official contracted for $1 million worth of satellite equipment with an Atlanta com-
pany because of introductions made by Young.[56] Hoping to develop more such
ties, Young was instrumental in opening a Nigerian Consulate General in Atlanta in 1983. He would continue working to build such bridges between Atlanta
and Africa throughout his eight years as mayor. His staff expected him to be
involved in foreign relations. Louise Suggs, who served for seven years as Mayor
Young's special assistant for protocol, recalled that "we always called him
ambassador."[57]

Young also continued to participate in the national dialogue about foreign
relations and was particularly active in the fight against apartheid. In spring
1985 the Senate Foreign Relations Committee held extensive hearings regarding
possible sanctions against South Africa. Young provided insight into how sanctions could facilitate change there, arguing that there were progressive elements
in the white government who wanted to end apartheid but couldn't for political reasons. Strong sanctions would give them an excuse to do what they
thought was right. He concluded, "In difficult matters of social change, some
outside idealistic authority is needed. I think the U.S. Senate in this case becomes that kind of authority . . . to say to the people of South Africa that they
must change quickly in order to avoid chaos and bloodshed."[58] The Congress
eventually imposed tough sanctions over President Ronald Reagan's veto, contributing to the downfall of apartheid. The sanctions represented the high point
of the influence of race on U.S. foreign relations and an extension of King's philosophy onto the global stage.[59]

Meanwhile, in early 1986 Young and former president Jimmy Carter em-
barked on an agricultural mission to Africa. Their first stop was the Sudan,
where they talked about better ways to grow wheat. In Tanzania they discussed
peanut farming with President Julius Nyerere. In Zambia they met with President Kenneth Kaunda, who told them that, although corn prospered in his nation, the people imported wheat to make bread. This prompted Young to pro-

pose an interesting way to promote cornbread to the Zambians—a television show featuring Mrs. Carter and Mrs. Kaunda concocting the southern staple. "Cornbread will be in," he predicted.[60]

Young had a strong interest in policy toward Angola, where the Reagan administration supported the rebel forces of Jonas Savimbi in their fight against the government. Young flew to Luanda in August despite a travel warning issued by the State Department and the lack of official diplomatic relations between the countries. The Angolan government warmly welcomed the mayor and arranged for him to visit the site of a recent battle and an oil rig.[61] Young decried official American policy as "a tragic mistake."[62] This was one of many instances in which Young blasted Reagan's foreign policy in the 1980s.[63]

In 1986 Young spent more than one hundred days outside Atlanta. He spent more than half that time in foreign countries during nine overseas trips. Some Atlantans criticized his absenteeism, but he defended his travels as good for the city's economy. Even the mayor felt 1986 had been a little too frantic, however, and so he hoped to travel somewhat less in 1987. Nonetheless, a few days after his state of the city address he departed for a twelve-day journey to southern Africa.

He joined about two hundred other participants for a week-long African American conference in Botswana. Speaking in the capital city of Gaborone, he urged the people of Botswana and neighboring nations to seek help from private corporations such as Coca-Cola and Chevron. He compared their plight during the Reagan years to that of American cities, which also failed to receive sufficient federal aid. Like Atlanta, he believed, African nations should focus on attracting private investment. He hoped that the governments of the world's wealthy nations would someday make Africa a higher priority, but until then the best solution was through the private sector. The response to his procapitalism message was mixed. Some audience members denounced Young's speech as "Reaganesque." Paulino Pinto Joao, Angola's minister of information, described Young's ideas as "slightly unrealistic."[64]

Young met another ambivalent response a few days later when, in a speech to rural Botswanans in the village of Molepolole, he told them about Martin Luther King and the power of nonviolence. The crowd certainly liked Young and cheered when he joined kitchen workers in a traditional dance on stage. However, they were not convinced that nonviolence could solve the problems of southern Africa. David Magang, a member of Botswana's parliament, observed that Young's "expression for patience is about four years too late." A man in the crowd on crutches stridently repudiated Young's call for nonviolence: "You are already violent, you have Star Wars, you have enough arms to do the job."[65] Many Africans obviously viewed Young as just as American as Reagan. They saw the incredible distance separating the United States from nations in southern Africa, not the connection between Young's ancestry and theirs. In their view the cultural and class divides between African Americans in Georgia and black Africans in Botswana were too great to apply the strategies of King and Young usefully.

From Botswana the mayor flew to Zimbabwe, where his task proved no easier. The State Department sponsored Young's visit to celebrate the King holiday and also hoped he could assuage the tensions between Zimbabwe and the United States. Relations, in fact, had gotten very bad. After a Zimbabwean official lambasted American foreign policy at a July 4th ceremony attended by Jimmy Carter, the Reagan administration cut off aid, withholding some $13 million in payments through the end of 1986. In the same hall where the insulting speech occurred, Young explained that Congress was working to reinstate aid to Zimbabwe. He primarily discussed King's legacy and how it could be used to fight apartheid and other problems in the region. He delivered a similar message in a sermon before an overflow crowd at a Methodist church and again during official ceremonies for King at the U.S. Embassy on January 19. His three days in Harare, which also included a meeting with Mugabe, received mixed reviews. As in Botswana, Young himself was popular among Zimbabweans, but his emphasis on nonviolence and capitalism was met with "polite disbelief." [66]

Soon after returning to Atlanta, Young joined a group formed by attorney Billy Payne to attract the 1996 summer Olympics to Atlanta. In December 1988 the Atlanta Organizing Committee for the Olympic Games officially appointed Young as its chair. Addressing the International Olympic Committee's (IOC) annual meeting in late 1989, Young emphasized the worldwide influence of King's philosophy and characterized Atlanta as "a capital of the human rights movement." [67] In the final IOC vote in September 1990, Atlanta triumphed over Athens, Greece, and Young had been a key player in the victory. The *Atlanta Journal Constitution* characterized Young as "the city's most eloquent and most effective representative on the world stage." [68]

Helping to secure the Olympics was the crowning achievement of Young's tenure as mayor and capped off his efforts to transform Atlanta into an international city. Young's eight years of globe-trotting redefined the potential role of a mayor in foreign relations and greatly increased Atlanta's international recognition. His impact was evident in many concrete ways. During his tenure, Hartsfield Airport gained direct flights to Italy, Japan, Switzerland, Ireland, Germany, and France. (Young played a key role in getting direct flights to South Africa in the late 1990s, too.) In 1989 the number of official consulates in Atlanta reached a record high of sixteen, up from thirteen when Young took office, and included the Nigerian one he had done so much to establish. The total of honorary consulates reached thirty-nine, including Liberia's, which was managed by Young's brother, Walter. As Young left office Atlanta boasted fifteen foreign chambers of commerce, whereas there had been only two a decade earlier.[69] Overall exports from Georgia rose from just over $3 billion in 1987 to $5.7 billion in 1990, and Young's boosterism certainly contributed to that growth.[70] Direct foreign investment in Georgia had increased from $4.6 billion in 1981 to $13.9 billion in 1989, also due in great part to Young's endeavors.[71]

Young's efforts while mayor to make Atlanta an international city were part of his overall attempts to promote economic development. Working closely with the business community he fostered a major overhaul of the city's downtown. The big-ticket items, such as the Georgia Dome and Underground Atlanta, helped make the city more attractive to tourists.[72] By applying affirmative action to the construction and management of these and other facilities, Young aided the black middle class. His emphasis on development delivered few benefits to the city's poor, however. Tyrone Brooks, a state representative, observed that "the downside has been that under his administration the city has realized a larger poverty population."[73] As was true in the nation at large, the 1980s prosperity for middle- and upper-class Americans did not trickle down to Atlanta's lower class. Furthermore, the experience of poor black Atlantans resembled another larger trend in the 1980s: although blacks across the South enjoyed political and legal equality after the civil rights movement, many challenges remained regarding their economic status.[74]

At the conclusion of his mayoral tenure Young retained his belief that capitalist development was the best way to improve the lives of people both in the United States and in Africa.[75] After an unsuccessful run for governor of Georgia in 1990, he entered the private sector as a consultant for the Law Engineering firm. He climbed quickly up the company ladder, first to chair of the international branch of Law Engineering, then to vice chair of the entire organization. Initially much of his work dealt with Africa, where the Law Company had many offices. In addition to his work for Law, Young built many other kinds of bridges to Africa.

One of the most exciting stories of the twentieth century unfolded in South Africa in the early 1990s, and Young followed the events closely. In February 1990, after some ten thousand days in prison, Nelson Mandela was released. In June he toured the United States, including a stop in Atlanta. Young welcomed Mandela when he visited the King Center and laid a wreath at King's grave. In July 1993, Mandela returned to Atlanta in search of backing for his presidential campaign. Young participated in a ceremony in which Mandela received an honorary degree from Clark Atlanta University, and he urged his fellow Atlantans to support the South African leader. Young lauded Mandela as "a reason for hope for the future" and added that the "survival of multiracial democracy is on trial in South Africa."[76] Multiracial democracy triumphed in May

1994, when Mandela celebrated his election to the presidency. His victory represented an incredible extension of King's vision of racial equality onto the international stage, a vision Young had advocated for over thirty years.

The connections were not just philosophical. Young was a key player in developing economic links between Atlanta and postapartheid South Africa, both in his work for Law Engineering and in his role as an unofficial diplomat. He encouraged Georgians to support Mandela and get more involved with South Africa, and they did. Exports from Atlanta to Africa in 1994 totaled just under $91 million and by 1996 had increased to over $115 million. A dramatic rise in trade with newly free South Africa was the key to this change. Atlanta sent $35 million worth of goods to Mandela's country in 1994 and that nearly doubled to $64 million in 1996.[77]

Young's ongoing involvement with Africa caught the eye of President Bill Clinton. In October 1994 Clinton appointed Young to oversee the $100 million Southern Africa Development Fund. Clinton, who made the announcement during a White House reception for Mandela, chose Young because he had "long worked to improve conditions in the region." Clinton instructed him to find promising small businesses in southern Africa and to award them grants from the fund. Furthermore, Young envisioned the grants serving as seed money to attract much larger contributions from private investments. "It's basically to help southern Africans develop business opportunities," he explained.[78]

While Young welcomed Clinton's appointment as another way to work on African development, he continued to focus on the upcoming Olympics. As cochairman of the Atlanta Olympic Organizing Committee, he participated actively in the effort to facilitate a successful event. He coordinated a program whereby foreign athletes could spend time training in Georgia and paid particular attention to African athletes. The city of LaGrange hosted over four hundred athletes from fourteen different countries, including South Africa, Mozambique, and Zambia. The athletes not only trained but also took college courses and visited elementary schools. They befriended locals through an adopt-an-athlete program, and these hosts took them to church dinners and high school football games.[79] Young believed the benefits of hosting the Olympics were more than just monetary, and this program proved him right. It represented a new version of traditional southern hospitality.

In summer 1996 Young helped with the final preparations for the Olympic onslaught: over ten thousand athletes, fifteen thousand journalists, and two million spectators from two hundred countries descended on Atlanta. Festivities began on July 19 when the Olympic torch toured the city. In midafternoon Coretta Scott King carried the flame past the Martin Luther King Chapel and then handed it to her son, Dexter. From there the Olympic symbol went to City

Hall. Young pronounced the official welcome: "Behold the flame!"[80] The opening of the Atlanta Games represented a triumphant moment for Young. While in city hall he had worked to transform Atlanta into an international city, and hosting the Olympics signified the realization of that goal. Young also experienced a deep personal gratification, as he was a lifelong sports fan with a special affinity for the Olympics.

More importantly, Atlanta's hosting of the Olympics symbolized the complete reversal of the worldwide reputation of the South. Atlanta and the South embraced the Olympic spirit of internationalism and cooperation. This fit with the new image of Atlanta and the South that Young had done much to craft during his years with King, in Congress, at the UN, and as mayor. The new image revolved around the legacy of King and the civil rights movement, and linked the South to the progression toward racial equality in Africa. The new image reflected a remarkable turnaround, and Young was probably the single most important architect of the renovation.

Young characterized southern culture as a model for the rest of the nation and even the world. Peter Applebome defined this vision of southern culture as the "redeemed interracial south." At the close of the twentieth century, it competed with another leading vision of southern culture, the one espoused by Lewis Grizzard. In his columns Grizzard pined for the good old days and snarled "y'all take Botswana." The biggest problem with Grizzard's vision, as Applebome rightly pointed out, was that it failed to address the challenges of the twenty-first century. At issue was the future of the United States. Applebome warned that "what kind of nation we become will depend in large part on which Southern vision becomes the nation."[81]

If Andrew Young had any say in the matter, the triumphant vision of southern culture would not be Grizzard's narrow-minded version. In Young's view, the South represented interracial cooperation, nonviolence, and economic growth. As the United States attempted to assert leadership in the twenty-first century in a world made ever smaller by ongoing technological advances, Young offered a creative alternative to traditional reliance on military force and old-fashioned attitudes of American exceptionalism. American politicians, diplomats, and businesspeople needed flexibility, compassion, and a willingness to listen to the concerns of their counterparts from the rest of the world. The difficult environmental and health crises of the modern world, not to mention the threat of terrorism, required unprecedented cooperation by people from all races and religions. As Americans searched for a successful approach in such a climate, they need look no further for useful models than Andrew Young's South.

Young himself continued working to build bridges between the South and Africa long after the 1996 Olympics. In July 2003 he chaired the Leon Sullivan

Summit in Abuja, Nigeria. Before, during, and after the summit he elucidated his ongoing belief in the potential for African nations such as Nigeria to achieve prosperity. He believed that Atlanta held the key to the success of Nigeria, both as a model and as a point of contact. To facilitate the latter, he espoused direct flights from Atlanta to Nigeria, citing the positive impact of the recently established service between Atlanta and Johannesburg. He portrayed Atlanta as a model in several respects: The first step toward black prosperity there was gaining the right to vote in the 1960s. Political power eventually led to increased economic opportunity. He pointed in particular to Hartsfield Airport, which had 2,500 flights per day and generated as much wealth as Nigeria's oil. The airport was an extremely complex and profitable operation that had been built and was being operated to a great extent by blacks. If blacks could succeed with such an endeavor in Atlanta, he concluded, they could similarly succeed in Nigeria.[82]

In spelling out his prescription for prosperity in Nigeria, Young nicely reiterated his contribution to the globalization of the South. First, he had been a leader of the civil rights movement that returned the right to vote to African Americans. Then, by emphasizing the positive accomplishments of the movement, he helped transform Atlanta into an international city. As a place where blacks enjoyed considerable economic success, moreover, Atlanta could serve as a model for future development in African nations. In Atlanta, because blacks had first solidified political rights and power, they could be confident of ongoing prosperity, even if most of the South became Republican and returned to traditional southern values. Young's key contribution to the globalization of the South—the prescription of democracy, then prosperity—was fittingly also his greatest gift to the less-developed world.

Notes

I would like to thank Bill Stueck and Jim Cobb for inviting me to participate in their symposium on the South and Globalization. This essay is an expanded version of the paper I presented there. Insightful comments and suggestions by Bill, Jim, Robert Pratt, and Michael Krenn helped me improve my analysis. Many of the details in this essay are drawn from my book *Andrew Young: Civil Rights Ambassador* (Wilmington: Scholarly Resources Press, 2003). Thanks to Andy Fry and Rick Hopper for all of their support on that project.

1. President Bill Clinton's address at the National Summit on Africa, Washington, D.C., February 17, 2000, author's personal typescript and tape recording; Nora Boustany, "U.S. Ties Key, Say Africans," *Washington Post,* February 19, 2000.

2. For an insightful analysis of African views regarding Young, particularly South African views, see G. C. Moremi, "South African Responses to Ambassador Andrew Young, 1977–79," master's thesis, University of Pretoria, 2002. Thanks to Dr. Jackie Grobler, Moremi's advisor, for providing me with a copy.

3. For an insightful discussion of Ali's success in increasing Americans' awareness of

Africa, see Alfred Eckes and Thomas Zeiler, *Globalization and the American Century* (Cambridge: Cambridge University Press, 2003), 198; see 222–23 of the same for analysis on Turner's accomplishments. For Jordan's role, see Walter LaFeber, *Michael Jordan and the New Global Capitalism* (New York: Norton, 1999).

4. James C. Cobb, "Preface to the Second Edition," in *The Selling of the South: The Southern Crusade for Industrial Development, 1936–90,* 2nd ed. (Urbana: University of Illinois Press, 1993).

5. Wilson's appointments, especially Davis, discussed in Tennant McWilliams, *The New South Faces the World: Foreign Affairs and the Southern Sense of Self, 1877–1950* (Baton Rouge: Louisiana State University Press, 1988), 92–93.

6. For an excellent analysis of this, see Joseph Fry, *Dixie Looks Abroad: The South and U.S. Foreign Relations, 1789–1973* (Baton Rouge: Louisiana State University Press, 2002), 223.

7. Joseph Fry, *Dixie Looks Abroad,* 4, 233–5, 238–40.

8. Numan Bartley, *The Creation of Modern Georgia,* 2nd ed. (Athens: University of Georgia Press, 1990), 213–4, 223–5.

9. Gary Pomerantz, *Where Peachtree Meets Sweet Auburn: The Saga of Two Families and the Making of Atlanta* (New York: Scribner, 1996), 502–3.

10. Andrew Young, *An Easy Burden: The Civil Rights Movement and the Transformation of America* (New York: HarperCollins, 1996), 43–44, 57; Andrew Young, *A Way Out Of No Way: The Spiritual Memoirs of Andrew Young* (Nashville: Thomas Nelson, 1994), 15–16.

11. There is a growing body of work on the intertwining of civil rights and foreign policy in the 1950s, particularly toward Africa. For example, see Mary Dudziak, *Cold War Civil Rights: Race and the Image of American Democracy* (Princeton: Princeton University Press, 2000); Cary Fraser, "Crossing the Color Line in Little Rock: The Eisenhower Administration and the Dilemma of Race in U.S. Foreign Policy," *Diplomatic History* (Spring 2000); Brenda Plummer, *Rising Wind: Black Americans and U.S. Foreign Affairs, 1935–60* (Chapel Hill: University of North Carolina Press, 1996); Penny Von Eschen, *Race against Empire: Black Americans and Anticolonialism, 1937–57* (Ithaca: Cornell University Press, 1997); Andrew DeRoche, "Establishing the Centrality of Race: Relations Between the U.S. and the Rhodesian Federation, 1953–1963," *Zambezia* (1998).

12. For details and analysis of Young's role in these events, see Taylor Branch, *Pillar of Fire: America in the King Years, 1963–1965* (New York: Simon and Schuster, 1998), 312–40; David Garrow, *Bearing the Cross: Martin Luther King, Jr., and the Southern Christian Leadership Conference* (New York: Vintage, 1986), 223–430; Adam Fairclough, *To Redeem the Soul of America: The Southern Christian Leadership Conference and Martin Luther King, Jr.* (Athens: University of Georgia Press, 1987), 111–251; and Young, *An Easy Burden,* 185–371.

13. Andrew DeRoche, "A Cosmopolitan Christian: Andrew Young and the Southern Christian Leadership Conference, 1964–68," *The Journal of Religious Thought* 51 (Summer–Fall 1994): 67–80.

14. Andrew Young, "An Experiment in Power," p. 12, August 11, 1965, folder 1, box 12, SCLC Papers, Martin Luther King Center, Atlanta, Ga.

15. Andrew Young, letter to Bill and Jean van den Heuvel, March 10, 1967, folder 19, box 38, ibid.

16. Connections between the civil rights movement and international relations in the 1960s are explored in Thomas Borstelmann, *The Cold War and the Color Line: American Race Relations in the Global Arena* (Cambridge: Harvard University Press, 2001); Michael Krenn, *Black Diplomacy: African Americans and the State Department, 1945–1969* (Armonk: M. E. Sharpe, 1999); Dudziak, *Cold War Civil Rights;* and the author's *Andrew Young: Civil Rights Ambassador.*

17. Fry, *Dixie Looks Abroad,* 223–43.

18. Laughlin McDonald, *A Voting Rights Odyssey: Black Enfranchisement in Georgia* (Cambridge: Cambridge University Press, 2003), 129.

19. The percentage of black voters in the Fifth District and its relationship to Young's success in 1972 was a complicated case that reflected more than just the impact of the Voting Rights Act. In 1964 residents in the district filed suit requesting redistricting based on the argument that they were not getting equal representation because the district was too large. According to the 1960 census, the Fifth had twice as many residents as the average size of the other nine districts in Georgia and was 26.5 percent black. In Wesberry v. Sanders the Supreme Court ruled in the residents' favor, concluding that they were being denied their right to equal representation because the district was so large. After the 1970 census the Georgia legislature proposed a redistricting plan that decreased the size of the Fifth District. The plan increased the black percentage in the district to 38 but did not include Young's home. The Georgia attorney general rejected this first attempt. The revised version, which took effect in 1972, raised the black percentage in the Fifth District to 44 and did include Young's home. For analysis of these events see McDonald, *A Voting Rights Odyssey,* 89–90 and 148–50.

20. William Clay, *Just Permanent Interests: Black Americans in Congress, 1870–1992* (New York: Amistad, 1993), 356–57.

21. 93rd Cong., 1st sess., *Congressional Record* 26192 (July 26, 1973).

22. Ibid.

23. Benjamin Pogrund, *Sobukwe and Apartheid* (New Brunswick: Rutgers University Press, 1991), 325–26.

24. 94th Cong., 1st sess., *Congressional Record,* 39397 (December 9, 1975).

25. Ibid.

26. Ibid.

27. 94th Cong., 1st sess., *Congressional Record,* 41096–7 (December 16, 1975).

28. 94th Cong., 2nd sess., *Congressional Record,* 1041–3 (January 27, 1976).

29. The best analysis of U.S. policy toward Angola is in Piero Gleijeses, *Conflicting Missions: Havana, Washington, and Africa, 1959–1976* (Chapel Hill: The University of North Carolina Press, 2002).

30. Robert Massie, *Loosing the Bonds: The United States and South Africa in the Apartheid Years* (New York: Nan Talese, 1997), 490–91.

31. 94th Cong., 2nd sess., *Congressional Record,* 28706–7 (August 31, 1976). For discussion of Soweto and the American response, see Massie, *Loosing the Bonds,* 393–403.

32. Randall Robinson, *Defending the Spirit: A Black Life in America* (New York: Penguin, 1998), 96–98; Massie, *Loosing the Bonds,* 404–6.

33. John Dumbrell, *The Carter Presidency: A Re-Evaluation,* 2nd ed. (Manchester: Manchester University Press, 1995), 88–89.

34. Andrew Young, interview with the author, March 2, 1994, Atlanta, Georgia.

35. Ibid.

36. Bartlett Jones, *Flawed Triumphs: Andy Young at the United Nations* (Lanham, Md.: University Press of America, 1996), 77–79. Also see Robert Shepard, *Nigeria, Africa, and the United States: From Kennedy to Reagan* (Bloomington: Indiana University Press, 1991).

37. Jones, *Flawed Triumphs,* 58.

38. For Smith's praise of Young's honesty see Ian Smith, *The Great Betrayal: The Memoirs of Ian Douglas Smith* (London: Blake, 1997), 251–52, 272.

39. Andrew DeRoche, "Standing Firm For Principles: Jimmy Carter and Zimbabwe," *Diplomatic History* 23 (Fall 1999): 667.

40. G. C. Moremi, "South African Responses To Ambassador Andrew Young, 1977–1979," 23.

41. Massie, *Loosing the Bonds,* 412–13.

42. Moremi, "South African Responses," 26–27.

43. Jones, *Flawed Triumphs,* 82–83; Biko quoted in Massie, *Loosing the Bonds,* 421.

44. Moremi, "South African Responses," 28–29, 42.

45. Young quoted in *Washington Post,* October 25, 1977, A1.

46. The Malta talks and especially Young's friendly relationship with Nkomo are described in a report from Steve Low, the U.S. ambassador to Zambia, to the State Department, February 4, 1978, on microfiche acquired by the author via the Freedom of Information Act, request number 8802607. Malta's significance is analyzed in Jones, *Flawed Triumphs,* 63–64, and DeRoche, "Standing Firm," 671–74.

47. Hal Gulliver, "Young: Conservative? Radical?" *Atlanta Constitution,* December 4, 1978; Stephen Rosenfeld, "Andrew Young at Work in Africa," *Washington Post,* December 8, 1978; Gilbert Cranberg, "Andrew Young earning respect as 'defender of African rights,'" *Des Moines Register,* December 6, 1978.

48. DeRoche, *Andrew Young,* 102–3.

49. See "Remarks of the President in an Announcement on the Zimbabwe-Rhodesian Sanctions," June 7, 1979, Staff Offices—Louis Martin, box 109, folder "Zimbabwe," Jimmy Carter Library, Atlanta, Ga.

50. For a detailed discussion of Carter and Zimbabwe, see Andrew DeRoche, *Black, White, and Chrome: The United States and Zimbabwe, 1953–1998* (Trenton: Africa World Press, 2001), 243–309. For another interpretation see Stephen Stedman, *Peacemaking in Civil War: International Mediation in Zimbabwe, 1974–1980* (Boulder: Lynn Riener, 1991).

51. Young's resignation is detailed thoroughly in Jones, *Flawed Triumphs,* 129–51. The impact on black-Jewish relations is considered in Jonathan Kaufman, *Broken Alliance: The Turbulent Times Between Blacks and Jews in America* (New York: Simon and Schuster, 1988), 245–47.

52. James Cobb, "An Epitaph for the North: Reflections on the Politics of Regional and National Identity at the Millenium," *The Journal of Southern History* 66 (February 2000): 3–24, citation at 15.

53. Election statistics from David Harmon, *Beneath the Image of the Civil Rights Movement and Race Relations* (New York: Garland, 1996), 302 and Frederick Allen, *Atlanta Rising: The Invention of an International City, 1946–1996* (Atlanta: Longstreet Press, 1996), 214–16. Also see Clarence Stone, *Regime Politics: Governing Atlanta, 1946–1988* (Lawrence: University Press of Kansas, 1989), 109–10.

54. Pomerantz, *Where Peachtree Meets Sweet Auburn*, 438, 446–51.

55. Dan Sweat quoted in Jacoby, *Someone Else's House*, 409.

56. *Atlanta Journal-Constitution*, December 19, 1982, C1.

57. Louise Suggs, phone interview with the author, October 4, 2002.

58. Senate, *U.S. Policy toward South Africa*, hearings before the Committee on Foreign Relations, 1st sess., 99th Congress, April 24, May 2 and 22, 1985 (Washington: United States Government Printing Office, 1985), 283.

59. For discussion of the Comprehensive Anti-Apartheid Act see DeRoche, *Black, White, and Chrome*, 340–42. For detailed analysis of the impact of the sanctions in South Africa see Massie, *Loosing the Bonds*, 620–71.

60. *Atlanta Journal-Constitution*, January 30, 1986, A2.

61. The Angola trip was described to the author by Carol Muldawer, Mayor Young's liaison to the business community, during an interview with the author in Atlanta, August 15, 2000.

62. *Atlanta Journal-Constitution*, August 8, 1986, A14.

63. For discussion of African American criticism of Reagan's policies toward Angola and South Africa, as well as the decreasing number of black ambassadors in the 1980s, see Krenn, *Black Diplomacy*, 166–68.

64. *Atlanta Journal-Constitution*, January 13, 1987, A3.

65. Ibid., January 16, 1987, A1 and A12.

66. Ibid., January 18, 1987, A17.

67. Ibid., August 29, 1989, A1.

68. Ibid., September 19, 1990, A10.

69. Ibid., April 3, 1988, H1; May 22, 1988, M4; June 3, 1989, C6; and July 11, 1990, A9.

70. Georgia export statistics from U.S. Department of Commerce, cited in "Arkansas Statistical Abstract," April 2000, http://www.lexis-nexis.com.

71. U.S. Department of Commerce, *Statistical Abstract of the United States 1992* (Lanham, Md.: Bernan Press, 1992), 787.

72. For a thorough summary of Young's domestic accomplishments as mayor, see Alton Hornsby, "Andrew Jackson Young: Mayor of Atlanta, 1982–1990," *The Journal of Negro History* 77 (Summer 1992): 159–82.

73. Ronald Bayor, "African-American Mayors and Governance in Atlanta," in *African-American Mayors: Race, Politics, and the American City*, ed. David Colburn and Jeffrey Adler (Urbana: University of Illinois Press, 2001), 178–99, citation at 190.

74. Cobb, *The Selling of the South*, 261.

75. For an insightful explanation as to why Young has put so much faith in capital-

ism, see Michael Dyson, *I May Not Get There with You: The True Martin Luther King, Jr.* (New York: The Free Press, 2000), 90–94.

76. *Atlanta Journal-Constitution,* July 11, 1993, A1.

77. Table on "Metropolitan Merchandise Export Totals" prepared by the Office of Trade and Economic Analysis, International Trade Administration, Department of Commerce, http://www.ita.doc.gov/td/industry/otea/metro/destinations/Atlanta.txt.

78. *Atlanta Journal-Constitution,* October 6, 1994, E1.

79. *New York Times,* October 11, 1995, B9 and B11.

80. *Atlanta Journal-Constitution,* July 20, 1996, S23.

81. Peter Applebome, *Dixie Rising: How the South Is Shaping American Values, Politics, and Culture* (New York: Random House, 1996), 341–43.

82. "Nigeria: How to Reposition the Country for Development: Interview with Ambassador Young," *Vanguard,* July 1, 2003; "Chairman of Sullivan Summit Andrew Young Addresses Africa Development," *Vanguard,* July 10, 2003; "Nigeria: Showcasing Lagos Investment Potentials in Atlanta," August 31, 2003. These articles were all retrieved through LexisNexis, and I am indebted to Bill Stueck for sharing them with me.

James C. Cobb, B. Phinizy Spalding Distinguished Professor of History at the University of Georgia, has written widely on the interaction between economy, society, and culture in the American South. His books include *The Selling of The South: The Southern Crusade for Industrial Development, 1936–1990* (1993), and *The Most Southern Place on Earth: The Mississippi Delta and the Roots of Regional Identity* (1992). He recently completed *Old South, New South, No South: A History of Southern Identity* (forthcoming 2005).

Peter A. Coclanis is associate provost for international affairs and Albert R. Newsome Professor of History at the University of North Carolina at Chapel Hill. He is the author of many works in economic and business history, including *The Shadow of a Dream: Economic Life and Death in the South Carolina Low Country, 1670–1920* (1989), and, co-authored with David L. Carlton, *The South, the Nation, and the World: Perspectives on Southern Economic Development* (2003).

Andy DeRoche teaches history and serves as social science department chair at Front Range Community College in Longmont, Colorado. He received his Ph.D. in diplomatic history from the University of Colorado, where he is an adjunct professor of international affairs. His publications include *Andrew Young: Civil Rights Ambassador* (2003) and *Black, White, and Chrome: The United States and Zimbabwe, 1953–1998* (2001). He is currently researching the role of Kenneth Kaunda in southern African international relations.

Alfred E. Eckes is Ohio Eminent Research Professor in Contemporary History at Ohio University in Athens. His most recent book, coauthored with Thomas Zeiler, is *Globalization and the American Century* (2003). He is a past president of the International Trade and Finance Association and from 1981 to 1990 served as chairman and a commissioner of the U.S. International Trade Commission. His books include *Opening America's Market* (1995), *The United States and the Global Struggle for Minerals* (1979), and *A Search for Solvency: Bretton Woods and the International Monetary System, 1941–1971* (1975).

Sayuri Guthrie-Shimizu is associate professor of history at Michigan State University. Her current book-length projects include "Pacific Crossings: The United States and Japan in a Changing World" and "Trans-Pacific Field of Dreams: Baseball and Modernity in U.S.-Japanese Encounters, 1872–1952."

Marko Maunula is a Ph.D. candidate in American history at the University of North Carolina at Chapel Hill. A native of Finland, Maunula has studied the South and globalization both as a journalist and as a scholar. Currently, he is completing his dissertation on the arrival of foreign corporations in the South Carolina Piedmont.

Raymond A. Mohl is professor of history at the University of Alabama at Birmingham. He has a Ph.D. in history from New York University and works in the fields of U.S. urban and immigration history. He is the author or editor of numerous books, including most recently *The New African American Urban History* (1996), *The Making of Urban America* (1997), and *South of the South: Jewish Activists and the Civil Rights Movement in Miami, 1945–1960* (2004). He is currently working on a book entitled *Cities in Flux,* a study of the post–World War II American city.

David M. Reimers is professor emeritus at New York University. He is the author of *Still the Golden Door: The Third World Comes to America* (2nd ed., 1992), *Unwanted Strangers: American Identity and the Turn against Immigration* (1998), and, forthcoming in fall 2004, *Other Immigrants: The Global Origins of the American People.*

William Stueck is Distinguished Research Professor of History at the University of Georgia. Most recently he is the author of *Rethinking the Korean War: A New Diplomatic and Strategic History* (2002).

Apparel industry: effects of NAFTA on, 56; job losses in, 53; move of, overseas, 54–57; and protectionism, 53; and responsiveness of U.S. firms, 61; and rural work forces, 3, 54; and terrorist threats, 61

Applebome, Peter, 202

Arab oil embargo, 140, 146

Arkansas: business climate of, 52; as business headquarters, 47, 49; European immigration to, 100; foreign-born residents of, 43–44; Hispanic population of, 71, 73, 78; income in, 39; regional development of, 149; and service economy, 41

Arlington County, Va., 114

Arlington, Va., 70

Armstrong, Louis, 20

ASDA, 9–11

Ashland, Ala., 82

Asia, xiv

Asian Indians. *See* Indians

Asian-American Hotel Owners Association, 112

Asians: and advanced education, 116; as business owners, 118, 120; church membership of, in southern U.S., 125; cultural assimilation by, xiv; effect of, on politics in southern U.S., 126–27; effect of, on U.S. foreign policy, 126; extended equal protection, 109; family incomes of, 120; and immigration laws, 105–6, 108, 118; immigration of, to U.S., xiii, 100, 110–11, 123–24; intended place of residence in U.S., 107–8; and job creation, 124; and knowledge of English, 120; occupations of, in U.S., xiv, 109, 110, 115–16; and other ethnic groups, xiv; participation of, in Small Business Administration programs, 109, 119–20; as replacements for freed slaves, 103; in southern U.S., xiii, 101–2, 106–7, 111, 121–22, 154; as undocumented aliens, 120–21

Askew, Reubin, 145

Association of Southeast Asian Nations (ASEAN), 142

AT&T, 45, 59

Atlanta Business Chronicle, 87

Atlanta, Ga.: as air travel hub, 47; Asians in, xiv, 116, 118–19; as banking headquarters, 49; downtown renewal of, 200; high-tech industries in, 68, 110; Hispanic population of, 70–72, 78; immigration enforcement in, 82; and international business, 139, 187; links of, to South Africa, 201; during mayorship of Andrew Young, 198; media industry in, 46; as model for success in Nigeria, 203; and Olympics (1996), xv, 185, 187, 199, 201, 202

Atlanta Journal-Constitution, 82, 119, 125, 195, 199

Atlanta Junior College, 190

Attalla, Ala., 67

Augusta, Ga., 149

Austin, Tex., 68

Automobile corridor, 148

Automobile industry, 56, 61

Aviation, 46

Ayoub, Sam, 149

Balance Agriculture with Industry (BAWI), 144

Bangkok, Thailand, 142

Bangladesh, 4, 56, 117, 118, 123

Bank of America, 49, 58, 59

Barnes, Roy, 126

Bartley, Numan, 106

Baton Rouge, La., 114

Baylor University College of Medicine, 115

Bayou La Batre, La., 113

Beamesderfer, Thomas, 114

Belafonte, Harry, 196

Bellagio, Italy, 14

Bentonville, Ark., 9, 10, 48, 49

BET (Black Entertainment Television), 6

Central Intelligence Agency (CIA), 191
Chandler, Alfred, Jr., 44
Chapel Hill, N.C., 82
Charleston, S.C., 74, 78, 137, 171
Charlotte, N.C.: as air travel hub, 47; and Asian refugees, 113; as banking headquarters, 49, 58; Hispanic population of, 70, 72, 78
Chatham County, N.C., 86
Chevron, 198
Chicago Council on Foreign Relations, 122
Chicago, Ill.: as air travel hub, 46; Asian immigration to, 102, 106, 114; as banking headquarters, 49; Hispanic population of, 68
Chilhowie, Va., 54
China: and currency adjustment, 60–61; economic similarity of, with southern U.S., xiii, 11; external cultural influences on, 7, 12; and granite business, 7; low cost of labor in, 36, 56, 60; manufacturing sector growth of, 62; shift of technology-related employment to, 59; shift of textile industries to, 54; as source of foreign adoptions in U.S., 111; as source of U.S. immigration, 106; tariff increases on, 61; U.S. missionaries to, 102; and Wal-Mart, 58. *See also* Chinese
Chinese: early immigration of, to southern U.S., 102, 103–4; immigration of, to U.S., 103, 106; as students in U.S., 117. *See also* China
Chinese Exclusion Act of 1882, 105, 123
Chinquapin, N.C., 6
Christian Science Monitor, 70
Cincinnati, Ohio, 49
Citibank, 59, 174
City University of New York (CUNY), 125
Civil Rights Act of 1964, 109, 188
Civil Rights Commission, 109, 121
Civil Rights Institute, 81
Civil rights movement: and African

Americans' influence on foreign policy, 187, 190; and business investment in southern U.S., 52; impact of, on presidential election, 192; involvement in, by international community, xv; northern U.S. response to, xi; participation of Andrew Young in, 185, 188; similarity of, to apartheid, 193
Civil War: and commerce in southern U.S., 25, 26, 27, 28; and postwar decrease in southern income, 39; and postwar emergence of Spartanburg, S.C., 166; and postwar recruitment of Chinese, 103; and postwar southern immigration, 100–101; and prewar southern outmigration, 24; and Reconstruction, 28
Clark Atlanta University, 200
Clarkston, Ga., 113
Clemson University, 170
Cleveland, Miss., 103
Cleveland, Ohio, 49
Clinton, Bill, 52, 185, 201
CNN (Cable News Network), 46
Coal, 27
Cobb, James C., 185
Coca-Cola, 10, 12, 149, 152, 198
Coclanis, Peter A., 36, 37
Cohen, Warren, 154
Cohn, Deborah N., 6
Collins, Martha Layne, 146
Collinsville, Ala., 67, 75
Colombia, 6
Columbia, S.C., 143
Columbia (S.C.) Record, 178
Columbus, Christopher, 36
Commentary, 152
Commerce, Ga., 148
Communist Manifesto, 21
Communist Party, 85
Community Foundation of Greater Birmingham, 81
Computer Sciences Corporation, 59

Georgia Department of Industry, Trades, and Tourism, 126
Georgia Poultry Alliance, 84
Georgia Public Television, 154
Georgians for Immigration Reduction, 86
Germany, 2, 164, 172, 178, 190
Girl Scouts, 153
Global economy, 12, 21, 22, 23
Global market, 27
Globalism, 174
Globalization: American features of, 11; and capital, 21, 42, 68; and capitalism, xv, 22; and corporate headquarters, 47; and cost cutting, 55; definition of, xii, 20, 24; effect of epidemics on, 61; effect of, on production and consumption, 20; four categories of, 36; and identity politics, 15; and individual networking, 37; influenced by human decisions, xv; and information, 44; and international currency, xiii; and labor, xiii, 21, 42, 68; as mutual and incremental phenomenon, 10; origin and popularization of term, 36; origin of, 21–22; and racial issues, 52, 187; regionalism versus, xii, xv, 8, 10, 180; role of, in democracy and prosperity, 203; and services, 21, 42, 68; sustainability of, 60; and synergism, 37; and terrorism, xiii, 61; and tourism, 44; and transnational flows, 23; and urban areas, 3; and U.S. economy, 36; U.S. government role in, 52; and U.S. national policy, 55; and warfare, 61
Globalony, 20
Glocalism, 10
Gold Kist, 66, 70, 82
Grady, Henry, 28
Grand Ole Opry, 8
Granite, 7
Great Britain, 111
Great Depression, 50, 68, 102
Greenfield investment, 146, 158 (n. 27)

Greensboro, N.C., 47, 70, 79, 109
Greensboro–Winston-Salem, N.C., 72
Greenville, S.C., 70, 171, 176, 180
Greenville (S.C.) News, 75
Greider, William, 21
Grizzard, Lewis, 202
Group of Ten, 173
Guatemala, 77, 79
Guinea-Bissau, 189
Gujarat, India, 112, 120, 126
Gulliver, Hal, 195

Hall County, Ga., 77
Harper's Weekly, 101
Harris County, Tex., 102
Harris, Green, 105
Hart-Arthur Act, 168
Hart-Celler Act, 123
Hartford Theological Seminary, 187
Hartsfield, William, 187
Harvard University, 36, 165, 192
Harvey, David, 22
Hasegawa, Norishige, 149
Hawaii, 126
Hayato, Ikeda, 138
Hearden, Patrick, 27
Helms, Jesse, 186, 191
Henegar, Ala., 83
Hill, Michael, 15
Hispanic Center for Social Assistance, 84
Hispanic Interest Coalition of Alabama, 84
Hispanics: church membership of, 125; cultural heritage of, 86–87; dangerous working conditions for, 78–79; employment of, xiii; extended equal protection, 109; immigration of, to southern U.S., xiii, 42, 66, 70–72, 75–77, 83, 88; and labor unions, 79; and other ethnic groups, xiii, 71, 78–81; and politics, 87–88; in rural versus urban settings, 71–73; school systems' response to, xiii; in small businesses, 119; in southern U.S., xiii, 72–74, 78,

Isolationism, 180
Isuzu, 147
Italy, 13
Iyer, Pico, 7, 12

J. C. Penney, 49
Jackson, Andrew, 186
Jackson, Maynard, 196
Jacksonville, Fla., 102
Jacksonville, N.C., 59
JaLog Industries, 171
Japan: and apparel manufacturing, xiv;
    and automobile industry, 2, 139;
    commercial and service sector
    investment of, 140; early agricultural
    settlement in Florida, 102; and
    European investors, 138; exports of,
    to U.S., 135, 141; and food production,
    157 (n. 20); and foreign exchange
    restrictions, 153; and foreign
    investment, xiv, 139; as member of
    African Development Fund, 190; and
    protectionism, 146; and pursuit of
    compatible labor force, 142; reliance of,
    on outside suppliers, 148; reparation
    payments of, to Southeast Asia, 140;
    resolution of, against racism, 186; and
    shipping industry, 136, 138, 139; and
    southern U.S., 3, 110, 124, 135–37, 152–
    54; and technical training, 144; and
    textile industry, xiv, 168, 173, 180; and
    U.S. corporate operations, 139; and
    U.S. investment, 140, 141, 144; and U.S.
    manufacturing sector, 141. See also
    Japanese
Japan Chamber of Commerce of Georgia,
    152
Japan Development Bank, 138
Japan External Trade Organization
    (JETRO), 135–37
Japan-America Society of Georgia, 152
Japanese: civic life of, in southern U.S.,
    152; family life of, in southern U.S.,
    153–54; as foreign students, 117;

immigration of, to U.S., 105; social
    status of, in southern U.S., 139. See also
    Japan
Java, 19, 30
Jazz, 20
Jefferson Parish, La., 101
Jefferson, Thomas, 186
Jekyll Island, Ga., 20
Jian, Zemin, 11
Jim Crow system, 108
Joao, Paulino Pinto, 198
Johannesburg, South Africa, 188, 193
Johnson, Lyndon B., 39, 52, 53, 109, 186
Johnson-Reed Act of 1924, 105
Jones, Fob, 2
Jordan, Barbara, 190
Jordan, Michael, 185
Just-in-time (JIT) production/inventory
    system, 148
JVC, 58

Kannapolis, N.C., 47
Karadzic, Radovan, 15
Karl Mentzel Maschinenfabrik, 169
Kaunda, Kenneth, 197
Keidanren (Japan Association of
    Economic Organizations), 149
Kempner, Matt, 82
Kenan, Randall, 6, 7
Kennedy, John F., 52, 53, 109, 186
Kennedy Round, 53
Kentucky: in automobile corridor,
    148; business climate of, 51; foreign
    automobile manufacturers in, 56,
    68; and greenfield investment, 50;
    and investment incentives, 151; and
    regional development, 149
Kentucky Fried Chicken (KFC), 10, 12
Kenya, 112, 190
Khartoum, Sudan, 195
Khmer Rouge, 114
Kikkoman, 157 (n)
Kim, Hochan, 118
Kimberley, South Africa, 190

Marcus, Sidney, 196
Marianna, Fla., 59
Marshall Fund, 122
Marshall Space Flight Center, 120
Marshall, Thurgood, 188, 192
Martin Luther King Jr. Resource Center, 81
Marx, Karl, 21, 22
Marysville, Ohio, 146, 147
Mashinini, Tsietsi, 194
Massey, Douglas S., 69
Matsushita, 146
Maus, Teodoro, 82
May Department Stores, 49
Mazda, 178
McCarran-Walter Immigration Act, 107, 123
McCoy, Drew, 24
McDonald, Larry, 195
McDonald's, 5, 9, 11, 12, 13
McKinney, Cynthia, 126
McMillion, Charles, 56
Memphis Chinese Labor Convention, 105
Memphis, Tenn.: Hispanic population of, 70, 73, 78, 84; as home of Piggly Wiggly stores, 37; immigration enforcement in, 82; Japanese manufacturing in, 146
Mercedes-Benz, 1, 2, 54, 148
Merion, Va., 37
Mexican American Legal Defense and Educational Fund, 84
Mexico: economic crises of, 68, 75; Filipino migration to, 101; historic connections of, to Texas, 71; and job shifts from southern U.S., 60; and migration to U.S., 69, 77, 106; as supplier for manufacturers in U.S., 56, 146
Miami, Fla.: as air travel hub, 44, 46, 47; Asian population of, 106, 114; Cuban refugees in, 113; as early Japanese export site, 137; foreign-born residents in, 43; as major urban center, 110

Michelin, 175, 178, 179
Michelin, François, 178
Middle Easterners, xiv
Middle Tennessee State University, 122
Migrant Head Start, 84
Milliken, Roger, 168, 169, 177, 178, 180
Ming, Yao, 124
Minolta, 58
Mississippi: African American political impact in, 192; automobile industry in, 2, 68, 148; Balance Agriculture with Industry (BAWI) program, 144; business climate of, 52; Chinese immigration to, 103–4; as corporate headquarters, 47, 49; effects of NAFTA on, 56; European immigration to, 100; foreign-born citizens in, 43; income in, 39; and regional development, 149; service industry in, 41
Mississippi Immigrants Rights Alliance, 84
Mitsubishi, 19, 146
Mitsui Senpako, 138
Mobil Oil, 153
Mobile, Ala., 75, 137
Mobile, N.C., 83
Moesha, 6
Mohl, Raymond A., 102
Molepolole, Botswana, 198
Monde, Le, 5
Mondlane, Eduardo, 187
Montana, 44
Montgomery, Ala., 75, 109, 148
Morgan City, La., 78
Morgantown, N.C., 77, 79, 114
Morita, Akio, 153
Motorola, 146
Mount Pleasant, Tenn., 149
Mozambique, 187, 189
Mugabe, Robert, 194, 199
Mulder, Connie, 194
Multiculturalism, 12
Munich, Germany, 175
Musgrove, Ronnie, 3

and textile industry, 165, 167; wages and benefits in, 171; and welfare capitalism, 178

Voluntary religious and state refugee
   organizations (VOLAGS), 113–14
Vorster, Balthazar Johannes, 192
Voting Rights Act of 1965, 109, 188, 189,
   192

Wachovia, 49
Wall Street Journal, 115, 116
Wallace, George, 15, 186
Walley, Pete, 73
Wal-Mart: and Chinese imports, 58; as
   corporate employer, 49; as global
   marketer, 9–10; and immigration
   enforcement, 83; national presence
   of, 38; origins of, in southern U.S., 8,
   48, 110
Walton, Sam, 49
Wang, You-Xiong, 117
Warwick, 146
Washington, D.C., 72, 106, 114, 118
Washington Post, 70, 195
Washington (state), 126
Weaver, Thomas, 68
West Columbia, S.C., 171
West Indies, 19
West, John C., 145, 172
Westmoreland, William, 186
Wheat, 26, 27
Whirlpool Corporation, 146
Whitfield County, Ga., 77
Wilkinson, Wallace, 175
Williams, Don, 8
Williamson, Jeffrey G., 22
Williamson, Joel, 6, 9
Wilson, Pete, 123
Wilson, Woodrow, 186
Winterthur, Switzerland, 168
Wipro Ltd., 59
Wolfe, Thomas, 11
Woods, Walter, 87
Woodward, Baldwin and Co., 27
Woodward, C. Vann, xi, 1, 28
Woolco, 49
World Bank, 194

World trade, 21
World Trade Center, 117, 122, 127
World Trade Organization (WTO), 60
World War I, 5, 47, 100
World War II: and African Americans, 42;
   farm labor demands during, 68;
   Japanese relocation camps during, 102;
   and Japanese reparation agreements,
   140; northern U.S. workforce during,
   42; and postwar anti-immigration
   sentiment, 123; and postwar
   immigration, 103; and postwar increase
   of exports, 50, 136; and postwar
   prominence of Atlanta, 187; and return
   of military to workforce, 38; and
   southern U.S. economy, 39, 110; and
   southern U.S. militarism, 188
Worldviews, 122
Wright, Gavin, 52

Yamota Colony, Fla., 102
Yesmin, Farhana, 117
YKK Industries, 143, 145
Young, Andrew: and Africa, xiv, 187,
   189, 192–93, 197, 198; and African
   Development Fund (ADF), 191; and
   Anglo-American plan, 195; and Angola,
   191; and Atlanta Olympics, xv, 199, 201;
   and black Africans, 194–95, 198, 199;
   and Carter, Jimmy, 192; and civil rights
   movement, 188; and Congressional
   Black Caucus, 189; and development
   of TransAfrica, 192; foreign relations
   philosophy of, 188; and Georgia's
   foreign business, 200; in Khartoum,
   195; and King, Martin Luther, Jr., 192,
   202; as mayor of Atlanta, 187, 196, 197,
   199, 200, 202; and militarism, 186, 189;
   and Nigeria, 193; and Rhodesia, 193;
   and South Africa, 189, 191–92, 194, 197,
   201; and Southern Africa Development
   Fund (SADF), 201; and southern U.S.
   traditions, 185; in United Nations, 186,
   192, 196, 202; in U.S. Congress, 186, 189,

202; and U.S. foreign policy, 198; and U.S. international investment, 190; vision of, for multiracial democracy, 188; and Young Ideas consulting firm, 196

Young, Walter, 200

Zambia, 190, 197

Zamora, Lois Parkinson, 6

Zenith Corporation, 146

Zimbabwe, 8, 196